SILENT
WARRIORS,
INCREDIBLE
COURAGE

SILENT
WARRIORS,
INCREDIBLE
COURAGE

The Declassified Stories of
Cold War Reconnaissance Flights
and the Men Who Flew Them

WOLFGANG W. E. SAMUEL

Colonel, United States Air Force (Ret.)

Foreword by R. Cargill Hall

University Press of Mississippi / Jackson

The University Press of Mississippi is the scholarly publishing agency of the Mississippi Institutions of Higher Learning: Alcorn State University, Delta State University, Jackson State University, Mississippi State University, Mississippi University for Women, Mississippi Valley State University, University of Mississippi, and University of Southern Mississippi.

www.upress.state.ms.us

The University Press of Mississippi is a member of the Association of University Presses.

First printing 2019

∞

Library of Congress Cataloging-in-Publication Data

Names: Samuel, Wolfgang W. E., author. | Hall, R. Cargill, author of foreword.
Title: Silent warriors, incredible courage : the declassified stories of Cold War reconnaissance flights and the men who flew them / Wolfgang W. E. Samuel ; foreword by R. Cargill Hall.
Description: Jackson : University Press of Mississippi, [2019] | Includes bibliographical references and index. |
Identifiers: LCCN 2018041329 (print) | LCCN 2018045460 (ebook) | ISBN 9781496822802 (epub single) | ISBN 9781496822819 (epub institutional) | ISBN 9781496822826 (pdf single) | ISBN 9781496822833 (pdf institutional) | ISBN 9781496822796 (cloth : alk. paper)
Subjects: LCSH: United States. Air Force—Airmen--Interviews. | Aerial reconnaissance, American. | Aerial observation (Military science)—History—20th century. | Cold War—History. | LCGFT: Personal narratives.
Classification: LCC UG626 (ebook) | LCC UG626 .S27 2019 (print) | DDC 358.4/54097309045—dc23
LC record available at https://lccn.loc.gov/2018041329

British Library Cataloging-in-Publication Data available

Dedicated to the brave men who flew alone
into harm's way to ensure the survival
of our country in the nuclear age.

In memory of all those who could talk to no one
about the dangerous missions they flew
and who perished serving our country,
resting in their watery graves.

I wrote this book so we
do not forget what a few
did for the many—
at the risk of their lives.

CONTENTS

TERMS AND ABBREVIATIONS

AAA	Antiaircraft artillery
AAF	Army Air Forces
AC	Aircraft commander in SAC
AFB	Air Force Base
AGL	Above ground level
Aileron	Moveable wing control surface to bank an airplane
ATC	Air Training Command
CFC	Central Fire Control RB-29/RB-50
CG	Center of gravity
CIA	Central Intelligence Agency
CO	Commanding Officer
CP	Copilot
DFC	Distinguished Flying Cross
DIA	Defense Intelligence Agency
DMZ	Demilitarized Zone
ECM	Electronic countermeasures
EGT	Exhaust gas temperature
EOB	Electronic Order of Battle
EW	Electronic warfare
EWO	Electronic warfare officer
FAA	Federal Aviation Administration
FEAF	Far East Air Forces
GCA	Ground control approach radar
GCI	Ground control intercept radar
Heart Throb	RB-57A-1 reconnaissance aircraft
HF	High frequency
IFF	Identification friend or foe (responder)
IFR	Instrument flight rules
Indicated	Airspeed as shown on an airspeed indicator; not necessarily the actual speed of the aircraft
IP	Instructor pilot

LSO	Landing ship officer
Mach	Speed in relation to the speed of sound
MiG	Russian aircraft designed by the Mikoyan and Gurovich Design Bureau—MiG-15, -17, -19, and -21
NCO	Noncommissioned officer
NRO	National Reconnaissance Office
NSA	National Security Agency
PARPRO	Peripheral Reconnaissance Program
POW	Prisoner of war
PRC	Peoples Republic of China (Communist China)
RAF	Royal Air Force
Raven	Electronic warfare officer (55th SRW)
ROK	Republic of Korea (South Korea)
SAC	Strategic Air Command
SAM	Surface-to-air missile
SENSINT	Sensitive Intelligence Program
Slick Chick	F-100A aircraft modified into an RF-100A-1
SRS	Strategic Reconnaissance Squadron
SRW	Strategic Reconnaissance Wing
Stall	The point at which a wing no longer produces lift
TAC	Tactical Air Command
TDY	Temporary duty
TRS	Tactical Reconnaissance Squadron
TRW	Tactical Reconnaissance Wing
UHF	Ultrahigh frequency (radio)
USAF	United States Air Force
USAFE	United States Air Forces Europe (USSTAF)
USSTAF	United States Strategic Air Forces
USSR	Union of Soviet Socialist Republics
VFR	Visual flight rules

FOREWORD

In the work of intelligence, heroes are undecorated and unsung, often even among their own fraternity. Their inspiration is rooted in patriotism; their reward can be little except the conviction that they are performing a unique and indispensable service for their country and the knowledge that America needs and appreciates their efforts.

—**President Dwight D. Eisenhower,** November 3, 1959, at the cornerstone laying ceremony for CIA headquarters, Langley, Virginia

Serving as Supreme Commander of Allied Expeditionary Forces in Europe during World War II, Dwight David Eisenhower oversaw the invasion of France in 1944 and subsequently led Allied forces to victory over the Axis powers on the Western Front. A General of the Army, he is now recognized as one of the most notable American military leaders in our history. Elected president of the United States in 1952, on taking office in January 1953 he directed his attention to ending the Korean War and secured an armistice in July between United Nations forces and those of Communist China and North Korea, which ended hostilities if not the war itself.

A few years before, in August 1949, the Soviet Union exploded a nuclear device and followed in August 1953 by exploding a thermonuclear device. With TU-4 long-range bombers that could deliver these weapons against America, the need to know with assurance of Soviet economic resources, nuclear capabilities, and military preparations had never been greater. Given his wartime experience, President Eisenhower knew that periodic overflights could collect reliable intelligence of Soviet strategic forces and arms facilities, and provide indications and warning of impending nuclear surprise attack. Moreover, the intelligence product would also permit him to size American military forces to meet real instead of imagined threats—with a corresponding savings of national treasure. In early 1954, the president authorized, and a few trusted advisers established, a clandestine project in compartmented channels to acquire precisely this kind of strategic intelligence by conducting in peacetime periodic, high-altitude aerial overflights of potential foreign adversaries. By doing so, however, the United States most definitely would be violating the terms of international aerial navigation treaties to which it was a High Contracting Party. Because of the international repercussions certain to occur should an airplane be brought down, the president could not have come to his peacetime overflight decision lightly.

The first of these efforts, the Sensitive Intelligence Program, known as SENSINT, contained within it a separate WIND FALL compartment for air force–acquired photographic products, products shared with the Central Intelligence Agency. Conducted between early 1954 and the end of 1956, SEN-SINT missions, directed by the Department of Defense, relied on available navy and air force military reconnaissance aircraft or modified versions of them. Deep penetration overflights employed air-refuelable reconnaissance bombers of the Strategic Air Command, the RB-45C and RB-47E. The air force modified high-performance reconnaissance fighter airplanes, the RF-86 and supersonic RF-100 in particular, to mount cameras and extra fuel tanks for shallow penetration missions. Finally, the service contracted for reconnaissance versions of the British Canberra bomber, which were built in America under license. Air force and navy pilots who flew SENSINT missions and the military and CIA photo-interpreters who analyzed their WIND FALL product would know only that piece of the puzzle with which they were directly associated. The participants directly involved did not discuss these missions with anyone, not even with their fellow flyers.

The second of President Eisenhower's overflight programs, which he approved in November 1954, produced the high-flying U-2 reconnaissance aircraft operated by the CIA with air force logistical assistance and piloted by "sheep-dipped" air force pilots who represented themselves as civilians. The U-2 program was shrouded within its own Secret Compartmented Information (SCI) cocoon between 1955 and mid-1960. Fewer than 350 people in the country, including the Lockheed designers, maintenance personnel, and pilots, knew about the U-2 and its actual use. Known to these few as AQUA-TONE, when overflight operations approached in 1956, it was subsumed in the TALENT access and control system, a Top-Secret compartment whose imagery products were separated into two additional access-limited compartments called CHESS (European Theater) and CHURCHDOOR (Asian Theater). Indeed, the SENSINT and TALENT programs were so closely held that neither ever appeared in the deliberations of the National Security Council—at least not until the U-2 "tore its britches," as one participant phrased it, in May 1960 and acquired thereby the unwanted international attention that these missions risked.

The president approved each U-2 mission, and the first two of them occurred on July 4 and 5, 1956, when U-2s flew over the Soviet cities of Leningrad and

Russian MiG-21s ran frequent intercepts on PARPRO mission aircraft, along with older MiG-15s, MiG-17s, MiG-19s, and two-seat Yak-25 interceptors, some resulting in shootdowns, always over international waters. Although RB-45C and RB-47B/E/H aircraft on several occasions overflew the Soviet Union, the only overflight loss was that of Francis Gary Powers on May 1, 1960, flying a high-altitude U-2 reconnaissance aircraft brought down not by fighters but by SA-2 surface-to-air missiles. The introduction of the SA-2 fundamentally affected not only high-altitude reconnaissance overflight operations but also the very nature of aerial warfare, a lesson yet to be learned.

Moscow, respectively, among other regions of European Russia. The last flight, however, ended rather more dramatically when, on May 1, 1960, the Soviet Union shot down a U-2 deep inside its territory. The resulting international furor mightily embarrassed the administration. The president at first offered a "plausible denial"—a weather research airplane over Turkey had strayed off course—a cover story that collapsed after the Soviets produced the pilot and charged him with espionage. The U-2 shootdown also ended a summit conference almost before it had begun, with Soviet leaders demanding a personal apology from Eisenhower, one that would not be forthcoming. Nevertheless, Eisenhower announced publicly that the United States would not, in the future, conduct clandestine aerial overflights of the Soviet Union, a pledge that he and his successors would keep. Fortunately for the United States, Eisenhower's earth-orbiting strategic reconnaissance satellites (not covered in this volume) succeeded aerial overflights and began successful operations in August 1960.

This work serves well those interested in early Cold War aerial overflight intelligence programs. Colonel Samuel's *Silent Warriors, Incredible Courage* surveys, describes, and explains these crucial, highly classified programs told through declassified records and the recollections of their participants, a history fine-tuned by his own experience as a flying member of the US Air Force Peripheral Reconnaissance Program, PARPRO. It is an important history of the United States' application and first wide-scale use of technical intelligence collection using overhead assets to acquire secrets hidden within "denied territory." And it underscores President Eisenhower's immense contribution to America's security during the Cold War. To my knowledge, there is no overall history of these early classified endeavors like this one available in the "open literature." I recommend it to you.

—R. Cargill Hall
Emeritus Chief Historian
National Reconnaissance Office
Department of Defense

PREFACE AND ACKNOWLEDGMENTS

We found thousands of families huddled in the debris of buildings and in bunkers.
There was a critical shortage of food, and thin faced, half-dressed children approached,
not to beg but to sell their fathers' war medals or to trade them for something to eat.
Nixon was profoundly moved by the spirit of the children who would not beg.

—Lucius Clay on Congressman Richard Nixon's visit to Germany in 1947,
in Jean Edward Smith, *Lucius Clay: An American Life*

The first overt Cold War confrontation between the United States and the Soviet Union, the Berlin blockade in 1948, was surely not the beginning of the Cold War but rather a manifestation of long-simmering conflict between the West and the Soviet Union. As early as April 1945, before World War II came to its final end in Europe, Marshal Konstantin K. Rokossovski's Second Belorussian Front swept across the northern German plain, driving before it what remained of a once powerful German army. Rokossovski had encountered more German resistance crossing the Oder River than expected and was behind schedule. I was a ten-year-old boy at the time, fleeing with my mother Hedy and my little sister Ingrid with a German army unit, heading west. We survived dive bombers and strafing, artillery and rocket attacks, SS troops not willing to give up, attempting to block our way, Russian tanks, and the general mayhem of war. I had no idea where we were going, when to my great surprise, on a brilliant morning in late April 1945, we surrendered near Wismar to soldiers of the 82nd Airborne and the 7th Armored Divisions.

Where did the Americans come from? I later learned that American and British Intelligence had intercepted Russian communications revealing their intention to make a grab for Denmark. General Matthew B. Ridgeway's XVIII Corps cut the Russians off. "We moved at least 30 miles eastward of the line which originally had been set as the point where Allied and Russian forces would meet—and on Montgomery's orders I clung to that 'Wismar cushion,' so that it could be used for negotiating purposes.... We made contact with the Russians on the Baltic on the 2nd of May. I saw my first one, a Russian general, a day later." Ridgeway and one of his division commanders, General James M. Gavin, met with their counterpart on May 3. The Russian seemed displeased. The furtive attempt to grab Denmark had failed.[1]

As World War II in Europe ended, a new conflict between the two former allies had already begun. It would in time be called the Cold War, not so cold after all for many of us who participated in it. Its major way stations were the Berlin blockade (1948–1949), Korea (1950–1953), the Cuban Missile Crisis (October 1962), and Vietnam (1961–1974). The fall of the Berlin Wall in 1989 signaled the end of the Cold War, and the Soviet empire ceased to exist two years later.

In 1955, only four years after immigrating to the United States, I found myself an American airman at RAF Sculthorpe, England, assigned to an air base from which American and British airmen flew night reconnaissance over the Soviet Union. I knew nothing about it. I got out of the air force in 1958, went back to college, and in July 1960 was commissioned a second lieutenant in the United States Air Force. A dream come true. Soon thereafter, I entered flight training at bases in Texas and Mississippi. I ended up in a reconnaissance wing at Forbes Air Force Base near Topeka, Kansas, just in time for the Cuban Missile Crisis. There, I met up with men who had flown B-17 bombers in World War II, bombers that I had watched with great fascination as a child and survived when I lived in Berlin. I flew with men who in 1948 had flown their coal-laden C-54 transports to save Berlin, a city they had bombed only three years earlier. I was a young refugee boy then, living in a down-and-out camp near one of those airlift bases. The Berlin airlift flyers were the men who became central to my life. I wanted to be like them, and in time I was.

The super-secret world of reconnaissance that I suddenly found myself a part of was an eye-opener. It was a war of reconnaissance, a war of secret flights and overflights, that the American public knew little or nothing about. But out there, high above the Barents Sea, the Baltic Sea, the Sea of Japan, and the Sea of Okhotsk, places few would care to go, over international waters mind you, the Russian MiGs would confront us—and shoot down all too many of our aircraft. When we came home, we didn't talk to our wives about where we had gone, nor did we talk to other crews about the missions we had flown or the encounters we had survived. This book is all about the men who served our country in that secret war of reconnaissance, men who so readily put their lives on the line because their country asked them to, who maintained years and years of silence, asked no questions, knowing full well that their missions were all about the survival of the country we all love and had the privilege to serve.

After the Director of Central Intelligence (DCI) declassified the early USAF overflights images in 1996, an Early Cold War Overflights Symposium

Captain Wolfgang W. E. Samuel, US Air Force, 355th Tactical Fighter Wing, Takhli Royal Thai Air Force Base, Thailand, 1968.

was held at the headquarters of the Defense Intelligence Agency (DIA) in Washington, DC, on February 22–23, 2001, where pilots and aircrews, for the first time in their lives, had the opportunity to talk freely about missions they had flown so long ago, and to hear what others had done. None of them, including myself, were aware of the scope of the Cold War overflights program, nor did we know at the time who planned or authorized the missions we flew. I participated in the symposium, and it was a privilege and an honor to listen to these men who had come together to share their experiences. General Andrew J. Goodpaster, who for years worked with President Eisenhower on overflight issues, remarked at the symposium as he ended his presentation: "I wish to recognize the incredible courage and bravery of a handful of

Americans and Britons who were prepared to do these intelligence collection jobs, who put their lives, their very existence, on the line under the utmost security and secrecy. For reasons of national security, no public credit could be given to them for the job they did. But let me say now it has been a privilege to serve with you."[2] And so it was for me a privilege to serve my country in the company of men of skill and courage, and to be part of the occasion that for the first time revealed the full scope of their accomplishments.

All of the stories in this book are based on personal interviews or presentations made by the men who flew reconnaissance missions, including numerous overflights of the Soviet Union, during the early Cold War years. I personally interviewed Sam Myers, Hal Austin, Hack Mixson, John Crampton, Charles Phillips, Francis Martin, Arthur Lidard, Joe Gyulavics, George Back, Hank Dubuy, Joel Lutkenhouse, Bob Rogers, David Holland, Frank Robison, and Joe Grace, who flew F/RF-86, RB-45C, RB-47E, RB-47H, RB-66B, or P2V-7 aircraft. Roger Rhodarmer, Jerry Depew, Stacey Naftel, Mele Vojvodich, Samuel Dickens, Joseph Guthrie, Robert Hines, LaVerne Griffin, Louis Picciano, Robert Morrison, Cecil Rigsby, Gerald Cooke, Roy Kaden, Donald Hillman, Lloyd Fields, George Brown, Barton Barrett, and Richard Koch, who flew RB-17, RB-26, RB-47B/E/H, RB-50, RF-80, RF-86, RF-100, and the various versions of the RB-57, were participants in the 2001 Early Cold War Overflights Symposium.

I would like to note that I made only minor editorial changes to interviews and presentations in the interest of readability, brevity, and clarity, including providing brief explanations of unfamiliar terms and jargon and adding other supplementary information. In no case did I alter the essence of any story. The photographs in this book came from my own collection, from the collections of those interviewed, from fellow flyers in the 55th Strategic Reconnaissance Wing, and in large part from some of our great aviation historians such as Dr. Richard Hallion and R. Cargill Hall. Dr. Hallion, a former NASA and USAF historian, held the General Harold Keith Johnson Chair of Military History at the Army War College and served as senior adviser on aerospace technology and policy for the secretary of the air force. Cargill Hall served as deputy command historian at Headquarters Military Airlift Command, followed by a tour of duty as historian at Headquarters Strategic Air Command, then as chief historian at the Jet Propulsion Laboratory, and finally as chief historian at the National Reconnaissance Office. Both were kind enough to review the manuscript for this book. I would also like to thank and express my appreciation to Brigadier General Regis Urschler, United States Air Force (Ret.), former commander of the 55th Strategic Reconnaissance Wing, and Al Stettner, a career Intelligence officer and current docent at the National Air and Space Museum, for reviewing the manuscript.

My personal praise for Cargill Hall cannot come close to doing him justice for all he has done—preserving and helping make public the story of the men who in great secrecy risked their lives to ensure that our senior leadership had the essential information on which to base decisions regarding force structure, deployments, and alliances. The 2001 Early Cold War Overflights Symposium was made possible by the contributions of many people in the Intelligence community, but it was the focused effort of Mr. Hall that made it all happen. The entire reconnaissance program conducted in the early years frowned on keeping records of any kind. So the symposium was critical to help reveal what happened before the memories of men were lost to the passage of time.

The Early Cold War Overflights Symposium was a difficult and indeed memorable undertaking led by R. Cargill Hall, then the Chief Historian of the National Reconnaissance Office. As noted in the stories to follow, it was frowned upon by those responsible for planning, approving, and executing overflights to keep records. There are no archives one can go to, no histories of participants or organizations that detail to any depth the decision-making process or the actual execution of the overflights. The missions were flown, and the participants were told never to talk about them to anyone—no pilot talk, no talk to family or friends, no talk to anyone—ever. In my conversations with Mr. Hall, he noted: "When I was organizing the symposium with the DIA History Office, I had no aviator roster to go by. SAC headquarters had destroyed whatever overflights records it had after the Francis Gary Powers shootdown in 1960. So it was a tedious task, mostly by word of mouth. One flyer would tell me the names of others, and I would use his name by way of introduction to others. I would explain to them that the Director of Central Intelligence had declassified the early Cold War overflights experience and that I was the National Reconnaissance Office historian, and we would like you to participate in . . . I remember calling a retired colonel in California and going through my introductory routine. When I finished, there was a pause before he replied, 'I don't know you and I don't discuss activities like that.' Click. End of call." In spite of all the difficulties encountered, the effort was rewarded by the attendance at the symposium of flyers of all the aircraft types flown in those very dangerous years.

On April 17, 1995, President Bill Clinton signed Executive Order number 12958, authorizing the review and declassification of US aerial imagery collected prior to January 1, 1976. After that review, the DCI responded on July 3, 1996, declassifying more than six million feet of film imagery in the National Airborne Archive including film taken by U-2, A-12, and SR-71 aircraft, and military aircraft from 1950 to December 31, 1975. The imagery is maintained, not indexed, at the National Archives Records Administration in College

Park, Maryland. Although the symposium proceedings, published by the National Reconnaissance Office in 2003, were available to the general public, their distribution was limited. I hope that this book remedies that situation and provides insight and understanding of the essential nature of our search for information about a closed society that had the capability to end life for our nation as we knew it.

—Wolfgang W. E. Samuel
Colonel, US Air Force (Ret.)
Fairfax Station, Virginia

SILENT
WARRIORS,
INCREDIBLE
COURAGE

WHEN PEACE CAME TO AMERICA (1945)

Nothing will contribute more to an understanding of the needs of future security
than a clear understanding of what has occurred in this war, the strategic
decisions, the reasons for them, and the operations by which they were executed.
—**George C. Marshall,** "General Marshall's Victory Report," 1945

War came to America in December 1941 in the form of four hundred Japanese aircraft launched from six aircraft carriers off the Hawaiian Islands, inflicting serious but not war-critical damage, which was soon repaired. That ill-chosen war was effectively terminated on August 9, 1945, when a single B-29 bomber, named *Bockscar*, of the 20th Air Force dropped on the city of Nagasaki the second of two atomic bombs dropped on Japan. Emperor Hirohito bowed his head to the inevitable, and the surrender of all Japanese forces was officially signed on September 2 onboard the battleship USS *Missouri* anchored in Tokyo Bay. Every major combatant of the Japanese fleet involved in the attack on Pearl Harbor on December 7, 1941, had been sunk. Japan's cities had been burned to ashes by the unrelenting firebombing of B-29 bombers of the 20th Air Force—and the drop of two atomic bombs marked the final act ending a war, the outcome of which was preordained. Adolf Hitler's "thousand-year Reich" had suffered a fate similar to that of the Empire of the Rising Sun a few weeks earlier, in May 1945. Its armies destroyed, its cities in ruins from relentless bombing by fleets of British and American bombers. The destruction was of such magnitude that rebuilding of Germany's cities was estimated to possibly take 50 years. In addition, Germany was diminished by the loss of territory east of the Oder and Neisse Rivers. If one of the aims of Hitler's regime was to expand the territory of the Reich, which it was, the outcome of the war had exactly the opposite effect. Neither Japan, nor a Germany divided into four occupation zones, were likely to have a military future for years to come.

In August 1945 it appeared to many Americans that the world was finally at peace, able to go ahead and rebuild itself. The most optimistic even thought that the rest of the world might just be ready for the ultimate human

OCCUPIED AREAS OF GERMANY

Only three zones of occupation were agreed to at the Yalta Conference in February 1945—the French Zone was carved out of the American and British Zones; the same approach was used to give the French a presence in occupied Berlin. The Russian position on the matter was that the French did not contribute to the defeat of Nazi Germany; therefore, they deserved none of the spoils of victory.

experience in government—democracy. Naïvely, this concept, that people of the world really are one and the same, and that all people wanted to be governed the way we governed ourselves, would lead America into future military conflicts, at this moment of victory totally unimaginable. General George

C. Marshall, in his "Victory Report to the Secretary of War" in 1945, wrote: "Never was the strength of the American democracy so evident nor has it ever been so clearly within our power to give definite guidance for our course into the future of the human race. And never, it seems to me, has it been so imperative that we give thorough and practical consideration to the development of means to provide a reasonable guarantee for future generations against the horrors and colossal waste of war. . . . If man does find the solution for world peace it will be the most revolutionary reversal of his record we have ever known. . . . Our diplomacy must be wise and it must be strong. Nature tends to abhor weakness. The principal of the survival of the fit is generally recognized. If our diplomacy is not backed by a sound security policy, it is, in my opinion, forecast to failure. We have tried since the birth of our nation to promote our love of peace by a display of weakness. This course has failed us utterly, cost us millions of lives and billions of treasure. . . . The world does not seriously regard the desires of the weak. Weakness presents too great a temptation to the strong, particularly to the bully who schemes for wealth and power. We must, if we are to realize the hopes we may now dare to have for lasting peace, enforce our will for peace with strength."[3]

General Marshall, one of our nation's greater statesmen, was to be greatly disappointed with the way things evolved in the postwar period. His plea for a "sound security policy," if at all remembered, was soon forgotten. The facts were that America at this moment in time was the undisputed military and economic superpower in the world, the sole possessor of the awesome and feared atomic bomb. With a weapon like that, who needs a standing army? Or so the reasoning went. The boys clamored to come home, to go on with their lives, and the nation's politicians saw nothing wrong with that. With over sixteen million uniformed men and women under arms at the height of the war, starting soon after August 1945, America's armed forces shrank to less than two million. The US Navy's battle fleet of 6,768 ships declined to a mere 634.[4] Disarmament was the very first postwar task politicians threw themselves into with a vigor difficult to imagine unless you were there to see it happen for yourself. Colonel Marion "Hack" Mixson, one of my future wing commanders, vividly remembered his own experience in those halcyon postwar days. Born in 1918, a South Carolina boy, he, like so many youngsters of his generation, always wanted to fly. Hack soloed in a little 45-horsepower Aeronca in 1939 at age twenty-one. "What a thrill it was to soar above Charleston on my very own," he recalled; "I'll never forget that first flight." By 1944, Hack Mixson found himself piloting a B-24 bomber out of Italy against targets in Germany, Austria, Hungary, and Czechoslovakia. Hack flew thirty-five combat missions, some so brutal, he wondered how he survived.

After war's end, Mixson remained in Italy for another year and recalls: "Many of those B-25, B-24, and B-17 bombers in Italy were destroyed. For

Lieutenant Colonel Marion "Hack" Mixson, second from right, with his navigator Henry Wilson, far left; copilot John Lightbedy, to his left; and Howard Kadow, bombardier, to his right, in front of their B-24 bomber in 1944, at Foggia Air Base, Italy.

a while I flew a brand-new B-25. German POWs took the armor out of it, stripped the paint, and polished the airplane to a high gloss. Although I had orders to turn the plane in to be destroyed, I kept stalling for about two months. Finally, I got a message that if I didn't turn in the plane I was to be court-martialed. I flew it down to the Pomigliano depot. My buddy flew down in a C-47 to pick me up. By the time we finished filing our clearance for our return trip, they had drained the gas out of that beautiful B-25, cut the engines off, cut holes in the crankcase and into the propeller blades. That airplane was completely smashed in about an hour."[5]

In Landsberg am Lech, in bucolic Bavaria, a former Luftwaffe airfield was filled with B-26 bombers of the 1st Tactical Air Force (Provisional). The planes were lined up wing tip to wing tip by the hundreds to be burned and turned into scrap metal by Germans who only weeks earlier had tried hard to shoot them down. Most of the 1st TAF's P-47 Thunderbolts were simply stripped of their instruments and destroyed, smashed, buried in place. John Hay, while stationed at Holzkirchen, Bavaria, in 1946, remembers removing radios and batteries from 186 brand-new B-17 bombers, never flown in combat, then placing one-and-a-half pound TNT charges in their cockpits and blowing them up.[6] The downsizing of the United States military establishment starting

Holzkirchen, Germany, 1946: 186 B-17 bombers destroyed without ever having flown a combat mission. Bavarian chicken coops sported B-17 bullet-resistant windows in their aluminum sheds constructed from the wings of those hapless B-17s.

in late 1945 fed on its own momentum and seemed headed to take the country back to where it was in the late 1930s—militarily weak. Other than for the mystique of the atomic bomb, there was in fact little combat capability left when the process finished. On August 7, 1945, two days before *Bockscar* dropped the second atomic bomb on Japan, the United States Strategic Air Forces in Europe (USSTAF) had the word "Strategic" removed from its name and became the United States Air Forces Europe (USAFE)—during the Cold War years, yet to come, I served for four years at Headquarters USAFE, still in Wiesbaden, the site selected for the headquarters by General Spaatz and his staff in 1945. The air power available to General "Tooey" Spaatz on August 7, 1945, was spread over 152 airbases and 226 supporting installations, manned by 450,000 airmen supporting a fleet of over 17,000 aircraft of all types.

Disarmament proceeded at a rapid pace after the surrender of the Japanese. The 12th Air Force inactivated on August 31, 1945; the 15th that September; and the famed 9th Air Force followed suit in December 1945. The 8th Air Force had been transferred to the Pacific region under the command of General Spaatz, who by this time had received his fourth star. At year's end, the US Air Force in Europe was down to 64,349 officers and men, and the number of airfields was down from 152 to 31 with a commensurate reduction of combat aircraft. The US Army in Europe followed a similar regimen and quickly lost its combat capability, turning into a police-type occupation force.[7]

General Henry H. Arnold, commanding general of the Army Air Forces, certainly understood that the overwhelming combat capability he had amassed during the war years consisted almost totally of dated equipment largely designed in the 1930s. As a matter of fact, he had a brigadier general assigned at Headquarters USSTAF/USAFE whose only job was to track and report the weekly total of military aircraft destroyed or transferred to the United States or its allies. "Possession of large stocks of war equipment at the end of a war affords a serious temptation to continue to use that equipment in training peace time forces.

"We must depend on scientific and technological advances requiring us to replace about one-fourth of our equipment each year. . . . The Weapons of today are the museum pieces of tomorrow. So, tomorrow, the B-29, the Super-fortress of today, will belong in the Smithsonian Institution, with the Wright and Lindbergh planes, its place on the line to be taken by bombers that will carry 50 tons of bombs, planes with jet or rocket motors capable of flying around the world at supersonic speeds."

General Arnold was not displeased with seeing yesterday's air power vanish—hoping to replace it with air power of the future, the jet-powered fighter and bomber, "manless or remote controlled radar or television assisted precision military rockets." Looking to the future, as early as 1944, General Arnold had tasked his technical adviser, the Director of the Army Air Forces Scientific Advisory Group, Dr. Theodore von Karman of the California Institute of Technology, "to investigate all the possibilities and desirabilities for postwar and future war's development as respects the AAF." Dr. von Karman, a refugee from Hitler's Germany, didn't waste time, assembled a group of the finest scientists available, including many immigrants like himself, and by December 1945 presented General Arnold with his findings and recommendations in the form of a concise and simply worded study titled "Toward New Horizons: Science, the Key to Air Supremacy."

The study, in the simplest of terms imaginable, yet visionary, called for the achievement of "supersonic flight, pilotless aircraft, all-weather flying, perfected navigation and communication, remote-controlled and automatic fighter and bomber forces, and aerial transportation of entire armies. . . . A global strategy for the application of novel equipment and methods, especially pilotless aircraft, should be studied and worked out. . . . As new equipment becomes available, pilotless aircraft units should be formed and personnel systematically trained for operation of the new devices. . . . The men in charge of the future Air Forces should always remember that problems never have final or universal solutions."[8]

Arnold's and von Karman's vision for the future of a United States Air Force using supersonic aircraft, precision-guided munitions, even fleets of unmanned aircraft, was not to go unopposed. Of all people, Dr. Vannevar Bush, vice president and dean of engineering at the prestigious Massachusetts Institute of Technology, MIT, in Cambridge, Massachusetts, appointed by President Franklin Roosevelt in 1940 as chairman of the National Defense Research Committee, later renamed the Office of Scientific Research and Development, was charged to "coordinate, supervise and conduct scientific research on the problems underlying the development, production, and use of mechanisms and devices of warfare, except scientific research on the problems of flight." That latter caveat exempting "research on the problems of flight" in effect set it aside to be pursued by Dr. von Karman and General Arnold, which rankled Bush. Bush had a low opinion not only of foreign scientists, meaning Dr. von Karman and the group of scientists he had assembled, but especially of military officers—meaning General Arnold and his attempts to define the requirements for a future air force. As an example, in his book *Modern Arms and Free Men*, Bush scoffed at the development of "guided missiles spanning thousands of miles and precisely hitting chosen targets. The question is particularly pertinent," he asserted, "because some eminent military men," meaning Arnold, Spaatz, and others, "exhilarated perhaps by a short immersion in matters scientific, have publicly asserted that there are. We even have the exposition of missiles fired so fast that they leave the earth and proceed about it indefinitely as satellites, like the moon, for some vaguely specified military purposes. All sorts of prognostications of doom have been pulled from the Pandora's box of science, often by those whose scientific qualifications are a bit limited."[9] Quite a mouthful for a scientist of the stature of Dr. Vannevar Bush, and a warning to proceed with caution to those doing "research on the problems of flight," because Bush had significant influence in high places. However, what was really going to inhibit the prognostications of von Karman and Arnold more than Bush and his allies was the big bully on the block—the atomic bomb. The Manhattan Project, coincidentally, fell under Bush's purview—but no one knew, neither Bush nor Arnold nor von Karman, how instrumental the bomb was going to be in shaping the future air force.

As early as 1942, General Arnold had attempted to bring jet aircraft into the Army Air Forces' inventory. The Bell XP-59 flew for the first time in 1942, as did the German Me 262. The Bell Aircomet was anything but a comet, and proved to be a major disappointment. Nathan "Rosie" Rosengarten, a Wright Field flight test engineer, in his evaluation of the Aircomet, noted: "It could hardly be considered a combat airplane—at best it was a good safe airplane, a training vehicle for indoctrinating pilots into the jet age."[10] That's not what

Only fifty P-59 Aircomets were built before the project was abandoned. Colonel Kenneth Chilstrom, then a major and chief of fighter test operations at Wright Field, can claim the honor of crashing the first American jet, a YP-59, on February 16, 1945.

General Arnold had in mind when he turned to the Bell Aircraft Company to build him a combat jet to take on the German Me 262 jet fighter.

Arnold turned to Clarence "Kelly" Johnson at Lockheed Aircraft Corporation, the innovative designer of the twin-tailed P-38 fighter. A contract was signed for one XP-80 jet fighter in June 1943 to be delivered in 180 days for testing at Muroc Field, later renamed Edwards Air Force Base, in the desert of southern California. That first XP-80 arrived at Muroc on November 13, 1943, 150 days after the contract was signed. Some additional YP-80 test aircraft were procured, and soon thereafter the Army Air Forces ordered five hundred P-80s, betting on the come, eventually increasing the contract to one thousand. In July 1944, a German Me 262 made its combat debut, attacking an RAF Mosquito, and two Me 163 rocket planes attacked a formation of P-51 fighters. The United States still didn't have anything on the tarmac to match the Germans, yet things appeared to be looking up—but this was about as good as it was going to get. In October 1944, an RP-80 crashed, killing its test pilot. To reassure the combat crews in Europe that, yes, we too are developing a jet-powered fighter aircraft, the decision was made to send four YP-80As to Europe for demonstration flights. In January 1945, one of the four exploded in flight, killing Major Fred Borsodi, a Wright Field test pilot. A second P-80 was diverted for engine testing at a British facility. The remaining two flew several demonstration flights with the 15th Air Force in Italy. That was it. As the war in Europe ended on VE Day in May 1945, there were no American jet fighter squadrons sitting on airfields ready for combat. The P-80 continued to have more than its share of setbacks. In July 1945, a production P-80A crashed

A T-33 trainer version of the P-80 on display at the National Air and Space Museum in Chantilly, Virginia.

on takeoff, killing the pilot. That August, a YP-80A exploded, killing its pilot. And on August 6, 1945, Major Richard Bong, America's top ace and Medal of Honor holder, died in a P-80, again on takeoff. The public and most anyone else knew very little about German or American jet programs—but Bong's death resulted in an outcry that jet flying was much too dangerous and should be stopped. It took all the imagination of General Arnold to keep the P-80 program alive and continue funding for the Army Air Forces to have a chance to enter the jet age. In time, the P-80 made a limited contribution during the Korean War of 1950–1953, but it is best remembered by generations of flyers as the T-33, the trainer version of the P-80, on which American flyers and our allies cut their teeth in the 1950s and 1960s.[11]

The P-59/P-80 experience, while World War II was still in progress, had General Arnold searching for solutions. With the help and guidance of his technical adviser, Dr. Theodore von Karman, General Arnold had his European air commander, Lieutenant General "Tooey" Spaatz, develop plans for the acquisition of advanced German technology as soon as the war came to a close—known as Operation Lusty. Under Operation Lusty, led by a capable and out-of-the-box thinker, Colonel Harold E. "Hal" Watson, later Major General Watson, the United States acquired all that was wanted and tasked by the Wright Field scientific establishment. Aside from several Liberty ships stuffed with everything from advanced wind tunnels to jet and rocket planes, and a thousand tons of technical papers, Watson had thirty-eight former enemy

HMS *Reaper* in Cherbourg harbor, France, July 1945, loaded with German aircraft. Cocooned Me 262s in the foreground.

aircraft loaded onto a British aircraft carrier, HMS *Reaper*, which arrived in Newark, New Jersey, on July 31, 1945. Among the German aircraft were ten Me 262 jet fighters, three He 219 night fighters, two Dornier 335 push-pull fighters, four Arado 234 jet reconnaissance bombers, one Dh 243 Doblhoff jet helicopter, nine FW 190 fighters, and others.[12] Watson was appalled by how far behind the United States was in aviation technology compared with the Germans and vowed that he would do whatever it took to ensure this is never going to happen again. The result was the establishment of the National Air Technical Intelligence Center (NATIC), of which he was the first commander, at Wright-Patterson Air Force Base in Dayton, Ohio, later renamed the Foreign Technology Division (FTD), which I had the privilege to serve in. The former FTD is currently known as the National Air and Space Intelligence Center (NASIC). Name changes for the center have been prolific in the past, and will probably continue to occur in the future—to what purpose I do not know.

Probably more important than the actual delivery of German jet-powered aircraft was a meeting arranged by Colonel Donald Putt, later Lieutenant General Putt, between Dr. von Karman and Germany's Dr. Adolf Busemann. Don Putt, like Hal Watson, was assigned to the Exploitation Division at Headquarters USSTAF, the later USAFE. It was Putt who, in April 1945, would lead a group of Exploitation Division personnel to a totally unknown German research laboratory just captured by General George Patton's troops. Hurrying to get there before the British, because the Hermann Goering Aeronautical Research Center at Völkenrode, near Braunschweig, was located in what would become the British Zone of Occupation—and the Brits would have every right for its exploitation, not the Americans. The center's facilities, located in a forest, were so expertly camouflaged that from the air it appeared to be no more than an ordinary farmstead. After surveying the facility and talking to some of its senior research staff, such as Professor Dr. Busemann, an expert in wind tunnel testing and jet aircraft design, Colonel Putt decided this was something Dr. von Karman needed to get involved in. Putt was a former student of Dr. von Karman's in 1938 at Caltech, where he studied to obtain his master's degree in aeronautical engineering. Putt was sent to Caltech after recovering from injuries suffered in an aircraft accident in 1935. He was the copilot on a flight crew testing the new X-299, which would become the B-17 bomber of World War II. The aircraft, rather than using wooden shapes to lock the aircraft's flight controls when parked, such as the rudder, flaps, ailerons, and elevators, used a mechanical locking device. The crew, in a hurry, this was before checklists, forgot to unlock the flight controls, and the aircraft on its takeoff roll went into a vertical climb, did a wing-over, and crashed, killing many of its crew. Putt survived with serious injuries and after recovering found himself studying under Dr. von Karman at the California Institute of Technology.[13]

Dr. von Karman was leading a group of scientists through varied German research establishments when he received an urgent call from Colonel Donald Putt, his former student, to come to Völkenrode immediately. "Just before I went overseas in 1944," Putt recalled, "I was running a jet bomber competition at Wright Field in Dayton, Ohio. It included the B-45, B-46, B-47 and B-48. All were straight wing aircraft, very conventional looking." At Völkenrode, Putt's ATI (Air Technical Intelligence) team found wind tunnel models with swept-back wings. Busemann and von Karman knew each other well from pre-Hitler days when both worked at the same research laboratory in Trier. Now they were to meet again. Also present at this crucial meeting was George Schairer, the chief design engineer of the Boeing Aircraft Corporation. According to Putt, Busemann and von Karman met like two "long-lost buddies." Their greetings were mutually cordial. "Busemann," von Karman asked as the meeting progressed, "why the swept wings?" Busemann explained: "By sweeping the wings you fooled the air into thinking that it was not going as fast as it really was, or not so fast as the airplane itself was moving through the atmosphere, and therefore, you delayed the onset of compressibility drag. When you get close to the speed of sound, drag just takes off and goes up like that [moving his hand up vertically], but by sweeping the wing back and fooling the molecules of air, they don't think they are going so fast, and you delay that great rise of the drag curve."

Professor Dr. Adolf Busemann pointing at the 35-degree wing sweep of the F-86 fighter.

This was a revolutionary concept, at a time when many scientists still believed that what they had dubbed the sound barrier could not be penetrated by aircraft. Colonel Watson, while getting his master's degree in aeronautical engineering at Ann Arbor, Michigan, in 1940, wrote his thesis on the very subject: "Why Man Will Never Be Able to Fly Faster than the Speed of Sound." George Schairer listened intently to the conversation between Busemann and von Karman, two of the world's leading scientists in matters aeronautical, and immediately after the meeting wired his company to hold up on the design that was to be the B-47 bomber until he got home.[14]

The B-47 bomber took the US Air Force into the jet age, and it became the design baseline for the 707 airliner, which led to the KC-135 jet tanker and to subsequent Boeing Company commercial aircraft designs. The B-47 put Boeing on the road to becoming one of the world's premier military and commercial aircraft companies. Dr. von Karman wrote to General Arnold that "probably 75 to 90 percent of the technical aeronautical information in Germany was available at this establishment and that information on research and development which had not previously been investigated in the United

A B-45A bomber of the 47th Bomb Wing on the flight line at RAF Sculthorpe in County Norfolk, England, during an open house in 1954. Note the glass nose of the aircraft; the reconnaissance version had a solid nose.

States would require approximately two years to accomplish in the United States with the facilities available there." Dr. von Karman further noted that "the information on jet engine development available at this establishment would expedite United States development by approximately six to nine months." This was important information for an Army Air Forces chief who was struggling with the introduction of America's first jet fighter, the P-80.[15]

As a result of the Busemann–von Karman meeting, the B-47 had swept-back wings and podded engines hung beneath its wings, like the Me 262. Hanging the engines below the wings provided easy access, unlike engines built into an aircraft's wing. Other aircraft manufacturers soon followed suit, and the F-86 fighter incorporated not only the 35-degree wing sweep but leading edge slats as well, and other innovative features gathered from German scientific data were incorporated into its design. Plans for the production of America's first jet bomber, the B-45, were ongoing, and the decision was made to go ahead with a limited production run of 140 aircraft, 33 of them built as RB-45C reconnaissance aircraft. More than 2,000 B-47 and RB-47 aircraft were built to replace the limited number of B-45 jet bombers and dated, conventionally powered aircraft such as the B-29, B-50, and B-36. The RB-45C would fly some of the most daring reconnaissance missions of the Cold War era, until it was replaced by the RB-47E/H reconnaissance aircraft.

THE PEACE THAT WOULDN'T TAKE (1947)

I think the Russians felt we were very foolish to demobilize as fast as we did. I don't
think we would have had a Cold War if we'd kept a strong army in Europe in 1945.
—**Lucius Clay,** in Jean Edward Smith, *Lucius Clay: An American Life*

The partition of Germany into four occupation zones soon revealed that the
western border of the Russian zone of occupation did not welcome trespass-
ers; and the same lack of Russian cooperation became evident in the equally
divided city of Berlin. As early as March 5, 1946, former prime minister Winston Churchill, in a presentation at Westminster College in Fulton, Missouri,
said: "From Stettin in the Baltic to Trieste in the Adriatic, an Iron Curtain
has descended across the continent. Behind that line lie all the capitals of the
ancient states of Central and Eastern Europe. Warsaw, Berlin, Prague, Vienna,
Budapest . . . all these famous cities and the populations around them lie in
what I must call the Soviet sphere, and all are subject . . . not only to Soviet influence but to a very high and in some cases increasing measure of control from
Moscow." If there is such a thing as a specific event or occurrence to mark the
beginning of the Cold War, this might be it—or maybe not. Certainly it wasn't
recognized as such at the time. On August 9, 1946, a European Air Transport
Service C-47 on the Vienna–Udine, Italy, run strayed into Yugoslav airspace
and was fired on and forced down by Yugoslav fighters. Ten days later, another
C-47 was shot down in the same area. From then onward, USAFE F-9/RB-
17s, capable of defending themselves against attackers, flew the endangered
route.[16] A Communist-inspired insurrection in Greece soon followed, making
Western statesmen uneasy. President Harry Truman, supported by a remarkably capable team of men including Dean Acheson, Clark Clifford, George
Kennan, and General George Marshall, put in place a proactive foreign policy
to thwart Communist expansion. The Strategic Air Command (SAC), established on March 21, 1946, as one of three major combat commands of the
Army Air Forces, initiated a series of deployments with B-29 bombers to
Giebelstadt and Fürstenfeldbruck Air Bases in Germany—the same aircraft

type that in 1945 had bombed Japan into submission dropping two atomic bombs. A hint to the Soviet Union and its aggressive tactics in Europe.

The Truman Doctrine was enunciated as a direct response to Russian pressure on Greece and Turkey. And what eventually became known as the Marshall Plan was set in motion in June 1947, when Secretary of State George Marshall outlined a European recovery plan in a speech at Harvard University. In the meantime, USAFE, in support of the president's commitment to Greece and Turkey, flew AT-6 and C-47 aircraft to Greece; and President Truman and the Congress authorized $400 million in aid to Greece and Turkey. Greece did not turn Communist. However, the Soviet Union kept pushing in other vulnerable places, and in February 1948, in a communist-orchestrated coup, Czechoslovakia was added to the growing list of Soviet satellites. Berlin was to be next, or such was the Russian plan.

On June 1, 1948, Russian troops stopped rail traffic between Berlin and the West for two days. On June 12, they closed a highway bridge "for repairs," and on June 24 the Soviet Union imposed a full blockade of Berlin. There was no doubt now that this event was the beginning of a long-term and dangerous confrontation between the West and the Soviet Union. The former World War II ally, who unlike the West had largely maintained its troop levels beyond what was reasonable for national defense, was now using its military advantage to exploit Western military weakness. The options for the Western Allies were indeed limited. Recalled then Lieutenant General Curtis E. LeMay, the Commander in Chief, CinC, of the United States Air Forces in Europe, USAFE: "When they clamped down on all surface traffic and transportation, we in the occupation needed suddenly to consider something beyond the demolition and housekeeping duties which had concerned us during previous months. It looked like we might have to fight at any moment, and we weren't self-assured about what we had to fight with. . . . At a cursory glance it looked like USAFE would be stupid to get mixed up in anything bigger than a cat-fight at a pet show. We had one fighter group and some transports, and some radar people, and that was about the story."[17]

In fact, in June 1948 General LeMay's fighter group consisted of ninety aging P-47s. The Allied option to go to war over Berlin in reality was not an option at all, although discussed by some. What was agreed to between American and British military officers, and supported by British Foreign Secretary Ernest Bevin and President Truman, was to attempt to supply the city of Berlin by air. An audacious undertaking—never successfully done before, and by many detractors deemed a failure in the making. That August, the 36th Fighter Bomber Wing activated at Neubiberg Air Base with a complement of seventy-five F-80 jet fighters, and SAC moved two B-29 groups to bases in England. These aircraft had not had the Silverplate modification and were not

A B-29 of the 28th Bomb Group on final approach to Giebelstadt Air Base in the American Zone of Germany, 1946.

nuclear capable, a fact not known to the Russians. The Berlin airlift proved to have been the right choice and was a stunning success. It also served to bring together America and its allies, forming in August 1949 the North Atlantic Treaty Organization, NATO. Peace, however, was not in the cards for America without the military strength that a farsighted General George C. Marshall had called for in his 1945 "Victory Report to the Secretary of War": "Weakness presents too great a temptation to the strong, particularly to the bully who schemes for wealth and power." Joseph Stalin had just proven this point.

By 1949, America's senior military and political leaders no longer had any doubt that the Soviet Union represented a major threat to the United States and our allies. To make matters worse, that September a US reconnaissance plane off the Kamchatka Peninsula picked up signs of aerial radioactivity. The Russians had exploded an atomic device, and the United States could reasonably assume to be threatened by atom-bomb-carrying Russian aircraft. In Asia, developments were equally ominous. Chinese Communist forces appeared on the verge of completing their conquest of mainland China. Although the United States responded to these concerns and had created NATO as a defensive alliance to thwart further Russian expansion in Europe, American military strength had not grown commensurate with the threat in either Europe

US Air Force C-54 aircraft at RAF Fassberg, Germany, in 1949, flying coal to the city of Berlin. Nearby Celle Air Base C-54s also flew coal to Berlin; food flights were principally flown out of Rhein-Main and nearby Wiesbaden Air Bases, near Frankfurt.

or Asia. Granted, the air force was reorganizing the Strategic Air Command under the driving leadership of General Curtis E. LeMay, but even LeMay had to make do with aging B-29 bombers. The air force of the future was evolving very slowly. At a time of military weakness and political uncertainty, the United States needed accurate and verifiable information about the military and nuclear posture of the Soviet Union and its satellites. While a foreigner could easily travel throughout the United States to view military installations and purchase any number of publications regarding the location, strengths, and weaknesses of the US Army, Navy, and Air Force, no equivalent access was available in the Soviet Union. The Soviet Union remained a closed society. The only practical option at the time, other than human intelligence, with its many shortcomings, was aerial reconnaissance.

The Strategic Air Command, created in 1946, wasn't going anywhere under the leadership of General George C. Kenney, with a rather motley group of dated aircraft assigned. As far as reconnaissance was concerned, the command in 1946 had some F-2s, Beech C-45s assigned (F during this period stood for photo; P stood for pursuit or fighter—all that changed in September 1947 when the United States Air Force became an independent service), and a squadron of F-13s/RB-29s. By 1947, a second reconnaissance group, the 55th, was added, equipped with F-9s/RB-17s and F-2s, all of which were photo reconnaissance aircraft. No significant reconnaissance operations were flown, other than the mapping of Greenland and surveying an Iceland-to-Alaska air route.[18] SAC, in general, was a collection of dated aircraft, and its crews were poorly trained. That was to change dramatically with the assignment of Lieu-tenant General Curtis E. LeMay on October 19, 1948. The Berlin airlift was just beginning when LeMay left USAFE and assumed command of SAC. He took over a mixed bag of crews and aircraft who, in his opinion, were totally incom-petent to execute their assigned mission, that is: to conduct long-range offen-sive operations worldwide, and to conduct maximum-range reconnaissance over land and water.[19] Soon after his arrival, he ran a maximum simulated bombing effort against Wright-Patterson Air Force Base near Dayton, Ohio, with the small force of B-29 aircraft then at his disposal. He wanted to see how bad it really was. "Our crews were not accustomed to flying at altitude," he wrote in his biography. "Neither were the airplanes. Most of the pressuriza-tion wouldn't work, and the oxygen wouldn't work. Nobody seemed to know what life was like upstairs [above 15,000 feet]. . . . Not one airplane finished that mission as briefed. Not one." Not only that, but during an inspection of a SAC mess, LeMay found low quality even there."[20] By the time LeMay relin-quished command, in 1957, to his personally trained and chosen successor, General Thomas S. Power, SAC was as deadly as a cat at a mousehole, an air force within an air force, an envy of those not part of it, and an intimidating presence to the Soviet Union and its aging leaders.

Photo and electronic reconnaissance, the latter initially at a fairly rudimen-tary level, received increased interest with the start of the Berlin airlift—and certainly after the Russians became an atomic power in 1949. The playing field had changed, and the Soviet Union was no longer a hermit kingdom but a power that potentially could threaten the very existence of the United States. Both the US Air Force and the US Navy began flying peripheral recon-naissance missions against the Soviet Union and Communist China. For the Strategic Air Command to be effective, it had to know what the opposition's combat capability was, where it was located, how it trained—anything and everything that defined the potential enemy was of interest. There was very little reliable intelligence on hand, and so began the peripheral reconnaissance effort by the US Air Force and Navy. These border flights, of which I person-ally flew over one hundred in RB-47H electronic reconnaissance aircraft in later years, were referred to as PARPRO missions—Peacetime Aerial Recon-naissance Program. Such missions were flown under serious restrictions pro-hibiting overflights of Russian territory, although actual navigation errors did occur under difficult meteorological conditions, remembering that navigation aids for this sort of activity were nonexistent. Even the best navigator at times had to fall back on the most rudimentary form of navigation—dead reckon-ing. In today's sophisticated electronic environment, with satellites positioned around the globe providing GPS directions to anyone able to buy a simple smartphone, it is difficult to imagine the rudimentary means then available to our aviators. PARPRO missions collected photographic and electronic intelligence to determine the location of Russian and Chinese forces and to assess their equipment's capabilities to the degree possible. Other missions specialized, as the Cold War progressed, on monitoring communications—verbal and electronic—along with nuclear tests and missile shots. Anything done by our adversary was monitored in one way or another. Ground stations, from Norway down to Turkey, provided a twenty-four-hour means of keeping tabs on our Russian "friends," but in many ways the reach of such stations was limited by geography. The airplane provided the high ground to look really deep into our adversary's backyard.

Cargill Hall, former chief historian at the National Reconnaissance Office, described the situation as it existed in the early years in an article for *Military History Quarterly*: "PARPRO missions collected electronic and photographic intelligence, but their intelligence coverage was limited to peripheral regions. Before long, commanders of the United States Air Force . . . sought permission to conduct direct Overflights of Soviet territory, especially those regions closest to Alaska. The Joint Chiefs of Staff, JCS, however, after consulting with the director of Central Intelligence, CIA, and the secretaries of defense and state, consistently denied these requests. Indeed, in 1948 . . . the Department of State restricted PARPRO missions approaching Soviet borders to standoff distances of no closer than forty miles. Overflights remained out of the question. In receipt of one request for such a mission from SAC headquarters in Omaha, Nebraska, in October 1950, the USAF director of intelligence, Major General Charles P. Cabell, replied that he would have to recommend against it. But, Cabell added, 'I am looking forward to a day when it becomes either more essential or less objectionable.'"[21] That day was close at hand.

On June 25, 1950, North Korean troops crossed the thirty-eighth parallel. In three major columns, with one headed for the South Korean capital, Seoul, they advanced rapidly with the aim of uniting Korea under the Communist banner. "The outbreak of that war came to me as a complete surprise, as it did to all our military men—from Seoul to Washington," wrote General Matthew B. Ridgeway in his memoir. The first military surprise had come at Pearl Harbor, less than ten years earlier—here we were again, SURPRISED by a military attack. Ridgeway continued: "Under the policy of retrenchment forced upon us by Secretary [of Defense] Louis Johnson, we had reduced the infantry battalions in the regiments from three to two. The firing batteries in the artillery battalions had been reduced from three to two. All of the medium tanks had been taken out of both the infantry regiments and the divisions, and placed in storage—partly because they were not needed in police duty, but mainly because, when we ran them on the roads of Japan, they broke the bridges down. We were, in short, in a state of shameful unreadiness when the Korean

The RAF Special Duty Flight in front of an anglicized RB-45C reconnaissance aircraft at RAF Sculthorpe, England. Colonel Marion "Hack" Mixson, the senior USAF coordinator for the planned overflights project, is standing number six from the right. Squadron Leader Crampton, the RAF senior project officer, is standing to his left.

War broke out, and there was absolutely no excuse for it. . . . The state of our Army in Japan at the outbreak of the Korean War was inexcusable."[22]

By December 1950, with the American army now positioned in North Korea, and with the possibility of a Soviet attack in western Europe a distinct possibility, President Truman approved the concept of selected overflights of the Soviet Union. In other words, overflights of "denied" territory in peacetime became national policy, a policy driven by the ongoing war in Korea, which at the time was defined as a "police action," not really a war. President Dwight Eisenhower in 1954 formalized the effort and its continuation by establishing the super-secret SENSINT (Sensitive Intelligence) program. Every overflight mission required approval at the presidential level.

In December 1950, after the Chinese Communists entered the Korean War, meetings took place between President Truman and senior British political leaders—Prime Minister Clement Attlee and Foreign Secretary Ernest Bevin—and an agreement emerged to plan for and, possibly, jointly execute overflights of the western Soviet Union. In the spring of 1951, the Royal Air Force, RAF, formed a highly secret "Special Duty Flight" of three aircrews to fly American RB-45C reconnaissance aircraft over the western Soviet Union. All flights were to be night missions with the objective of obtaining radar photography of potential targets. Additionally, three RB-45C aircraft were deployed to Yokota Air Base near Tokyo to fly photographic reconnaissance against targets in North Korea, Communist China, and Soviet territory adjacent to the Sea of Japan. And, of course, PARPRO missions were flown in both Europe and the Pacific region using older and more vulnerable RB-29 and RB-50 aircraft assigned to the Strategic Air Command.

The Russians responded quickly to the increased level of American reconnaissance flights, shooting down an older PB4Y-2 US Navy reconnaissance aircraft over the Baltic Sea, flying over international waters near Latvia, with the loss of ten lives. The Cold War between the West and the Soviets had gone beyond rhetoric—and no one knew how it would end.

MORE SECRET THAN THE MANHATTAN PROJECT (1952)

Even though the story leaked out of the woodwork two or three years ago, I still
find it strange to talk and write about it. While it was happening it rivaled the
Manhattan Project for secrecy. In fact, I think, it outranked the Manhattan Project.
—**Squadron Leader John Crampton,** Royal Air Force,
in a letter to the Museum of the US Air Force

"I flew about thirty-five combat missions. Some missions counted double, giving me a total of fifty. Every week or so we would go up to Ploesti. Ploesti was
always bad—they had a lot of flak there. Munich was bad, as was anything
around Vienna. The Germans often put up a spotter plane to give their antiaircraft guns our altitude. That was World War II for me. Late in 1946 I returned
home to Charleston [South Carolina] and was discharged from the Army Air
Forces with the rank of lieutenant colonel. I was twenty-eight. In 1948 I got
a message from the air force offering me a regular commission, giving me
twenty-four hours to accept or decline. I accepted. I was assigned to the 343rd
Squadron of the 55th Reconnaissance Group at MacDill Air Force Base in
Tampa, Florida. They were flying B-17s, C-45s, and C-47s equipped for aerial
photography—a mapping outfit. Within weeks we transferred to Topeka, Kansas, and then in October 1949 the 55th Group disbanded. I was transferred
to the 91st Reconnaissance Group at Barksdale Air Force Base, Louisiana. In
December the 91st transitioned to the RB-45C, a four-jet reconnaissance aircraft, and I was given command of the 323rd Strategic Reconnaissance Squadron." That is how Marion "Hack" Mixson, the former B-24 bomber pilot, got
into the reconnaissance business—where he would remain for the rest of his
air force career, flying and directing the employment of RB-45, RB-47, and U-2
reconnaissance aircraft.

With the impetus of the Korean War, British prime minister Clement
Attlee and US president Harry Truman reached an agreement for a combined
reconnaissance program for flights over the western Soviet Union—a former
ally with a seemingly voracious appetite for further territorial acquisitions.

An RB-45C piloted by Colonel Howard S. Myers in 1952 making its takeoff from Yokota Air Base, Japan, a major reconnaissance base for the US Air Force throughout the Cold War years.

The only aircraft able to implement such a program was the RB-45C Tornado, the first four-engine jet of the newly created US Air Force. It, later joined by the RB-47 six-engine jet, would replace the much slower and more vulnerable RB-29, RB-50, and RB-36 reconnaissance aircraft. The RB-45C had a gross weight of around 111,000 pounds. Unlike the A-model bombers, the C-model was air-refuelable and in addition could carry 1,200-gallon wingtip fuel tanks. The range of the RB-45C was only limited by the endurance of its crew and the availability of aerial refueling tankers. The aircraft was powered by early-model J-47 General Electric engines with around 4,000 pounds of thrust each. By injecting a water/alcohol mixture on takeoff, engine power was increased by close to an additional 1,000 pounds of thrust per engine. The result was a very dirty engine that, after takeoff, left the runway shrouded in a black cloud of exhaust fumes. The J-47 engine, however, was the engine of choice at the time and powered the F-86 fighter as well as the B-47 bomber, still in development and undergoing testing. Colonel Howard S. Myers, who flew the RB-45C out of Yokota Air Base during the Korean War years, described it as "very nimble on the controls, much like a modern two-seat fighter. It had excellent visibility from its large canopy which, incidentally, could not be opened for ground operations. Both pilots had ejection seats; however, the navigator egressed through the left side entrance hatch which had spoiler deflectors just forward of the door.[23]

The RB-45Cs were equipped with a remarkable suite of high- and low-altitude cameras designed by the renowned Harvard astronomer James G. Baker. An incredibly capable airplane for the dangerous missions it was soon to fly

Airmen in the process of reattaching the nose cover for the low-altitude camera of the RB-45C. High-altitude cameras were located in the former bomb bay.

under both British and American colors. In late 1949, after flying the Berlin airlift, Colonel Harold R. "Hal" Austin, then a captain, was assigned to the 324th Reconnaissance Squadron of the 91st Strategic Reconnaissance Wing at Barksdale Air Force Base, Louisiana, equipped with the brand-new RB-45C. The other squadrons in the wing were the 322nd and the 323rd, the latter later commanded by Colonel "Hack" Mixson. Austin related: "Everyone of course had to see how high we could get in the airplane. We got it up to around 50,000 feet, it took forever. In the early days there wasn't anyone up at that altitude except for a few F-86s. So we flew cruise climb, that's what the contractor told us to do. We'd end up over Barksdale at 43,000 feet. Pull the power back and the aircraft hardly slowed down. We had no speed brakes, nothing to slow down the airplane. So you start pushing the nose of the airplane down and you are in a high speed buffet, and of course, once you start pulling it back up, you are in a high speed stall—or right between buffet or stall. Coffin corner. You couldn't get it out of the sky. The airplane had other problems, they never got fixed—we just learned how to manage them. When the Brits later flew the airplane they used to joke with us, 'Yank, we had to pull the power back over Archangel'sk to land at Sculthorpe.'" It was a very clean airplane, which, once airborne, didn't want to come down.[24]

Air force pilots fly whatever airplanes they are given. In a period of one year, the 91st SRW lost eight of its thirty-three RB-45C aircraft, 24 percent of the force. Each aircraft carried a crew of three. In most cases, all aboard the doomed aircraft perished. This was the sort of attrition flying experienced in combat. But this was routine peacetime flying in the early 1950s. Captain Harold Austin coped with day-to-day stress by focusing on those aspects of the airplane that gave him pleasure. And the RB-45C was a pleasure to fly when compared to most piston-engine aircraft. When the RB-45C was first put into service, in 1950, it was early in the jet age. If there had been time, the airplane would have been flight-tested sufficiently to discover more of its problems. But there was no time for testing. The Korean War had started. SAC needed a fast, high-altitude reconnaissance aircraft to complement the slow RB-29s. The RB-45C was that airplane.

"Soon after I checked out in the RB-45C at Barksdale, I was sent in May 1951 to RAF Sculthorpe," recalled Mixson during our interview. "Our presence at Sculthorpe consisted of the twelve aircraft of the 323rd SRS, which I commanded. By the time I arrived, RAF crews had already joined the squadron and flown one or two joint missions. By the end of July I returned to Barksdale accompanied by three RAF crews to continue their training. The three crews and a couple of extras were led by Squadron Leader John Crampton. Crampton was a tall, lean man with extensive World War II experience. His lead navigator, Flight Lieutenant Rex Sanders, had a similar combat background. Only those two were privy to the real purpose of their training at Barksdale. For the others, and anyone else asking questions, the story was that the RAF was considering acquiring a number of RB-45Cs on loan and wanted to conduct air refueling trials. B-29s had been provided to the Royal Air Force under a previous agreement, so this seemed like a reasonable explanation. Each RAF crew consisted of a pilot, a radar navigator, and a flight engineer. The flight engineer sat in the seat normally occupied by an American copilot. None of the RB-45Cs assigned to the Strategic Air Command carried defensive armament, so there were no gunners on the crew." The B-45A bombers assigned to the 47th Bombardment Wing, United States Air Forces in Europe, based at RAF Sculthorpe, did have 20mm tail guns installed and consequently carried a gunner. As far as SAC was concerned, the gun represented extra weight, which would diminish the range and altitude capability of the aircraft. So, they had them taken out and put in storage.

Mixson went on: "As for my role in this extremely sensitive and highly classified operation, I was in charge of the planned overflights of the Soviet Union as far as SAC was concerned. To a limited degree, I was involved in mission planning and accompanied Crampton and Sanders to Bomber Command Headquarters at High Wycombe, near London, to sit in on their

One of three RAF Special Duty Flight RB-45Cs refueling from an American KB-29 tanker over Denmark the night of April 17, 1952.

briefings. There, the routes were drawn up, and we met with Air Chief Marshal Sir Ralph Cochrane, vice chief of Air Staff, to discuss issues regarding the loan of the aircraft. I don't think SAC or anybody else on the American side had any real input into where the Brits were going. The RAF did the planning and provided the aircrews; the US Air Force provided the aircraft. We rotated the three 91st Wing squadrons into Sculthorpe. Because of my experience with the RAF crews and as the only one knowledgeable of the real purpose of their being there, I remained behind when my squadron rotated home. Meanwhile, plans were made for the first deep penetration of the Soviet Union. Four RB-45Cs at Sculthorpe were stripped of their US Air Force markings and repainted with Royal Air Force roundels on the fuselage and RAF colors on the tail fin. Aircraft numbers were omitted. On March 21, 1952, a night mission was flown into East Germany, east of Berlin, to find out how the Soviets would react to such an incursion. Their reaction wasn't sufficient to dissuade the planners from going ahead with the overflights planned for the night of April 17, 1952. In a letter to the Air Force Museum at Wright-Patterson AFB, Ohio, Squadron Leader Crampton recalled, 'Even though the story leaked out of the woodwork two or three years ago, I still find it strange to talk and write about it. While it was happening it rivaled the Manhattan Project for secrecy. While off base we weren't allowed to THINK about it. It was all well above top secret.'

"On the night of April 17, 1952, three RB-45Cs in RAF colors rose into the East Anglia sky and proceeded to their individual air refueling areas—one over the North Sea; another over Denmark. The three aircraft topped off their fuel tanks from US Air Force KB-29 refueling tankers and proceeded on their individual routes, flying at 35,000 feet in total radio silence into the heart of the Soviet Union. One plane photographed targets in the Baltic states of Estonia, Latvia, and Lithuania; Poland; and the former German province of East Prussia. The second aircraft flew across Belarus, as far as Orel. And the third, piloted by Squadron Leader Crampton, with Sanders as his radar navigator, flew the longest and most southern route, crossing the Ukraine and penetrating as far as Rostov on the Black Sea. Each route had frequent turning points to expose a maximum number of assigned targets."[25]

While Colonel "Hack" Mixson described this undertaking from the perspective of an American whose function was to serve as the SAC point man, provide the airplanes, and ensure the training of the British aircrews who would fly them into harm's way, his role was passive. John Crampton's perspective is that of a man who was to "do or die." "My experiences in overflights of denied territory grew from my World War II service with RAF Bomber Command," recalled Crampton at the 2001 Early Cold War Overflights Symposium in a lengthy memorandum. "I flew Whitley and Halifax bombers, and after the war I flew the first RAF jet fighters, the Meteor and the Vampire, for RAF Fighter Command. In 1952 I took command of the RAF's first Canberra unit, while also serving as the commander of the Special Duty Flight, flying the American RB-45C. In July 1951 I was the happy boss of 97 Squadron when the Commander in Chief of Bomber Command sent for me and said that I was to assume command of an RAF Special Duty Flight under conditions of utmost secrecy. This secret flight was to be equipped with the American RB-45C four-engine jet reconnaissance plane, and the RAF crews would proceed almost immediately to the United States to begin sixty days training in the aircraft. The other eight aircrews, as much in the dark as I was about our immediate future, joined me at RAF Sculthorpe for a flight on a SAC C-97 Stratofreighter for Barksdale AFB, Louisiana. There we spent ten days with a B-45 squadron, coming to grips with the airplane, before moving on to Langley AFB in Virginia for our indoctrination into the RB-45C reconnaissance version.

"On September 2 we flew to Lockbourne AFB, Columbus, Ohio, home of the 91st SRW, then operating the only three squadrons flying the RB-45C. In our second month of flight training at Lockbourne, one of my pilots made a very heavy landing one night. The airplane was written off but the crew was unhurt. The dramatic result of this incident was that Lockbourne's base commander along with myself and the pilot concerned were flown to Omaha, Headquarters of the Strategic Air Command, to be interviewed personally by

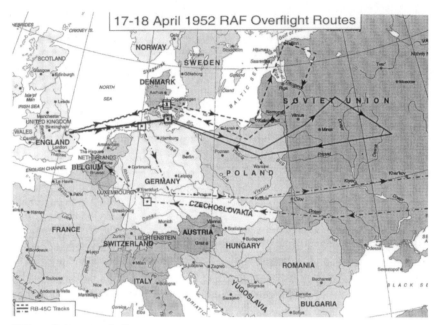

RAF overflight routes, April 17–18, 1952.

RAF Gloster Meteors, flown by Squadron Leader John Crampton of 12 Group at RAF Horsham St. Faith in 1948. Robin Olds at the time flew the Meteor with 11 Group at RAF Tangmere and became commander of Number 1 Squadron.

the Commander in Chief of SAC, General Curtis E. LeMay. The CinC SAC did not like people who destroyed his airplanes, and he left us in no doubt of that fact. His anger was directed mainly at the wretched RAF pilot, who departed for home shortly thereafter. I learned subsequently that he had been posted away from his unit, where he had a reputation as a 'Pranger'. He was immediately replaced by an RAF pilot who was on an exchange tour with a B-45 unit. We completed our training on December 1, 1951, and returned to RAF Sculthorpe. We still had no idea what was being planned for us. It was a tense time for us and our host, because having nine RAF aircrew flying with an elite US Air Force squadron raised eyebrows. The situation eased when Colonel Marion 'Hack' Mixson arrived in early 1952 as our liaison officer, fielding many of the difficult questions.

"In late February 1952 I was summoned to RAF Bomber Command headquarters at High Wycombe, with my navigator, Rex Sanders. This was the moment of truth, and I confess to some apprehension when the charts were unrolled to show three separate tracks from Sculthorpe to the Baltic states, the Moscow area, and central southern Russia. The deal was for the three routes to be flown simultaneously at night, departing Sculthorpe in rapid succession to rendezvous with tankers to the north of Denmark. After top-up we were to climb to the highest altitude the nighttime temperature would allow. Our targets were Soviet air bases and similar areas of strategic importance. We were to take 35mm photos of the aircraft's radar display. Timing was critical because our intelligence agencies would be listening for the Soviet air defense reaction to our deep penetration of their air space. And they had devised certain diversionary exercises to keep the Russians clear of our routes. We were of course to fly without navigational lights and maintain radio silence. It was a relief to finally know what was expected of us. However, I was concerned about my crews who were not volunteers. My fears were justified; on learning of the mission, one of the original pilots washed his hands of the whole affair and returned to his unit. This pilot was soon replaced by one posted to a B-45 squadron as an exchange officer.

"Before the date had been finalized, I took my crew on a gentle probe of the air defenses by flying over the Soviet Zone of Occupation of eastern Germany for an hour or so. Our Intelligence people monitored radio and radar activity. Nothing of consequence was noted and we judged ourselves ready for the big one. Four RB-45C aircraft had been allocated to us and were stripped of all USAF markings and repainted in RAF colors. With the approval of the Prime Minister presumably secured. [A very informal note marked 'Most Secret to the Secretary of State for Air, from Prime Minister Winston Churchill, dated 24 February 1952,' on Downing Street stationery stated, 'Operation JIUJITSU will be done by us if the Americans cannot be persuaded to do it. I am to be informed at least a week before it happens.' Signed.] Late in the afternoon of 17 April 1952, the three RAF RB-45Cs departed Sculthorpe and headed toward Denmark for refueling. All was going well, and Rex Sanders was getting good plots on his radar and feeding me with the courses to steer to the 126 air intelligence targets. We had the long-haul sortie across Russia. My most abiding memory of the route across the Ukraine is the apparent wilderness over which we were flying. There were neither lights on the ground nor any sign of human habitation, quite unlike the rest of Europe. We continued our gentle climb to 36,000 feet and covered our briefed route and photographed the assigned targets. It was all so quiet as to be distinctly eerie. We landed at Sculthorpe after ten hours and twenty minutes in the air. Farther to the north, the other two aircraft had covered their targets, making the operation a complete success. A few days later we flew our aircraft, still in RAF markings, to Lockbourne AFB, Ohio, and the following day we traveled to SAC Headquarters to again meet with General LeMay under much happier circumstances. He was most gracious in his compliments. It was all very heart warming. I assumed command of a Canberra squadron; the seat of the Canberra seemed very small after flying the RB-45C, not unlike driving a Ford Escort after having given up a stretch Cadillac."[26]

In October 1952, "Hack" Mixson was again alerted for a possible RAF mission planned for that December. "Four aircraft were repainted in RAF colors," Mixson recalled, "but at the last minute the mission was canceled. It was December 18, 1952, just before Christmas and everyone wanted to go home. I called Headquarters SAC in Omaha, and they decided to have us fly the airplanes home without first repainting them. While there were four airplanes, the RAF had not enough pilots to crew them. I flew one of them back with a British engineer in the back seat, and Rex Sanders as my radar navigator; Captain Naftel, one of my squadron pilots, flew another. It was a long and tiring ten-hour flight, since the engineer could not help me fly the airplane. We landed at Keflavik Air Base, Iceland, and Goose Bay, Labrador, to refuel. Snow was blowing at Lockbourne when we arrived. There were some surprised looks by the ground crew when we taxied in, resplendent in the colors of the Royal Air Force.

"In January 1953 SAC began transferring our RB-45Cs to the Tactical Air Command, and I left Lockbourne temporarily to get checked out in the new six-jet B-47. Between January and March 1953 I checked out in the B-47 at McCoy AFB, Orlando, Florida, along with Hal Austin and many others who once flew the RB-45C. Late in the year I received a message from General LeMay to come and see him immediately. Once I got to Offutt AFB, General LeMay instructed me to get down to Shaw AFB in South Carolina, pick up four RB-45Cs, take them to Wright-Patterson AFB in Ohio for modifications

RAF overflight routes, April 28–29, 1954. Flight routes courtesy of Rex Sanders.

to their radars, and then fly them over to RAF Sculthorpe. TAC crews flew the aircraft to Wright-Patterson. The modifications to their radars took about a month. The radar fix significantly improved the picture to very crisp and clear. When the aircraft arrived at Sculthorpe in early April 1954, Crampton and his bunch were there waiting for the airplanes. They were repainted in RAF colors, and we waited for a launch date on routes nearly identical to those flown in 1952. The date of the mission was April 28, 1954, ten days past the two-year anniversary of the 1952 flights."

"I was again summoned to High Wycombe and told that the Special Duty Flight was to be revived once again," wrote Squadron Leader Crampton. "By this time I had viewed the entire project as mine and would have been most upset if the job had been offered to anyone else. So, in March 1954, it was back to Sculthorpe. At this point, however, so many people knew we were up to something. Our flight line procedures under which crew chiefs could call stores or any other department using walkie-talkies to discuss our aircraft problems and movements in clear, unencoded language, was a worry. The least competent Soviet spy or sympathizer in the locality with a small radio tuned to the Americans' radio frequency could have written a manual on events at Sculthorpe. After a month of hard work the aircraft were again repainted; I again went to Bomber Command headquarters, accompanied by

Sanders, to collect the flight plans. The southern route this time around was much longer and required a different in-flight refueling location inbound as well as outbound."

Again, Squadron Leader Crampton took the longest, most southern route, extended to Volgograd, the former Stalingrad. In his letter, Crampton wrote of this mission, "The RB-45C squadrons who were our kind and courteous hosts during that very dicey period from which I have always thought we were very lucky indeed to survive, especially now that we know that the Ruskies knew we were to fly a second mission in 1954, and shot at us all 'round our route—and frightened the life out of me over Kiev when they finally got our height right and sent up a highway of predicted flak, a real highway, fantastic it was, but by the grace of God they got our speed wrong and chucked the stuff just ahead of us. Even the hot shards of shrapnel missed us. My reaction was instinctive. The throttles were opened wide and I hauled the airplane around on its starboard wing tip until the gyrocompass pointed west. I told Sanders to give me a heading for Fürstenfeldbruck, our refueling rendezvous over West Germany and emergency alternate. We had about 1,000 miles to go, and I urged Mac, flying as copilot, to keep his eyes peeled for fighters. Much later I learned that there were fighters about in the night sky, with orders to ram us on sight. Maximum speed was essential and I flew the RB-45C just on the right side of the buffet and it sort of trembled affectionately. The early firings had all misjudged our height, and thank God, the Kiev defenses misjudged our speed. They had chucked everything up a few hundred yards ahead of us. I thought for a moment of jettisoning our now empty 1,200-gallon wing tip tanks. Their absence might have added a few knots to our speed, but once found their maker's name and address would have revealed that they came from the United States and resulted in a major incident. Anyway, the thought of them bouncing down High Street of Kiev at two o'clock in the morning, disturbing the ladies and frightening the children, did not appeal. We were not flying over the USSR to do that. Moreover, based on past experience, General LeMay could be expected to object at my scattering expensive bits of his airplane over the Soviet Union. So I kept the tanks, and finally we met up with our tanker over West Germany. The refueling boom would not stay connected, so I decided to land at Fürstenfeldbruck and refuel the conventional way." Although all three RB-45Cs returned safely, it was a close thing. It was the last flight in the RB-45C for the RAF. Not for the RB-45C, though, it wasn't finished yet overflying the Soviet Union—this time under American colors and flown by American aircrews.[27]

Squadron Leader Crampton noted: "The story would not be complete without a tribute to the American and British leaders who set up the whole exercise, in particular the late Sir Winston S. Churchill, who agreed to RAF

RAF Special Duty Flight personnel, October 1952, RAF Sculthorpe, England. Left to right, Sergeant Donald W. Greenslade; Squadron Leader Gordon Cramer; Unknown; Squadron Leader Rex S. Sanders; Flight Commander John Crampton; Flight Lieutenant M. Furze; Unknown; Flight Lieutenant H. Currell; Flight Lieutenant G. Acklam.

participation, and to General Curtis E. LeMay, who was determined to get the best target information for his SAC aircrews. I found the operation a good example of real USAF/RAF get-togetherness. There was never anything quite like it." Squadron Leader Crampton died in June 2010. His daughter, Anne Turner, wrote to me about a moment in February of that year, when she asked her father, "'Given a choice of all the airplanes you've flown, which would you like to have up on the wall to look at?' In a faint voice my father replied, 'The RB-45C.' I am very proud of my Papa." And so are we, Anne, and of all the valorous men who kept our lands safe, at the risk of their lives.[28]

TO THE YALU RIVER AND BEYOND (1950)

The Korean imbroglio was a frustrating experience for the SAC strategist. The real and inviting targets lay in China, just across the Yalu River, industriously turning out war goods for the enemy without the slightest fear of reprisal.
—**Richard J. Hubler**, in Curtis E. LeMay, *Mission with LeMay*

On June 25, 1950, North Korean armed forces, including large numbers of T-34 tanks provided by the Soviet Union, launched a surprise attack against the South, aiming to unite the country under Communist rule. By that September, hastily assembled US Eighth Army elements were fighting for their lives at the southern end of the peninsula, in the Pusan Perimeter. American air power prevented a disaster, chewing up the attacking North Korean formations—and an audacious seaborne landing on September 15 at Inchon, near Seoul, by American forces under the command of General Douglas MacArthur drove the North Koreans back across the thirty-eighth parallel. That same September, a reconnaissance element of three RB-45C Tornado aircraft settled in at Yokota Air Base, Japan, to support the ongoing war effort. The detachment was commanded by Captain Charles E. McDonough. Another of the pilots assigned to the RB-45C detachment was Major Louis H. Carrington. Carrington and his crew, on July 29, 1952, would gain a measure of fame by flying an RB-45C aircraft 3,640 miles, in nine hours and fifty minutes, from Elmendorf Air Force Base, Alaska, to Yokota Air Base, Japan, made possible by two KB-29-supported in-flight refuelings. It was the first transpacific flight of that nature and was recognized as such by the award of the prestigious Mackay Trophy awarded by the National Aeronautic Association for the outstanding flight of the year.[29]

The RB-45Cs at Yokota were flown by aircrews provided by the Tactical Air Command in support of the Far East Air Forces (FEAF) combat operations against the North. Their objective would be to provide photographic intelligence not only of North Korea but also of China and adjacent Russia, who were supporting the North Korean war effort. China entered the Korean War

To the Yalu River and Beyond (1950)

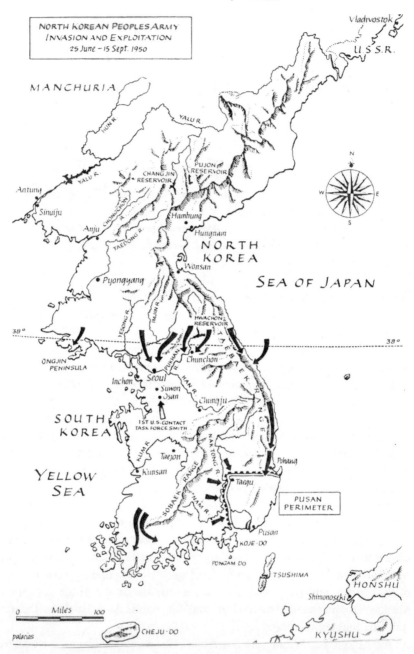

Military situation map, Korea, 1950. By November 1950, US forces had advanced deep into North Korea, when the PRC committed its armies to the conflict. Reconnaissance was flown over North Korea to support combat operations, and across the Yalu River to find the location of IL-26 medium bombers, which could threaten the fleet and US air bases in South Korea and Japan.

as a cobelligerent of the North in October 1950, and Russia provided active military support to North Korea. In recognition of those facts, President Truman in December 1950 authorized overflights of the Sino-Soviet block countries.[30] At noon on December 4, 1950, an RB-45C piloted by Captain Charles E. McDonough, the RB-45C detachment commander, rose into the sky above Yokota Air Base, headed for its reconnaissance targets beyond the Yalu River, the border between North Korea and China. The aircraft called in its position when it entered North Korean airspace—after that, silence. It was not a routine reconnaissance mission. On board the aircraft, besides the pilot, copilot, and radar navigator, was an air force colonel by the name of John Lovell, who was based at the Pentagon and directly involved in planning reconnaissance missions for the RB-45C. Why Colonel Lovell was on board this particular aircraft is unknown; however, for a man with his knowledge of highly classified and close-hold reconnaissance operations to expose himself to possible capture was indeed unusual and very risky. It just wasn't done. Certainly Moscow was aware of the RB-45C's capabilities, the most advanced photo-reconnaissance aircraft at this time in the world. Moscow may have even known more than that, regarding this particular flight. However that may be, the aircraft was intercepted by fighters as it entered Chinese airspace—and was shot down. According to documentation that became available after the demise of the Soviet Union in 1992, Russian fighters shot down McDonough's plane near the Yalu River. McDonough ejected from the plane but appeared to have been injured in the ejection and died en route to an interrogation facility. None of the others appeared to have survived.[31]

Only four months later, on April 9, 1951, a second RB-45C came close to sharing the fate of Captain McDonough's aircraft. Second Lieutenant Arthur L. O'Connor, assigned to the 4th Fighter Interceptor Group based at Kimpo Air Base near Seoul, South Korea, was lead of a flight of four F-86 aircraft escorting an RB-45C in the Sinuiju area. First Lieutenant James McGrath was the pilot of the RB-45C. The F-86s joined up with McGrath as he crossed into North Korea. A large formation of MiG-15 jet fighters attacked the RB-45C. The enemy leader, according to Lieutenant O'Connor's Distinguished Flying Cross citation, was in firing position behind the RB-45 when O'Connor shot him down. The F-86s, commanded by World War II ace John C. Meyer, were all MiG hunters and thrilled when they could get an RB-45 escort assignment, which nearly always guaranteed that MiG-15s would show trying to take down the RB-45.

Since all the RB-45C reconnaissance aircraft were assigned to the Strategic Air Command, and only the B-45A/C bombers were assigned to the tactical air forces, the decision was made in January 1951 to replace the RB-45C Tactical Air Command aircrews at Yokota Air Base with SAC crews. Captain Stacey

D. Naftel was assigned to the 323rd Reconnaissance Squadron, commanded by Lieutenant Colonel Marion C. Mixson of the 91st Strategic Reconnaissance Wing based at Barksdale Air Force Base, Louisiana. "I was asked if I would be interested in going to Yokota Air Base, and I was, provided I could select my crew," recalled then Captain Naftel at the 2001 Early Cold War Overflights Symposium. "I selected Captain Bob Dusenberry as my new navigator, and 1st Lieutenant Ed Kendrex as the copilot. Two crews from the 91st SRW went over. First Lieutenant James McGrath commanded the other SAC crew. Captain Lou Carrington, the former Tactical Air Command aircraft commander, checked me out on my first combat mission along the Yalu River in North Korea. We became Detachment 2, 91st SRW, at Yokota. For day-to-day missions we were briefed to avoid the corridor along the Yalu River. For sorties that penetrated that corridor we were provided F-86 escorts. For missions considered extremely sensitive, both Jim McGrath and I received our initial briefings at Far East Air Forces, FEAF, headquarters, also located at Yokota. Briefings and mission planning were conducted in a top-secret environment. On at least one occasion General Earl E. Partridge, the FEAF commander, sat in on the presentation. Jim and I both flew three of these highly classified missions. The first was over central China. I pointed out that we could not get there and back without aerial refueling. 'That's no problem,' the briefer replied. 'We'll get a tanker over here.' As I had not formally checked out on night refueling, I felt I would need a little practice before committing to the mission. Anyway, they got a tanker. I did know the tanker pilot, Captain Bob Hall. After working together a little I checked out on night refueling, and we were ready to go."

Captain Naftel was born in 1922 in Atlantic, Massachusetts. After graduating from high school in 1940, he enlisted in the Army Air Corps wanting to be an aerial photographer. The 33rd Pursuit Group was a P-40 outfit at Mitchell Field, Long Island. They had no positions calling for photographic skills, so they assigned him to the orderly room. In 1941, the Air Corps opened up the pilot program to high school graduates, and Naftel saw his chance. He graduated in class 42-G and was assigned to a B-25 outfit in Greenville, South Carolina, to train others in the B-25. Finally, in late 1942, he got a much sought after combat assignment. He picked up a brand new B-25 in Battle Creek, Michigan, to head overseas. There was a problem. He was a staff sergeant, and his newly assigned copilot was a flight officer—everyone on the crew outranked him. Policy at the time restricted enlisted pilots from combat assignments. Since he had more flying time in the B-25 than anyone else on his crew, they promoted him to flight officer. Naftel received a battlefield commission as a second lieutenant, and after fifty combat missions over Burma he returned to the United States. In 1949, he was assigned to the 55th SRW at Barksdale Air

Force Base, and after the wing's deactivation he found himself in the 91st SRW checking out in the brand new RB-45C reconnaissance aircraft. After being certified combat ready, Naftel was assigned to the 323rd SRS.

"This was shaping up to be a long, hairy mission. Some thirty minutes after penetrating Chinese airspace south of Shanghai, we received orders to abort, turn around, and get back out. The reason was that west of us the sky was filled with contrails. We could see the contrails at sunset, dead ahead, and assumed correctly that they were MiG fighters. The electronic intelligence aircraft, or whatever it was monitoring our mission, reported that there was no way we were going to get through the Communist Chinese air defenses that night. We were happy to turn around and hightail it out of there. My second mission was flown on July 4, 1951. It too was a moonless nighttime mission intended to gather radar scope photography of a military complex in the Harbin area of Manchuria. Taking off from Yokota Air Base, we headed west across the Sea of Japan, transiting North Korea just south of Pyongyang. Then we flew across the Yellow Sea, entering Chinese airspace in the area of Port Arthur and Dairen. Our flight plan called for us to follow the railroad line to Fushun, then on to Changchun, with our target in the Harbin area. About halfway up that line of flight, while cruising at about 34,000 to 35,000 feet near the city of Fushun, the copilot and I noticed what appeared to be Roman candles exploding off our right wing. I banked the aircraft sharply to check the ground, thinking that this must be hellish high antiaircraft fire. Nothing but blackness below us. The Roman candles kept popping off our right wing. I asked Kendrex to turn his seat around and see if there was anything behind us. I heard Ed exclaim, 'My God, Stacey, there are about seven aircraft back there in echelon. They've all got their navigation lights on.' Of course, we were all blacked out. They were in echelon to the right, and appeared to be firing in turn until each expended their ammunition, dropping off to the left to be replaced by the next in line. This went on for some time, while we went through a series of corkscrew maneuvers, varying heading and altitude, trying to shake them. We were riding the RB-45's Red Line, and whenever I felt the aircraft start to shudder due to our high speed, I would ease off or pull up some. The attack and our evasive maneuvers lasted for about twenty-nine minutes.

"When we did these penetrations, the special operations people would launch an electronic intelligence aircraft to monitor communications. They used, I believe, RB-29s or RB-50s, with the ability of monitoring and recording any Chinese air defense transmissions as well as ground radar transmissions. They were picking up that kind of intelligence while we were covering the area with radar scope photography. Of course the electronic intelligence aircraft did not penetrate hostile airspace. The MiG fighters we encountered had no problem staying right with us. According to the information I was

A typical RB-45C crew loaded down with their survival gear (chute and Mae West) ready to enter their aircraft for another combat mission over North Korea—or Communist China.

given, this was the first time the Chinese attempted a night airborne intercept. Our Roman candles probably were 20mm tracers or exploding shells. I do not know if they had proximity fuses or not. The only fireworks we saw that Fourth of July was provided by the enemy. After the MiG fighters broke off, Dusenberry gave me a revised heading into the target area of Harbin. With the mission completed, we took up a heading for North Korea, careful to avoid overflying Soviet airspace, then back over the Sea of Japan into the Yokota traffic pattern. The ceiling was down to 300 to 500 feet and we called for ground control radar assist. We lined up for final approach, and the operator started to give me reciprocal headings. After a night flight we had just had, it was almost too much. I aborted the approach and called for the senior supervisor to take over. Fuel at this point was critical. Brigadier General James E. Briggs, commander of FEAF Bomber Command, and Major Henry Walsh, our operations officer, were on the flight line to meet us and take us to the debriefing. Said Walsh after landing, 'When you pulled up, I watched the clouds, expecting to see three parachutes. What a relief it was to see you break out of the clouds on final approach.' We landed with less than 300 gallons of fuel at chock point—about enough fuel to fill the fuel lines.

"All the special missions we flew were nighttime operations, except for the last one over Vladivostok naval base in the Soviet Union. That was a low-level daylight mission flown on about August 10, 1951. The weather forecast called for a low ceiling of about 1,500 feet. We let down below the overcast to about 800 feet. At 440 knots, flying the length of the harbor, we sure caught the attention of a lot of deck hands on the Russian warships and freighters anchored there. They were really scrambling as we completed our run and pulled back up into the overcast. We detected no enemy fire during our low-level run. By late August 1951 our replacement crews arrived, were checked out, and McGrath and myself headed back to Barksdale, joining the 323rd SRS under the command of Lieutenant Colonel Mixson, just in time to make the move with the 91st SRW to Lockbourne Air Force Base near Columbus, Ohio."

Although only one of the three RB-45C photo reconnaissance aircraft deployed to Yokota Air Base, Japan, was shot down, very early in their deployment, on December 4, 1950, there were frequent encounters with MiG-15s intent on claiming a victory over the American spy planes. According to then Lieutenant Frank Robison, who flew the F-86E Sabre Jet, first with the 4th Fighter Interceptor Group out of Kimpo, then transferred to the 51st FIG commanded by Colonel Francis "Gaby" Gabreski, a World War II ace with twenty-six confirmed kills and another six added during the Korean War period, "I flew fighter escort for the RB-45Cs on several occasions, and every time we escorted them, the RB-45s attracted MiG fighters like flies heading for a honey pot. The MiGs never succeeded again to shoot down a 45, but the 45s picked up a bunch of shrapnel holes from exploding cannon shells. I talked to the chief of maintenance for the RB-45Cs at one time, a Major Simmons I believe was his name. He told me that they came up with an ingenious method of patching shrapnel holes, flattening out beer cans, which made great temporary patches."

Lieutenant Robison has the unique distinction of shooting down two MiG-15s without ever firing his guns. Two MiGs got into Robison's and his wing man's jet wash; each MiG was already near a high-speed stall, "burbling," snap-rolled twice, then went into a flat spin. "I put the pipper on the closer MiG's cockpit," Robison recalled. "Just as I started to pull the trigger, the pilot ejected. I put the pipper on the other MiG's cockpit, and that pilot ejected. The second pilot's chute didn't open properly. Both were Russians I later learned. We all suspected that many of the MiGs were flown by Russian pilots." Robison was given credit for the two MiG kills, and Colonel "Gaby" Gabreski, his group commander, pinned the Air Medal on Robison in a ceremony on January 17, 1951.

"One day in October 1952," continued Captain Stacey Naftel, "Colonel Mixson called me into his office and told me to take a three-ship formation of RB-45Cs to RAF Sculthorpe for a special operation. We departed Lockbourne on October 21, refueled in Goose Bay, Labrador, and Keflavik, Iceland, arriving at RAF Sculthorpe on the twenty-second. My assignment was to requalify

Lieutenant Frank Robison in the cockpit of his F-86E Sabre Jet right after engine start in September 1951 at Kimpo Air Base, K-14, near Seoul, on his way to "MiG Alley."

two Royal Air Force pilots in the RB-45C and check out a third, a Canberra pilot. The two pilots were exchange officers with the 91st SRW and had a fair number of hours in the RB-45C. The third pilot had no time in the aircraft. He was, however, one of the sharpest pilots I ever worked with, and after only seven training flights he was fully qualified, including day and night refueling. Then in late November the three planes I had brought over disappeared and reemerged with Royal Air Force markings. The overflight mission laid on for the RAF crews was canceled and the aircraft were released. In the meantime Colonel Mixson appeared at Sculthorpe and we flew the aircraft back to Lockbourne just in time for Christmas. Ground crews were surprised to see our aircraft in Royal Air Force markings—but they went into the hangar and came out shortly repainted with fresh US Air Force insignia." Stacey D. Naftel had started his air force career as an enlisted pilot and retired in the rank of colonel.

The Korean War was in its third year in November 1952 when Sam Myers's crew and another aircrew relieved two RB-45C crews from the 91st SRW at Yokota. It was the fourth rotation for the small RB-45C detachment at the sprawling Yokota airfield. Sam's navigator was Frank Martin, who, like Sam, was assigned to the 322nd SRS of the 91st Wing. "Our standard missions," Sam Myers recalled during our interview, "were day missions over North Korea. We were tasked by FEAF Bomber Command, and as soon as we returned from a mission, their intelligence specialists would retrieve our film, process it, look at the target area, and then task the B-29 bombers at Yokota and

The black RB-45C, tail number 48027, at Yokota Air Base, Japan, used almost exclusively for night reconnaissance missions.

Kadena, Okinawa, against the targets we had located. Some of our missions were deep penetrations into China and the Soviet Union. We flew other missions along Sakhalin and the Kurile Islands, often escorted for part of our flight by F-84 fighters. We had a 100-inch lens camera mounted at a 30-degree angle in the bomb bay. We could fly at 25,000 feet over water and shoot into the Soviet Union and get great pictures of their airfields. We used our powerful bomb bay camera for high-altitude photography and the nose camera for low-altitude work. Nearly 90 percent of our missions were day photography, the remainder were night radar photography.

"If our missions were flown at night, we always tried to use our black RB-45C, tail number 48027. There was a US Army searchlight detachment at Yokota. My predecessor, Major [Louis] Carrington, had run a test to determine how visible our aircraft was at night if we were picked up by a searchlight. The Koreans and Chinese used searchlights prodigiously. In the test Carrington ran, the RB-45C flew at 35,000 feet when it was picked up by the Yokota searchlights. The aircraft shone like a bright star. They then painted one aircraft black and flew the test again. The searchlights couldn't track the black RB-45C, so at night we flew aircraft number 48027. On December 17, 1952, I flew a deep penetration mission over the Soviet Union and China. We took off from Yokota, crossed the Sea of Japan, and coasted inland at 35,000 feet altitude, just south of Vladivostok. Then I turned northwest toward Harbin, then back south toward Mukden [Shenyang]. After passing an airfield near Mukden I made a programmed 90-degree banking turn, and I could see MiGs taking off below me. They didn't catch us. We crossed North Korea and headed toward Japan. When we flew over the battle lines, there were searchlights operating on both

F9F Panther of VF-72, from the USS *Bonhomme Richard*, piloted by Lieutenant Charles E. Myers, in 1952, over North Korea.

sides. The battle lines were lit up all the way across the peninsula, a spectacular sight from 35,000 feet. On other missions we staged first to K-13, Suwon Air Base in South Korea. There we refueled, and then we'd go out over the Yellow Sea, up the west coast of North Korea. We'd penetrate into China and took photographs of activity along the coastal areas, especially ships being loaded. Much of what was being loaded was going to North Korea. The B-29s then would try to catch the ships as they were unloading in North Korean ports.

"The closest I came to getting shot down was over Wonsan on the North Korean east coast, returning from a night mission over China. We had two 50-caliber machine guns mounted in the tail of this aircraft, not the black one. Although it looked like we carried a gunner back there, we didn't. The two guns in this particular aircraft were fixed. One gun pointed straight aft, the other pointed downward at a 30-degree angle. I could fire the guns from the cockpit. We were cruising along at 35,000 feet, heading for the Sea of Japan, when by chance I overheard a flight of two navy F9F Panthers calling their carrier, which was sitting right in front of us. The lead navy pilot was saying they had spotted an IL-28 bomber heading for the carrier and they were going in for the attack, thinking my RB-45 was an IL-28. Luckily, I happened to be on their frequency. My adrenalin level rose instantly, and for a moment I felt like the bull's-eye at a rifle range. I immediately called back to let them know that I was friendly. The shipboard radar had seen us coming from the

The second RB-45C at Yokota had two 50-caliber fixed machine guns mounted in its tail. The guns could be fired from the cockpit—there was no gunner. The black paint and the installation of the 50-caliber guns were local modifications, and they were removed once the aircraft transferred back to the United States. The RB-45C came with a set of tail guns; SAC decided they were not necessary for its reconnaissance aircraft and had them removed and put in storage. The guns were reinstalled when the RB-45Cs were transferred to the United States Air Forces Europe, USAFE.

north, assumed we were hostile, and launched the Panthers. The F9Fs finally got the word and broke off their attack, but not before making a pass at us close enough to rock the aircraft with their jet wash."

Lieutenant Frank Martin, Sam's radar navigator, sat in the nose of the aircraft and spent most of his time with his eyes glued to his radar scope. "I had none of the panoramic views of Korea or Vladivostok Sam had from the cockpit of the aircraft," Frank noted during our interview. "On several occasions we flew up the Yalu River from Antung until we could see Vladivostok. Those were daylight missions for which we had navy fighter escort. I recall one mission over Tsingtao [Qingdao], on the Yellow Sea. There were three MiG airfields in that area. I'll bet you there were a hundred MiGs sitting on the aprons. I could see them on my radar scope. They didn't have a clue we were there. They didn't have the radar to see us, nor, I presume, did they think we would do that in broad daylight. My crew flew a total of thirty-one missions over North Korea and the maritime provinces of China and the Soviet Union."

The World War II tradition of crews naming their aircraft and painting often gaudy images on the nose section was carried over into the Korean War period. Many bombers pulled out of storage still sported their World War II monikers and designs. SAC largely ended that practice after Korea.

"HONEY BUCKET HONSHOS" OF THE 91ST STRATEGIC RECONNAISSANCE SQUADRON (1952)

The B-29s were trained to go up there to Manchuria and destroy the enemy's potential
to wage war. They were trained to bomb Peking and Hankow if necessary. They could
have done so. The threat of this impending bombardment would, I am confident, have
kept the Communist Chinese from revitalizing and protracting the Korean War.
—General Curtis E. LeMay, *Mission with LeMay*

Over the years, Yokota Air Base, near Tokyo, Japan, hosted nearly every air
force reconnaissance aircraft imaginable, from the venerable RB-29 and
RB-50 to the jet-powered RB-45C, RB-47, and various versions of the RB-57
and RB-66; and, of course, the feisty little F-86 fighter turned into an amazing
reconnaissance platform. Master Sergeant Arthur E. Lidard in 1952, purely by
chance, found himself assigned to the 91st Strategic Reconnaissance Squadron
at Yokota Air Base, Japan, flying the RB-29 as a flight engineer. He had gener-
ously taken the place of a friend whose wife was expecting, but he didn't have
the faintest idea what he had gotten himself into. Lidard was better known
as "Lucky," and he was going to need all the luck he had in his account to
get him through this combat tour. In addition to a small SAC RB-45C photo
reconnaissance detachment at Yokota during the Korean War years, there was
a much more sizeable presence of aging RB-29 and RB-50 aircraft, both photo
and electronic reconnaissance. The ELINT aircraft were known as Mickey
ships, an old World War II label. Lidard's aircraft was a photo reconnaissance
version with the handle of "Honey Bucket Honshos."

"I was born in Baltimore, Maryland, on February 24, 1926," recalled Lucky
Lidard when I interviewed him. "My first flight in an airplane was with Colo-
nel Roscoe Turner, flying a Fokker monoplane. I was six years old. Roscoe
Turner was a well-known barnstormer, three-time winner of the Thompson
Trophy, and an experienced fighter pilot. My father admonished me, 'Don't
you tell your mother about this,' because he had spent five dollars to take me

on that flight. It was 1931 and times were bad. After that breathtaking flight, my dream was to become a pilot and fly airplanes when I grew up. When the war started, I was two years behind in school because my dad was crippled and I had to go to work to help my family. I attended Loyola High School in Baltimore. They sent me to take the aviation cadet examination. I finished in the top 10 percent. I enlisted in the Army Air Forces, waiting for a flying slot to open up, but as the war was winding down in 1944, they didn't need any more pilots. Instead, they sent me to B-17 armaments and electronics school at Lowry Field, near Denver, Colorado. Then I was sent to Maxwell Field, Alabama, where I flew as a scanner. When the war ended, I extended for a year because I had no job to go home to. I was transferred to Alaska, into air rescue, on a B-17E as a crew chief. We carried a twenty-foot wooden boat with twin inboard Packard engines slung underneath its belly. I never actually had to drop the boat to rescue anyone. In October 1946 I was discharged and went to work for the post office. Two days before Christmas I called a recruiting sergeant and asked him if it was possible for me to come back into the air service. The day after Christmas, they swore me back in. I missed being around airplanes, and they sure didn't have any at the post office. I came back in as a buck sergeant, a three-striper. Promotions were frozen and I stayed in that rank for five years—seventy-eight bucks a month for five long years. Hard to make a living on that. I was assigned to Bolling Field in Washington, DC. When I showed up, the line chief said, 'We need crew chiefs—I'm going to give you a T-6.' I said, 'No, Sarge, that's single engine. I've been crewing B-17s, multiengine aircraft.' He said, 'I'll fix that for you.' And I ended up with two T-6s. The most important tool in my toolbox turned out to be a can of metal polish. Man, we shined those things until you could see your face in them. All the brass at the Pentagon did their flying at Bolling. The chief came out one day and said to me, 'You've done a hell of a job, Lucky. I wish I could promote you, but I can't. But I can put you in a multiengine aircraft and you'll get some flying pay.'

"The chief gave me a C-45. It was my baby. I did everything including the twenty-five-hour inspections. The pilots came over from the Pentagon to fly. One old colonel I will never forget. He had four sets of different prescription glasses. He'd come out and say, 'Hello, Sergeant. A nice day today. Good day for flying. We'll take it up for a while.' I knew that 'for a while' meant four hours, to get his flying pay for the month. I got the crew chief next door to hold the fire bottle, because I had to sit in the right seat. The colonel never brought a copilot along. Then he would say, 'Start 'em up, Lucky,' and I'd crank 'em up. 'Read the checklist,' he'd say. I read the checklist for him. Ran up the engines, and he'd turn it onto the runway, take the power up, and we'd start to roll. That's when he switched glasses, scary. We'd roll, break ground, and he'd say, 'You've got such and such on the bird dog?'

B-17E air rescue aircraft, with boat beneath fuselage, flown by Colonel Eugene Deatrick, then a young lieutenant just out of West Point and flying school. He along with Lucky Lidard were assigned to the 10th Rescue Squadron at Adak. The squadron was commanded by the famed Arctic explorer, a Norwegian by birth, Colonel Bernt Balchen.

"'Yes, sir,' I'd reply.

"He'd say, 'Clean her up, and you got it. Take us up to 8,000 feet.' We'd get to our assigned quadrant in the local flying area and he'd say, 'Fly it around for a while, Sarge. When it's time to go in you wake me up. It's been a busy day in the Pentagon.' That's how things went, time after time. I flew around for a while, then woke him up when we got close to having four hours in the air. Going home was a rerun of what it's been before, only in reverse. This happened once or twice every month. I got to thinking, this isn't for me. I'm getting twenty days a month flying pay—not even a full month's pay—and I had to fly with anybody who came along. Some of the landings were pretty awful. I went to headquarters every day. There, they had a bulletin board on which they posted arrivals and departures as well as available assignments. Off to Alaska I went, to the 54th Troop Carrier Squadron flying C-54 transports. Our commander was Colonel Sammons, General Nathan F. Twining's son-in-law. The colonel had a southern drawl you could cut with a knife. He assembled all of us late one evening and told us that we were leaving on a thirty- to sixty-day TDY to Germany. 'I want them off the ground heading for Germany as soon as they're ready.' I worked all night changing an engine.

"We got off the following day with three crews aboard and a bunch of maintenance men, as well as their toolboxes, carbines, and helmets. We flew to Great Falls [Montana], then on to Scott Field and Westover, Massachusetts. There, we crew-rested for eight hours, then flew on to Lajes in the Azores,

The letter on the tail fin designated the bomb group the aircraft was assigned to and was a hold-over from WWII. Circle E was the 22nd Bomb Group, assigned to FEAF during the Korean War. A circle or a square displaying the group letter in its center designated the numbered air force an aircraft was assigned to; in this case, the circle represented the 15th Air Force.

where we stayed on the ground long enough to eat. Took off in the evening and landed at Rhein-Main the following morning, July 1, 1948, and the airplane went into Berlin that afternoon. During the Berlin airlift I flew almost entirely with my own airplane and kept it running. When I returned to Anchorage on February 7, 1949, I had made 185 round trips to Berlin. In 1951, a friend of mine got an assignment to RB-29s at Yokota Air Base, Japan. His wife had just gotten pregnant. So I volunteered to take his assignment, if they allowed me to do so. I had flown B-29s at Maxwell, so I knew the airplane and I liked it. A lot of people didn't like flying the B-29. So I put in my request and was informed that I could take the shipment. I reported to Randolph Air Force Base, near San Antonio, where I was assigned to a crew. We went through training together at Fairchild Air Force Base, Spokane, Washington, and then reported to the 91st Strategic Reconnaissance Squadron at Yokota. The 91st had RB-29s and a small detachment of SAC RB-45Cs attached. Our tail marking was a circle X for the 91st SRS; the 98th Bombardment Wing's B-29s, a SAC wing, also at Yokota, were circle Hs.[32]

"From 1951 until I left in 1952, I flew thirty-five photo missions, three of which were over Beijing; and eighteen Yoke missions, for a total of fifty-three. Yoke missions were sea lane surveillance flights off the coast of the Soviet Union. We'd fly out over the Sea of Japan at three hundred feet off the water and twelve miles off the coast. We'd take pictures of Russian ships. The Russian sailors waved to us as we passed. We'd wave back at them. The 91st SRS also had two B-29s without numbers on them and no tail markings. Those two B-29s, painted black, carried special equipment. When we briefed for those airplanes they sent some of our gunners back to the barracks. We still took our Central Fire Control (CFC) gunner, but the two waist gunners and the tail gunner we left behind. We also sent the photo men home, because the aircraft was a Mickey ship, full of all kinds of electronics. On those missions we turned in our identification except for our dog tags. They'd give each of us a little box, which we carried in the leg pocket of our flight suits. The box held several Mickey Mouse watches—the good ones. There also were several gold ingots in there, and a blood chit that said I was worth 25,000 American dollars in gold, and half that if dead.

"The Mickey airplane had Curtis electric props. The electrical motors changed the propeller pitch automatically. With them we could get up to altitude without a lot of prop problems. At high altitude, the conventional props would constantly change their pitch and hunt. Sometimes they would go so fast I thought they would spin off the airplane. Then I'd shut down the engine and feather the props. The Curtis props didn't hunt. They were steady even at 43,000 feet. We could get up to that altitude if we burned off enough fuel. We would go as high as the plane would go before we entered China. When we got what we had come for, the Mickey operators would tell us it was alright to turn around. Heading east, we'd pick up the jet stream, and all of a sudden that plane almost turned into a fighter. The trip into China took forever, but the trip back didn't take much time at all.

"My regular photo-recce plane was Honey Bucket Honshos. The name was painted across the nose of the airplane. My pilot was Captain Zimmer. I was the flight engineer. We would take off from Yokota and head out over the Sea of Japan, climbing all the time. We'd climb maybe two and a half hours, all the way across Korea if we were heading for China. We'd be at 40,000 feet when we penetrated. The Korean missions we flew around 20,000 to 25,000 feet. The DMZ, at night, was always lit up with searchlights. Pyongyang also had a lot of searchlights. When they shot at us, I could see the rounds coming up, looking like corkscrews. The old stuff glowed yellow and didn't get up to our altitude, but the new stuff, glowing silver, did. Sometimes single MiGs came up and paced us. They seemed to call the altitude down to the AAA. The AAA never shot a barrage at us, only single rounds.

"On June 13, 1952, we were to fly a Yoke mission, but it was canceled. I don't know why. We had already preflighted our airplane and were ready to go. They said that Captain English's crew could fly part of the Yoke and also do recce near Sakhalin. There was no need for two of us to go. Captain English's flight engineer came over and asked me if he could borrow my watch, since I wasn't flying—his had quit running. I said OK. He promised to return it as soon as they were down. It was a good automatic watch. It's probably still running on a skeleton in the Sea of Japan. They got shot down by a Russian fighter near Sakhalin with the loss of twelve airmen." It was grim news but not totally unexpected by the men of the 91st SRS, who knew that the Russians were touchy around Sakhalin. The navy had lost a P2V seven months earlier near Sakhalin, on November 6, 1951, with the loss of ten. The 91st would lose another RB-29 in October over the Sea of Okhotsk, near the Kurile Islands, with the loss of eight of its crew. The squadron started with twelve airplanes in late 1950, by 1954, when the remaining RB-29s were replaced with newer RB-50s, only eight of the original twelve remained. Lucky Lidard didn't think it could happen to him. "I was young and felt immortal." But there came a mission in 1952 over North Korea when Lucky nearly lost his belief in his immortality.

"That night we briefed for Pyongyang on Honey Bucket Honshos, aircraft number 929. It was supposed to be a paper route, leaflets. I helped load the paper bombs. When we got to the mess hall, we had a message waiting for us: Take your time. When we got back to the airplane, they had yanked the paper bombs and reloaded with M-15 flash bombs. We would follow the 98th Bomb Wing B-29s for a big hit on the railyards near Pyongyang and take poststrike pictures. Fifteen B-29s would be bombing in a bomber stream. By the time the fifteenth bomber was rolling down the runway, we had completed our taxi checklist and done our runup. Everything looked good on takeoff and climbout. As we turned west, I watched the sun set. Soon it was pitch black. We coasted out of Japan twenty-five minutes behind the bomber stream. Engine temperatures and pressures were in the green. We pulled the pins from the fuses of the M-15s and pressurized to 8,000 feet. The gunners test-fired the turrets and ran their in-flight ready checks over the Sea of Japan. We leveled off at 25,000 feet and took up a heading into our target. As we approached, we could see the flashes from the 98th bomb drops. We could also see the searchlights and the flashes from the North Korean flak. Over the initial point, we opened the bomb bay doors and started our photo run. We had some flak, dispensed chaff to mislead their radars, and the flak remained erratic. As we finished our run, the radio operator reported that one M-15 bomb was still in the forward bomb bay. The navigator checked the forward bomb bay and called the pilot over the intercom, 'The left rack in the forward bay still holds one M-15, hanging nose down from the rear latch.'

"'Roger, Nav,' was Captain Zimmer's response. 'Lucky, set up a descent. Depressurize the cabin. Send Sergeant Bjork [the radio operator] into the bay, and have him get rid of the bomb.'

"Honey Bucket Honshos" RB-29 AC #1929. Pilot Zimmer, copilot Hoyt, navigator LaFrancis, flight engineer Lidard, radio operator Bjork, L. gunner Padova, R. gunner Marshall, tail gunner Robinson, central fire control Riner, and instructor navigator Mickey.

"'Yes, Sir,' I replied. As the flight engineer, my responsibility was the supervision of the enlisted crew members. 'Sir,' I called Captain Zimmer, 'go ahead and head for home. We are in a descent, and I will slowly depressurize the cabin.' I told the radio operator to go into the bomb bay with the doors open. He started to shake and told me that he couldn't go out there with the doors open. I looked at him, and I knew the man was so afraid he would kill himself if I forced him to go out there. I called Captain Zimmer and told him that I would go into the bomb bay to get rid of the bomb. When I looked through the port into the bomb bay, I realized that things were worse than I expected. I walked up behind the pilot and told him what I had seen. Every once in a while, the vane on the flash bomb rotated. I had no idea how long that had been going on. If it went off inside our airplane, we would turn into a Fourth of July rocket. It was a magnesium—fifteen million candlepower—bomb. Captain Zimmer accelerated our descent and informed the crew to get ready for a possible over-water bailout. I asked the CFC gunner to come forward through the tunnel and ride in the flight engineer's seat and attend to the panel while I went into the bomb bay to get rid of the bomb. I then informed the rest of the crew of the situation and what I intended to do. Just then the number three engine started to take oil. I suggested to Captain Zimmer that we shut down number three and feather the prop. One emergency at a time was enough for me. He agreed.

"I had never been in the bomb bay at night with the doors open. I knew it would be a religious experience. I clipped an oxygen bottle to my flying jacket, adjusted my mask, put a big crescent wrench in one inside pocket, my Stanley screwdriver in the other, pulled on my nylon glove liners, and dropped my flashlight into a leg pocket. When I got to the bulkhead at the hatch into the bomb bay, I pulled a crash ax out of its straps, and I was ready as I was ever going to be. I looked into the bay and decided to walk along a narrow ledge between the bomb rack and the fuselage. I wasn't going to go down the middle of the bomb bay, over that black nothingness. I removed my backpack parachute. It was decision time. My heart was pounding in my throat. We were at 15,000 feet when I opened the hatch and stared into the black, endless chasm. There was some light from the bomb bay lights, and we were drawing ground fire, which helped to light up the blackness of the night. I went through the hatch slowly, onto the narrow sill, hanging onto handholds. I told myself, 'Don't look down.' Then I said it aloud over and over. About that time I noticed the vane on the huge bomb flipping over almost a full turn. It was windy as a hurricane in the bomb bay. I squeezed my way between the left front rack and the fuselage, hanging onto anything I could grab. I made it to the rear rack.

"I looked at the shackle holding the bomb and tried my screwdriver in the release slot. I couldn't turn it. I tried to turn the release with my crescent wrench. It wouldn't move. Then the wrench slipped from my grasp and dropped away into the dark. I hacked at the shackle three or four times with the crash ax before it too spun off into the night. I wedged my twelve-inch Stanley into the latch of the shackle, and, holding the shaft with my left hand, I planted my left foot on the handle. I hung on for dear life with my right hand and pushed with my foot. Suddenly, the shackle released, and the M-15 disappeared into the night. I started to count as the bomb left the shackle—one thousand, two thousand, three thousand. At the count of fifteen thousand, a brilliant flash of white filled the darkness below and behind us and stayed bright as the bomb fell away. I gave a hand signal to the navigator to close the bomb bay doors. When they whoosh-whumped closed, I struggled my way back through the hatch and into the ship. Once on the intercom, I informed Captain Zimmer that I was repressurizing to get some heat in the aircraft and to let us remove our oxygen masks. I suggested to Captain Zimmer that we restart number three so we would have four engines for landing, but it wouldn't turn. We were at 11,000 feet over the Sea of Japan. I set up three-engine cruise and realized I was shaking and soaked in sweat.

"By the time we arrived at Yokota, I had recovered my sense of immortality and joked over the intercom about having to pay for the crescent wrench and the crash ax. Captain Zimmer laughed and called for the before-landing

A B-29 bomber of the 19th Bombardment Group, 1950, based at Kadena Air Base, Okinawa, with typical nose artistry. After F-86 fighters, B-29s had the highest number of MiG-15 kills in the Korean War. However, the MiGs also took their toll of the bombers, forcing them to night operations only. Over the period of the Korean War from July 1950 until July 1953, the 19th SRS flew 1,995 reconnaissance sorties by RB-45C, RB-29, and RB-50 aircraft.

checklist, and then he added, 'We'll go to town tomorrow for dinner, Lucky, and I am buying.'"

Lidard indeed counts himself lucky to have survived this experience in the bomb bay of a B-29 bomber. After retiring from the air force, "Lucky" settled in California—until he was called "West" to join his flying buddies who had gone before him. Courage has so many faces—one of them was named Arthur "Lucky" Lidard, master sergeant, United States Air Force.

THE 19TH TACTICAL RECONNAISSANCE
SQUADRON (1955)

The RB-45C was powered by the early model of the J-47 engine. The engine had to be
pulled every 25 hours of flying time for a complete overhaul. I was right over the spot
where a friend of mine had crashed two weeks earlier. My number 3 engine seized. Flipped
us over. Scared the hell out of me. I rammed the power back up and rolled it level. My
navigator called, "You son of a bitch, what are you doing up there? I got her down safely.
—**Colonel Harold R. Austin,** in Wolfgang W. E. Samuel, *I Always Wanted to Fly*

In July 1953, with the signing of the armistice agreement leading to a ceasefire
in Korea, the RB-45C reconnaissance detachment at Yokota Air Base deactivated. The aircraft returned to their home base in Columbus, Ohio, and
shortly thereafter transferred to the Tactical Air Command. SAC's focus when
it came to reconnaissance was the new RB-47 configured to do both photographic and electronic reconnaissance. The RB-47E photographic version
of the B-47 bomber carried the same camera suite carried by the RB-45C,
so there was no loss in capability; and there were just too few of the RB-45s
for SAC to continue to operate them. However, USAFE's 47th Bombardment
Wing at RAF Sculthorpe in the United Kingdom was equipped with B-45
bombers, so it made sense for the tactical air force to operate this small number of reconnaissance aircraft and co-locate them with the B-45 bombers. The
former SAC aircraft first transferred to Shaw Air Force Base in South Carolina, where they had their tail guns reinstalled and the aircraft underwent an
inspection and repair cycle. Then the plan called for the aircraft to be flown
to RAF Sculthorpe, where they would be assigned to the 19th Tactical Reconnaissance Squadron, attached to the 47th Bombardment Wing.

In early 1954, the 19th Tactical Reconnaissance Squadron, Night Photo
Jet, from Shaw Air Force Base, South Carolina, flying former SAC RB-45Cs,
and led by its new commander, Major John B. Anderson, flew its aircraft en
masse via Goose Bay, Labrador, and Reykjavik Air Station, Iceland, to RAF

Sculthorpe. The planes arrived at Sculthorpe on May 8. Major Anderson and the 19th TRS aircrews were met and greeted by Colonel David M. Jones, the 47th Bomb Wing commander. Colonel Jones, soon to be promoted to brigadier general, was a World War II veteran of the Pacific and European Theaters of Operation. Jones, then a captain, was the pilot of aircraft number 5 of James Doolittle's Raiders—the air raid that changed the war in the Pacific. He later flew B-25s in North Africa, was shot down over Bizerte, Tunisia, and became a POW in Stalag Luft III, a camp near which I grew up as a little boy. The 19th was attached to the 47th Bomb Wing, with its three squadrons of B-45A/C bombers and one squadron of KB-29 tankers, probably the most powerful air wing stationed at the time in continental Europe. The attachment of the 19th was purely for reasons of aircraft maintenance and supply—operational control of the squadron resided with the 3rd Air Force, headquartered at South Ruislip Air Station, near London. Soon, the 19th TRS crews were involved in extensive photo mapping of Europe. One of its members was Captain Francis T. Martin Jr., a radar navigator with extensive combat experience in the RB-45C over North Korea, Communist China, and Russia. His former pilot, Sam Myers, entered RB-47 conversion training after their tour of duty in Japan ended. Frank chose to remain with the RB-45 program. A welcome assignment to England allowed Frank to take along his family, and made it an easy choice for him to stay with the RB-45.

Francis, who went by Frank, was a farm boy, born in 1928 in Roslindale, Massachusetts. "While I was still in high school, my family moved to the country, to Medway, where my father and I raised chickens for eggs and meat. We had a rabbi kill the chickens, and I had a delivery route in Boston where we sold kosher food. I continued to commute to Boston to finish my schooling. The war got everyone interested in aviation, particularly us youngsters. My father had been a torpedo man in submarines in the First World War, and several of my uncles served either in the army or navy during the war with Spain, in the Philippine insurrection, and the First World War. I wanted to become a navy flyer, so I joined the navy. Then the war ended, and they just discharged our whole class. At age eighteen I decided I wanted to start a career in photography. I heard that the Army Air Forces would give you your base of choice if you enlisted, so I did. In 1946, I was sent to the photo school at Lowry Field, in Denver, Colorado. When I graduated, I stayed there as an instructor. I really enjoyed air force life, so I decided to try again and applied for pilot training through the aviation cadet program. It turned out I had insufficient depth perception, disqualifying me, but I was offered a slot in the navigator aviation cadet program, which had just opened at Ellington Field in Texas. I graduated in 1951 and continued with my training, qualifying as a bombardier/radar navigator. Since I had expressed an interest in photography, I was assigned to the 322nd Reconnaissance Squadron at Barksdale Air Force Base, Louisiana. The squadron flew the new RB-45C photo reconnaissance jet. Within weeks of my arrival at Barksdale, the squadron transferred to Lockbourne Air Force Base near Columbus, Ohio.

"At Lockbourne I was quickly checked out in the RB-45. The Korean War was in full swing, and by December 1951 I was flying photo reconnaissance out of Yokota Air Base, Japan, over North Korea. That time I flew twenty-one combat missions. Upon my return to Lockbourne I ended up on Sam Myers's crew, and I went back to Yokota with him for a second combat tour. Our missions were pretty straightforward, mostly day photo missions over North Korea. There was a small percentage of special missions. On several of those we flew up the Yalu River from Antung [Dandong] until we could see Vladivostok. The pilots could actually see the MiGs taking off at Vladivostok, but the MiGs could never catch us. On the daylight missions up the Yalu we always had navy fighter escorts, F9F Panthers. Then we flew night-radar deep penetration missions into China as far as Mukden [Shenyang]. Other missions, day and night, we flew along the Kurile Island chain and along Sakhalin Island. For the night missions we flew aircraft number 8027—the black bird. Some of us got jumped by MiGs near the Kurile Islands and Sakhalin. The B-45s made out all right, but some of the others in our squadron, the slower RB-29s, didn't do so well." On June 13, 1952, an RB-29 flying out of Yokota Air Base was shot down over the Sea of Japan by Russian fighters with the loss of twelve crew members. Another RB-29 was downed on October 7 near the Kurile Islands with the loss of eight, followed by a third RB-29, downed on January 12, 1953, over Manchuria. Three more crew members died. The RB-29 reconnaissance crews from Yokota Air Base were taking a real beating, frequently not escorted by fighters, flying alone, and very vulnerable. In contrast, the RB-45 and RF-86 jets could usually out climb and outrun Russian and Chinese Communist fighters, as a result only losing that lone RB-45C on December 4, 1950.

Martin continued, "In January 1953 I transferred to TAC, along with our airplanes. Most of the RB-45 crews of the 19th TRS at Shaw Air Force Base came from Lockbourne. When all of the RB-45s finally arrived from SAC and had their tail guns reinstalled, the squadron went into an accelerated training program. In May 1954 we transferred to RAF Sculthorpe, and I stayed there until 1958. We had less than twenty airplanes in the squadron and had some supply problems with spare parts. Everybody was saying we couldn't do our mission. So, two or three times we got the entire squadron off the ground, every airplane, to show that we could do our mission. In June, only a month after our arrival at Sculthorpe, one of our aircraft set a record for the most flying time in the B-45 for a thirty-day period—108 flying hours. We did a lot of photo-mapping in Europe, Norway for example. That was very difficult

Sam Myers, Frank Martin's pilot, at Yokota Air Base, Japan, in 1951. Martin, as the navigator, sat in the nose of the aircraft and did not have an ejection seat, so it was nearly impossible for him to get out of the aircraft in an emergency.

because of the steep mountains rising sharply from sea level to thousands of feet. If we had a camera focused for sea level, it wouldn't be in focus for higher up. When you do mapping work, they get very, very stringent. It was a difficult mission for us, but we did it. We did some work in North Africa too, and we even did some archaeology work for some of the colleges in England to help them with their digs. From the air we could see outlines which were not readily discernible on the ground.

"On March 27, 1955, my squadron flew three deep-penetration missions over the Soviet Union. The pilots were Major John B. Anderson, our squadron commander, and Captains Howard B. Grigsby and Robert A. Schamber. I was the radar navigator on Anderson's aircraft. Our copilot was First Lieutenant John D. Flynn, and our gunner was Technical Sergeant Lee W. Bryant. The aircraft with the longest route, which was ours, had to recover in Germany for refueling. We didn't have enough fuel to make it back to Sculthorpe. Our routes were essentially the same as those flown by the Royal Air Force in 1952 and 1954. Our mission planning was highly classified, very secret. We did not know the routes of the other crews. It was all kept very quiet. Somebody else did all the map preparation and planning for us. We just took what Intelligence gave us. We didn't know until the last minute where we were going."

At the time when Anderson's crew was planning their overflight of the Soviet Union, I was assigned as an airman at Detachment 2 of the 28th Weather Squadron. My duty station was outside the air base in the small nearby village of South Creek, where the 47th Bomb Wing command post was located, and other essential wing elements necessary to command and control the wing during emergencies. Our weather detachment did not provide daily weather briefings to the aircrew; rather, our function was to look at the bigger picture and provide weather forecasts to commanders and planners, and to the B-45A bomber crews sitting on nuclear alert. So, being a German speaker, I found myself translating old German weather records for countries east of West Germany—of course having no idea why I was asked to do that. None of us at the detachment knew about the overflight when it took place, or learned of it afterward. No one talked about things like that.

"The three of us took off reasonably close together," Martin continued. "I remember a strange incident just as we were crossing the border into East Germany. We were not yet at our cruising altitude, still climbing to 35,000 feet. The night was pitch black. We had no lights on anywhere. Major Anderson said to the copilot, 'Did you see that? The plane going to the west.' There was a plane heading west as we were going east, pretty close to our altitude. His lights were out just like ours. I flew with my radar on for the entire mission. That was my primary means of navigation. I believe one of the things the Intelligence people were trying to do at the time, other than taking radar scope photography of assigned targets, was to find out what the Russians would do in the way of identifying and stopping us. I think it was important to find out if they would launch night fighters and what radars they would turn on to locate us. It was a coordinated effort to find out everything they had and could do. It was a dark night, and we didn't see any reaction other than the one airplane that passed us early in the flight. The same was true for the other crews; they encountered no hostile reaction from the Russians. Upon landing, we were met at the airplane by Intelligence personnel, who took the radar film and every scrap of paper we had in our bags."

In addition to the aircrew members already mentioned, Major Jessie B. Sutton, the squadron senior navigator, participated in this daring overflight of the Soviet Union, as did Lieutenants Robert S. Hedstrom, Wilbur V. Stephens and Kenneth G. Yerk. Sergeants Marvin N. Highsmith and Mercer E. Garrison were the other two gunners. On April 17, 1956, on General Order 22, the Department of the Air Force awarded each crew member the Distinguished Flying Cross for extraordinary achievement while participating in aerial flight. Like the RAF missions flown in 1952 and 1954, the three RB-45Cs from the 19th TRS did have an aerial refueling just prior to entry into Soviet-controlled airspace. Anderson's aircraft, flying the longer southern route, had to

Colonel Mixson, commander, 55th SRW, Forbes Air Force Base, Kansas, presenting Captain Wolfgang Samuel with his first Air Medal, January 1964. The 55th SRW in 1964 was flying the RB-47H/K, the ERB-47H, and several modified B-47E bombers, Tell Two, which monitored Russian missile launches.

recover at Fürstenfeldbruck Air Base near Munich and return to Sculthorpe the following day. Anderson's flight was the last time such mass reconnaissance flights were flown into the western USSR. Frank Martin's last flight in the RB-45 was on June 28, 1957. "It was a cool airplane. I liked the B-45," Frank told me when I interviewed him on his chicken farm on the eastern shore of Maryland. Before returning to the United States in May 1958, Frank transitioned into the new RB-66, which replaced the RB-45 in the TAC inventory. All B-45 aircraft versions were replaced by B/RB-66s, and those not flown back to the United States were parceled out to American air bases in Europe to be used for firefighting practice, a fate that saddened many an airman who had flown the B/RB-45. Frank was reassigned to the Strategic Air Command, flying as a radar navigator on the B-52 bomber in the early days of the Vietnam War. He and his wife retired to the Delmarva Peninsula in Maryland, near Salisbury—to raise chickens, of course.

Colonel Marion C. "Hack" Mixson continued to serve for many years in the secret world of strategic reconnaissance, commanding an RB-45C squadron, then converting to the newer RB-47. In 1955, Mixson transferred to a super-secret reconnaissance program run by the CIA, piloting Kelly Johnson's high-flying U-2. Mixson was involved in nearly every aspect of that program, from getting the U-2 operational, to hiring the aircrews, to flying them out of various locations in Germany, Japan, Thailand, and Pakistan. After five years of being constantly on the move with the U-2 program, he assumed command of SAC's 55th Strategic Reconnaissance Wing, in which he had once served as a young major flying converted C-47 and B-17 aircraft. The 55th still operated out of Forbes Air Force Base in Kansas, as the unit did when it deactivated in 1949, but by this time it flew highly capable RB-47H electronic reconnaissance jets. I served under Colonel Mixson when assigned to the 343rd SRS, his former squadron, when he was the 55th Wing commander, and he pinned on my first Air Medal after a successful overseas deployment. Colonel Mixson retired from the air force while commanding officer of the 100th SRW, a U-2 wing, at Davis-Monthan Air Force Base near Tucson, Arizona. He settled in Tampa, Florida, not too far from MacDill Air Force Base, where I interviewed him. As for so many of his generation, Mixson went from the little 45-horsepower Aeronca via the B-24, RB-45, and RB-47 to the U-2 spy plane. "I loved every minute of it," Mixson said to me, "and every airplane I ever flew." His favorite airplane though, his wife confided to me, was the RB-45C.

THE INCREDIBLE RF-86F SABRE JET (1952–1955)

The *Dayton Daily News* reported a mysterious explosion one afternoon in the spring of 1950. A young project engineer outside Dayton was recording F-86 dive tests. He read the article and remembered recording a dive at that time. The next day the same thing happened. The sonic boom was unknown at the time. The F-86 was not believed to have exceeded the speed of sound, but the Mach meter always hung up at 96%. We reported this phenomenon to higher authorities, and all hell broke loose. Everyone tried to schedule an F-86 flight to "boom" Wright Field. General [Benjamin Wiley] Chidlaw called me, "Another boom and you are fired." Just then another loud one occurred, and the good general said, "Oh—!" and hung up.

—**Bob Shaefer,** in Kenneth Chilstrom and Penn Leary, *Test Flying at Old Wright Field*

Aerial reconnaissance during the Korean War years really came into its own. Although RB-29 and RB-50 aircraft continued to fly the Sea of Japan, they were slow, and very vulnerable to the Russian's latest jet fighter, the MiG-15. The RF-80, although a jet aircraft, was no match for the MiG-15, but the United States had an ace up its sleeve, the F-86 Sabre Jet, which soon would make its mark over the Yalu River and produce a slew of American fighter aces. It turned out, with a few modifications, that the F-86 made one heck of a good reconnaissance aircraft. Demands for intelligence increased after Communist China entered the war in November 1950, resulting in the activation of the 67th Tactical Reconnaissance Wing on February 25, 1951, under the command of veteran World War II reconnaissance pilot Colonel Karl L. "Pop" Polifka. Polifka, who flew 145 combat reconnaissance missions in World War II, and who was the holder of the Distinguished Service Cross, was shot down by ground fire on July 1, 1951, flying one of his RF-51s. Pop did not survive. The 67th was stood up with three squadrons—the 12th, 15th, and the 45th. The 12th TRS flew all the night missions in RB-26 aircraft, and the 45th flew daytime missions in RF-51 and RF-80 aircraft. Only the 15th TRS was equipped from the start with the RF-80. The appearance of the MiG-15 jet fighter made unarmed RF-80 flights near the Yalu River extremely hazardous. So, in early 1951, the commander of the 15th TRS pushed for the installation of reconnaissance cameras in the F-86. In spite of some initial opposition at FEAF headquarters, Far East Command personnel installed cameras in six F-86A fighters at Tachikawa Air Base. They had cameras installed but retained four of their six 50-caliber machine guns. There was no wing modification, so they could carry only the usual two 120-gallon drop tanks. These six depot-modified aircraft were officially referred to as Ashtray aircraft, but the pilots came up with a more colorful name, Honey Bucket. Honey Buckets were a beginning.

Air Force Chief of Staff General Hoyt S. Vandenberg, on a visit in December 1951, found the Ashtray/Honey Bucket project interesting, and soon after his visit North American Aviation came up with six modification kits for the F-86 aircraft, relieving some but not all of the shortcomings of the Honey Bucket camera installation. The RF-86 Ashtray/Honey Bucket aircraft and the RF-80 continued to share missions near MiG Alley along the Yalu River, and the highly classified overflights of Communist Chinese and Russian airfields. In early 1953, the 15th TRS finally received four brand-new RF-86 aircraft, which would be referred to as RF-86F-30s, featuring a hardened wing that allowed the installation of four drop tanks, two 120-gallon tanks, and two 200-gallon tanks, extending the range of the aircraft significantly. It also lengthened the wings by six inches and extended the wing root by three inches. The -30s still carried the same camera suite as the Ashtray aircraft. The final modification, called Haymaker, was made at Tachikawa Air Base in 1953, replacing the camera suite and resulting in the removal of all the guns. The Haymaker represented a new aircraft type, and under the terms of the Korean armistice of July 1953, it could not be stationed in-country. So the RF-86Fs were moved to Komaki Air Base, Japan.

"Captain LaVerne Griffin, our operations officer, had me develop operational data on the new aircraft to determine the best drop tank configuration, speed, and altitude for flying maximum-range reconnaissance missions in the new 'hard-wing' RF-86Fs. At the time I was serving as assistant operations officer and A-flight commander. Our squadron commander was a major, while the rest of us were first and second lieutenants. The basic F-86 flight handbook was useless for our purposes. We knew that maximum thrust was obtained in the RF-86 at 690 degrees centigrade at full military power on takeoff. However, we wanted maximum speed at the highest possible altitude. From then on we estimated temperatures at altitudes above 40,000 feet, and placed a number of 'rats and mice,' small pieces of titanium, in the tail pipes to ensure achieving a 690 degree centigrade EGT, exhaust gas temperature, at full military power at 40,000 feet. Our technical representative assured us that maintaining full military power would not have a negative effect on engine performance on any given flight—but it would drastically reduce engine life. That was the answer we wanted to hear. We then planned our missions for

The "Wild Bunch" 15th TRS pilots in front of their tents at Komaki Air Base, Japan, March 1954.

maximum thrust throughout the entire flight envelope," recalls Colonel Samuel T. Dickens, then a young captain, at the 2001 Early Cold War Overflights Symposium. "We wanted maximum speed and maximum altitude to avoid interception by Soviet and Chinese MiGs.

"In the early overflights we retained the 120-gallon drop tanks throughout the mission, as they did not significantly affect the performance of the RF-86F. Later on, as the top-secret overflight missions continued, the tanks were jettisoned when empty and the aircraft was flown clean up to 50,000 feet, at times even a bit higher. Though a placard limited flying the aircraft to Mach 0.90, we found that at full military power above 40,000 feet the aircraft reached and maintained Mach 0.92 with ease. Since fuel was of such consequence to us, we had the aircraft towed out to the flight line and started the engine at the end of the runway. The mounting of twin 40-inch focal length cameras in the aircraft, with all six 50-caliber guns removed, required aircraft modifications to fit the camera magazines, resulted in a bulge on either side of the aircraft. Heavy lead panels were also added as ballast to provide the proper center of gravity.

"Late on March 21, 1954, less than three weeks after deploying to Komaki, we flew our six RF-86Fs to Osan, South Korea, where immediately they were moved into hangars to keep them from the roving eyes of United Nations inspectors. The next morning, we started engines at the end of the runway and prepared to take off. Six RF-86Fs. The pilots of the first 15th TRS top-secret overflight mission, after the signing of the armistice, were Major George H.

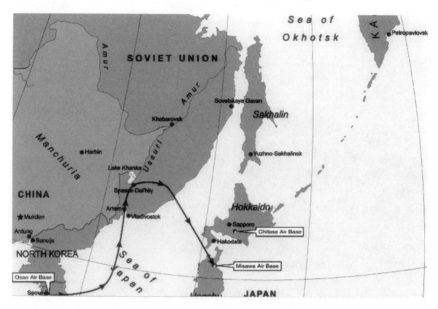

April 3, 1954, RF-86F overflights of Vladivostok by Samuel Dickens, returning to Misawa Air Base.

Saylor, our squadron commander; Captain LaVerne H. Griffin, the operations officer; and First Lieutenants Bill Bissett and Larry Garrison. My wingman, Lieutenant Peter Garrison, and I flew the two spare aircraft. We flew easterly from Osan for about seventy miles, then turned onto a northerly heading at about 25,000 feet. The primary four aircraft dropped their 200-gallon outboard tanks cleanly. No need for a spare, so Pete Garrison and I turned around and flew back to Komaki.

"The overflight of the Vladivostok area was successful. Upon seeing the photographs of the various airfields, General Otto P. Weyland, commander of the Far East Air Forces, immediately called the four pilots to Tokyo and personally pinned Distinguished Flying Crosses on their chests, saying, 'The paperwork will follow.' This successful overflight whetted the appetite of the Intelligence community, right up the chain of command to the Pentagon and the White House. New orders arrived, and on April 2, 1954, we were to do it all over again—same route, same target, Vladivostok, but without any spare aircraft. Off we went to Osan and went through the same routine as before, hiding our aircraft in hangars. The next day, April 3, I was flying as wingman for LaVerne Griffin, our operations officer, and Larry Garrison flew wing for Major George H. Saylor, our squadron commander. We climbed up to 42,000 feet after dropping our 200-gallon drop tanks. We maintained radio silence and had no visual contact with land. It was a beautiful day and visibility was outstanding. We were flying at full military power, maintaining our 690-degree tail pipe temperature and pushing Mach 0.92. At last we picked up landfall and realized we had to make a slight adjustment of our heading to the left to come over the first of our several targets, from Vladivostok north. Our cameras were working perfectly, taking photographs of TU-4 bombers on various airfields. It's easy to remember that day, not only for the thrill of taking photographs over Vladivostok on a beautiful day but also because our new aircraft with the new engines performed perfectly. It was always a joy to fly the Sabre."

Captain Larry Garrison, Larry retired from the air force in 1987 in the rank of major general, recalls that mission flying over Vladivostok. "We flew all four aircraft over the targets; however, we split up as we approached the target area and rejoined Griffin and Dickens on the way out. The CO, commanding officer, and I cut short our flight over Vladivostok due to contrails, but we did get good photos. Grif got the best pictures, though. Just prior to flying this mission, Captain Griffin, our operations officer, took me aside. Said he, 'I have two things to tell you Larry. One—keep your eyes open for MiGs because if they come after us they will likely go for Blue 4 first.' Since I was Blue 4, I listened closely to what he had to say. 'Two—for Ch--t sake, don't let the CO get lost!'" Continued Sam Dickens, "When it was clear that we did not have intercepting MiGs on our tails, Grif led all four of us into a descent into Misawa, rocking his wings.

"This was my only top-secret overflight mission, and soon thereafter I headed home to Shaw Air Force Base in South Carolina. No RF-86s were ever lost to enemy action. Our photography revealed not only the extensive bomber buildup around Vladivostok but also the deployment of MiG-17 fighters east of the Urals. Years later I learned that the FEAF commander was authorized to task missions north of the Yalu River to gain photographic intelligence in China during the Korean War years. Following the truce, however, authority for such missions was withdrawn and reverted back to the Joint Chiefs of Staff, with final approval by President Eisenhower.

"The top-secret overflight missions continued after my departure from Komaki for another year by the 15th TRS. During this period, at least one mission was flown over the Soviet-held Kurile Islands, photographing submarine pens. Another was a deep penetration to Khabarovsk on the Amur River. Numerous missions were flown over the Peoples Republic of China, PRC, and North Korea. Missions were staged out of South Korea; others were staged from Japan, including Okinawa. With the end of the Cold War and the declassification of these top-secret overflights, RF-86 pilots gathered in September 1999 in Arlington, Virginia. For the first time some twenty-five pilots told their stories of overflying the PRC, the Soviet Union, and North Korea from 1952 to 1955. Historians at the National Reconnaissance Office retrieved some of the

Soviet TU-4s, copies of B-29s, parked on hardstands at Spassk-Dalniy East Airfield north of Vladivostok; below, a closer look at some of the aircraft.

Lieutenant George Best being readied for takeoff by his crew chief at Komaki Air Base, Japan, March 1955. Note the film magazine bulge the crew chief is leaning on—an identifying feature of the RF-86F-30.

15th TRS overflight imagery from the Defense Intelligence Agency, had them declassified and posted on bulletin boards for all to see. Since such overflights were never discussed, pilots in the same squadron did not know what other missions had been flown.

"One of the RF-86 pilots told us of a bar encounter that took place in Japan in 1955, a conversation he had with an F-84 pilot also based at Komaki. The fighter bomber's mission was also top secret, because in the event of war his squadron had been assigned the mission of dropping tactical nuclear weapons on targets in the Vladivostok area. Confided the F-84 pilot, 'I know what you guys do because my target folder contains a photograph of my target with the words "15th Tactical Reconnaissance Squadron" at the top of the print.' The RF-86 pilot supposedly smiled and said nothing. It was nice to hear that his product had been put to good use." Samuel T. Dickens retired as a colonel and was a participant in the February 2001 Early Cold War Overflights Symposium sponsored by the National Reconnaissance Office and the Defense Intelligence Agency.

Major General Mele Vojvodich Jr. flew in the same squadron as Sam Dickens, although a bit earlier than Sam. "In 1950–1951 I was assigned to fly F-84s while assigned to the Strategic Air Command. I tried my best to get into the

Korean War action. I kept volunteering for fighter quotas, but none came open. The first one that did was a reconnaissance quota, so I said to myself, 'I don't know anything about reconnaissance, but I think I'll volunteer. At least I'll get to the war.' I ended up in a very short course at Shaw Air Force Base learning how to take pictures. I finally reached Korea in July 1952. The first thing I did when I arrived at Kimpo Air Base outside Seoul was to go over to the 4th Fighter Wing, even though I was assigned to the 67th TRW. I introduced myself to Colonel Harrison Thyng, the wing commander, and told him I wanted to fly fighters. He asked, 'Why?' I said, 'I want to shoot down MiGs.' He said, 'Man, you are just the kind of guy we are looking for. I'll work it.' The transfer did not work out because Colonel Russell A. Berg, 67th Wing commander, blocked it. Robbie Riesner had just pulled a similar stunt. Went through Shaw, volunteered to fly fighters after arriving in South Korea, and ended up an ace. Berg was determined that was not going to happen again. So, I ended up in the 15th TRS, which turned out great.

"During my time in Korea as a recce pilot, between July 1952 and July 1953, I flew about fifty to sixty missions, a number of them across the Yalu River in the RF-86A and RF-80. We had a classic mission which Fifth Air Force called 'Mission 2000,' flying over Chinese airfields at Fen Cheng, Tatung Kao, and Antung, among other places. When I was there, the reconnaissance pilot on a 2000 overflight mission would lead a group of anywhere from twenty-four to forty-eight F-86 Sabre Jets from the 4th Fighter Wing north to the Yalu River. These pilots allegedly flew as our escorts. As a rule, however, what they wanted to do was shoot down MiGs. The escorts used us for bait, because every time we went up there we would draw a hostile crowd. One time, in May 1953, flying across the Yalu near Mukden, we got into a heck of a dogfight. Jim Jabara shot down two MiGs while I was flying his wing, which was the standard procedure by a reconnaissance pilot if you got bounced. On a typical mission, we would go over to the 4th Fighter Wing and sit down for a recon briefing with perhaps a hundred eager fighter pilots. On a 2000 mission, we would have three fighters flying on our wing, and the rest of the escorts would patrol for MiGs up and down the Yalu River. Invariably our four aircraft would get jumped by about twenty-four to forty-eight MiGs, and there would be one heck of a dogfight. After one such mission I told my wing commander, 'I'm not getting any pictures. The F-86 guys are getting all these kills at my expense.' He said, 'What do you suggest?' I answered, 'We ought to let the F-86s go up there and patrol up and down the river, get involved in a dogfight with the MiGs, then two of us, one wingman and myself, will penetrate and head up north.' We started doing that and it worked like a charm.

"One of these missions was kind of humorous in retrospect. It was the longest mission I ever flew, March 1953, three hours and fifteen minutes. My

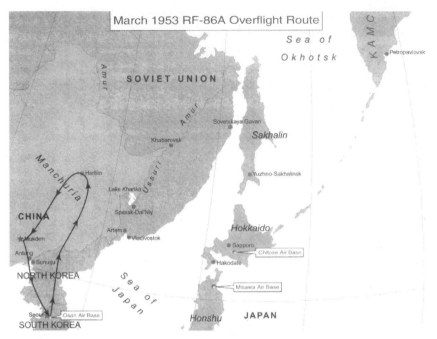

RF-86 overflight Harbin/Mukden, People's Republic of China, March 1953, by Mele Vojvodich.

escort, with more limited fuel capacity, had already returned and landed at Kimpo. I was up there all by myself but thinking I still had escorts loitering at the Yalu. I was approaching Mukden at 50,000 feet in my RF-86F-30 Haymaker, moving along at Mach 0.90, when I looked left, off my wing, there were four MiGs sitting there. I couldn't believe it. Here I am 350 miles from home, low on fuel, and I'm surrounded by the enemy. But they did not attack. They just flew along and looked at me, and I looked at them. I did not move. I was just frozen at the stick. The next thing, the MiGs popped their speed brakes, descended right underneath me, and headed down to land at Mukden. About ten minutes later, just as I made my turn to overfly Mukden, I discovered about twenty-four friends on my tail. I was at 50,000 feet, and those MiGs were about 4,000 to 5,000 feet above and behind me. They cut me off in the turn, and I thought, 'Boy, this is going to be a desperation act. You better come up with something quick.' I rolled over, split-S in the RF-86, and, in the dive, got terminal velocity at about Mach 1.05. I looked into the rearview mirror and saw the MiGs were really out of control. They were all trying to hit Mach 0.95 and were fishtailing and firing cannons like crazy. The good thing about being in a dogfight with twenty-four airplanes is that only one of them can get on your tail at a time—and they were all behind me. I broke radio silence, yelling like a wounded eagle, screaming for help because I thought my friends patrolling the Yalu River would come and rescue me. I dove for the deck and flew across Antung Air Base at about 100 feet, right down a ramp. I zipped across south to the Yellow Sea, which was only a short distance away. I knew that was my only escape. If I had to punch out, the US Navy would rescue me. The MiGs dropped off as soon as we passed the coast. I climbed back up on fumes, called Kimpo airfield, and told them that I was flamed out. They said, 'You are number six in the flameout pattern.' I thought they were joking. Here we had a 6,000-foot runway, 100 feet wide, and all these F-86s are coming back from missions over North Korea 'flamed out?' Finally I got there and down safely.

"My wing commander, Russ Berg, met me when I landed. The first thing he asked was, 'Where the heck have you been?' I was overdue by forty-five minutes and had been reported shot down over the Yellow Sea. I said, 'Colonel Berg, you won't believe it. Let me show you.' I laid the map out on the wing of the RF-86 and traced my altered flight path toward Harbin and vicinity, covering all these airfields. He turned white. He said, 'I am going to get court-martialed; and so are you. Grab that film.' They got the raw film out of the RF-86, put it in the colonel's staff car, with me sitting in the back, to go to downtown Seoul. The colonel was driving, and he intended to brief Lieutenant General Glenn O. Barcus, the three-star commanding the 5th Air Force. I used to smoke a pipe in those days, knocking the ashes out in what I thought was an ashtray. But the car didn't have an ashtray, and the red-hot embers were going into the back of the seat. About halfway to Seoul, smoke and heat started leaking out of the back of the seat. I said, 'Sir, we've got a problem. Better pull over.' He said, 'Why?' I said, 'The car is on fire.' There happened to be a Korean woman nearby, out in a rice paddy, with two honey buckets on her shoulders. I ran up to her, grabbed one of those honey buckets, and dumped it in the back seat. It was a heck of a mess, but finally the fire went out. Colonel Berg had just about had it with me at that stage, but we pressed on, only to have the fire start up again. We stopped in front of a Korean firehouse. They came running out with their machine guns at the ready as if they were going to fire on us. They finally put out the fire, and we arrived at 5th Air Force headquarters, smelly but with the film intact.

"General Barcus came into the room and said, 'Show me what you did, captain.' I said, 'Well, sir, here is where I went—up here, here, and here. And I saw these airfields and I saw Il-28 Beagles.' During the Korean War, we were really concerned that these aircraft could strike us as far as Japan. On these overflight missions, we were actually looking for these aircraft, not MiGs. We already knew there were lots of MiGs there. Colonel Berg was nervous as heck. I said, 'Colonel, let me brief.' General Barcus kept looking, then said,

'Let's go see what you did.' The wet film was still coming off the processor. You could see all the MiG airfields, and the Il-28s. He turned around, took my hand, and said, 'Congratulations captain.' Long story short—I got a medal and Russ Berg made general.

"I was the first to fly that RF-86F-30, which was the precursor to the RF-86F that mounted the twin K-22 cameras vertically. Most of our overflight missions were in the RF-86A models, Ashtray aircraft. Then we got five or six RF-86F models by boat at Komaki, Japan, and we flew them to Tachikawa for modifications. We flight-tested these RF-86F-30 aircraft up and down Japan in late 1952 to 1953, before they were delivered to the 15th TRS in Korea. The F-86F models were modified with hard wings that supported four drop tanks. They were not at all like the RF-86A models, which had two drop tanks, and all of them were different. As the project officer, I was supposed to go down to Tachikawa and help modify them. We took out all of the guns except the two on top. In the later F models, they got rid of the guns completely, but then you had a ballast problem. If you took out all of the guns, you had to offset that weight somehow, or your center of gravity would shift aft too far. When I first arrived in 1952, the ten to fifteen reconnaissance pilots already flying were using previously modified F-86A Honey Bucket and Ashtray aircraft. The RF-86F-30 I modified had bulges on the side. We mounted one 36-inch camera horizontally, that shot through a mirror, and had a little window to cover it all. We had to take the radar out to make room for the guns and put a dicing camera in the radar dome in the nose. There is a famous picture of Suiho Dam on the Yalu River taken with a dicing camera, which was one of the most dangerous missions I ever flew. That picture was taken at low level, at 600 knots indicated air speed. The heavy flak looked just like it did in the movie *The Bridges at Toko-Ri*. The Chinese were lowering their 120mm guns and firing across the canyon at us. The dicing pass produced one of the most spectacular pictures of the entire war.

"In recognition of our service, in May 1953, we had a big parade at Kimpo Air Base, where I received a Distinguished Service Cross, second to the Medal of Honor, and a couple of other guys also received medals. It was a big surprise to me. Most of the pilots that flew the 2000 missions received an automatic Silver Star because it was pretty hairy going up there alone, or even with a couple of escorts. I flew probably ten or fifteen of the overflight missions, and I had been recommended for five Silver Stars. I learned later that General Barcus instructed his staff to 'pick the best mission he flew, and the hairiest and upgrade this to a DSC.' General Barcus came out and presented the medal to me in person in the first parade we've ever had at the base. I couldn't believe it. I returned stateside that July. Some years later I took part in the development and flight testing of the YF-12/SR-71 aircraft in Nevada. And later still I

The F/RF-86 Sabre Jet was the airplane every pilot loved to fly. As the old saying goes, "If it looks good, it flies good." The F-86 did all of that. The RF-86F-30 shown here had no guns but had a reinforced wing that allowed it to carry four external fuel tanks, which greatly extended its range.

served as the director of operations for my old outfit, the 67th Tactical Reconnaissance Wing at Bergstrom Air Force Base, Texas." Mele Vojvodich, a true survivor, retired from the US Air Force in the rank of major general.

During the Korean War years, the glory went to the F-86 fighter pilots, whose exploits could be and were widely publicized. The daring reconnaissance missions of RF-86 flyers over Communist China and the Soviet Union, whose aircraft carried no guns, fell into a black hole of national security and received zero publicity. In essence, the pilots were told just to forget they ever flew those missions—certainly talking about them would have had dire consequences, so they never did. LaVerne H. Griffin, like Mele Vojvodich, Samuel Dickens, and Larry Garrison, all assigned to the 15th TRS, was one of those flyers. Above all, they loved to fly the RF-86, which one of Griffin's squadron mates referred to as a "dynamic ship—the hottest our country had in regular service."

"One thing that I remember," Colonel Griffin noted at the Early Cold War Overflights Symposium, "it was just before the ceasefire, when Vice President Richard M. Nixon visited our unit, the 15th TRS. I am sure he was sent over by President Eisenhower to see what was going on, because Ike had pledged during the presidential campaign that if elected he would go to Korea with the intention of ending the war. It was my job to brief the vice president on the capabilities of the RF-86. One of his questions was, 'Son, what do you need this airplane for?' This was a fair question, since the rest of the 67th TRW flew straight-wing RF-80As. I replied, 'Well, if we get caught up there in MiG Alley, we can get away from anything they have because the RF-86 is faster.' Nixon must have told President Eisenhower about the aircraft's capabilities, because after the Korean armistice we had a significant number of missions laid on. My first overflight was as the wingman of Lieutenant Tom Gargan flying the RF-80 over Shantung Peninsula, just across the Yellow Sea from North Korea. All we could see over the target area were a few rice paddies. We aborted the flight and returned to K-14, Kimpo. Tom Gargan was one of the best pilots around and received several medals during the war. He had so many medals and decorations that we got a little device to throw over his shoulder on his back just to balance the weight of all of those medals hanging on the front of him.

"My second overflight took place on July 27, 1953, the last day of the war. My targets were installations at Kirin and Harbin in Manchuria. My F-86 wingman was from the 4th Fighter Wing who already had four MiGs to his credit. During our briefing, he tried to reassure me about the MiGs we might encounter, saying, 'If we get into a problem up there, I'll take care of you.' I replied, 'If we get into trouble I'll get the hell out of there because those guns on my aircraft are only painted on.' We took off from Kimpo, climbing out through a low overcast. Radio silence was maintained, and navigation was strictly time and distance—hold the course, and pray that the forecast winds were accurate. We dropped our external fuel tanks before crossing the Yalu River; the weather began to clear. I remember the impressive sight of the Great Wall of China, which extended as far as the eye could see. I obtained photos of Kirin, then proceeded on to Harbin, picking up the airfield at Harbin. I banked 90 degrees to the right so that I could see half the airfield, then 90 degrees to the left so that I could see the other half—then I knew the airfield was directly below my line of flight and I turned on the cameras. On the way home, we flew over Mukden, where I photographed more airfields.

"About the time we crossed the Yalu I discovered I couldn't breathe. A quick glance at the oxygen regulator confirmed that the tank was empty. We were at 47,000 feet and did not dare to descend because we would not have enough fuel to reach home base. I was wobbling all over trying to extract my bailout bottle when my wingman, noting my erratic flying, broke radio silence to ask me if I had a problem. I told him that I did but thought I could handle it. We had no autopilot in the RF-86. I hooked up my bailout bottle, giving me about ten minutes of oxygen. We were at 47,000 feet, the cockpit was pressurized at 28,000 feet, so I figured if I let down at about 2,500 feet a minute for ten minutes I'd be at 22,000 feet and that would bring down the cockpit pressure to about 15,000 feet—where I could make the rest of the flight without supplemental oxygen. My plan worked. The best compliment I received from

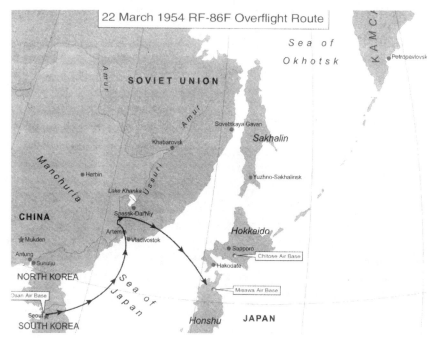

March 22, 1954, overflight route by LaVerne H. Griffin's RF-86 aircraft, launching from Osan Air Base, South Korea, and recovering at Misawa Air Base, Japan.

the fighter pilot was when he said, 'Did you get the pictures?' I said, 'Yes.' He replied, 'I didn't know where we were from the time we took off until we got back.' I was put in for the Silver Star for this mission, and my fighter pilot escort got some sort of a medal as well. But being the last day of the war, the awards and decorations officer soon transferred out, and the paperwork got lost in the shuffle.

"A decision was made at the highest level after the Korean armistice that we would be launched on top-secret overflight missions—Vladivostok, Port Arthur, Dairen, Shanghai, Mukden, and Khabarovsk. As the squadron operations officer, I was selected to select pilots and plan for these missions. We flew practice missions locally, using the same distances we would be required to cover on the actual flights. North American Tech Reps installed titanium inserts, called Rats and Mice, in the engine exhaust to increase the tailpipe temperature to maintain 640 degrees at 40,000 feet. On March 21, 1954, six RF-86 Sabers departed Komaki Air Base, Japan, for Osan, South Korea. The next morning was beautiful and clear; we checked out the en route weather and winds and briefed for the mission. The aircraft were towed out of the hangar, and fuel was added to the drop tanks until they overflowed. We cranked up the engines and taxied to the runway, using a green light from the tower for clearance. The climb to altitude was uneventful, and we successfully jettisoned our 200-gallon tanks when empty over the Sea of Japan. At this point the two spares returned to Komaki Air Base in Japan. Four of us pressed on. We climbed to 42,000 feet, our cruising altitude to the target area. As we approached Vladivostok we split up into two flights, heading for our respective targets. It was shortly after this I heard the transmission, Alabama, the code word of our companion element for pulling contrails—a dead giveaway revealing our presence. Our codeword was California. I looked over at my wingman, and he wasn't pulling any contrails. I continued to press on over the Vladivostok area, nervously I might add. I did not know this at the time, but the other element, pulling contrails, had aborted their mission and headed back for Misawa. We flew over the airfields at Vladivostok, proceeding as far north as Artem. My wingman's cameras had failed, so I was the only one out of four on this mission to bring back any pictures. We had no airborne aircraft sightings to worry about, and we proceeded to exit the area out over the Sea of Japan, toward Misawa. At Misawa, a C-47 met us and flew us to Tokyo. Someone else picked up our aircraft. We were not allowed to view the film, but it must have been successful. The next morning we were summoned to the office of the commander of the Far East Air Forces, General Otto P. Weyland, who pinned the Distinguished Flying Cross on the four of us. His exact words were, 'Boys, I'll take care of the paperwork later, but here is a little something for a job well done.' We would have done just about anything for General Weyland because of the time he took for that impromptu ceremony."

Griffin continued, "I was the leader for the next two missions in the same general area. Vladivostok on April 3, 1954, and another on April 21. We refueled as before at Misawa but flew the film down to Tokyo ourselves. I selected different pilots for these flights to ensure that all the qualified RF-86 pilots had a chance to get a mission and a Distinguished Flying Cross for their efforts. My wingman on April 3 was Lieutenant Sam Dickens, and on the April 21 mission Lieutenant Frank Halstead. On the last mission, we sighted two airborne MiGs about 5,000 feet below us as we were exiting the area, and I managed to take pictures of them. Upon examining the film, the photo interpreter rushed out of the lab and exclaimed, 'Do you know what you got on this film?' I said, 'You mean the MiG-15s that flew below us?' 'That is not a MiG-15,' he said; 'it is a MiG-17, and we didn't know that they were deployed east of the Urals.' I rotated back to Shaw Air Force Base in May 1954. At Shaw, I received two more Distinguished Flying Crosses for the last two missions I'd flown in April 1954. What was probably the highlight of a twenty-eight-year air force career I could not talk about for forty-six years. I am glad that this forgotten overflight reconnaissance is finally being documented and will take its rightful place in

The 15th TRS pilots, June 1954, the "Wild Bunch," at Komaki Air Base, Nagoya, Japan, in "moon suits" as they referred to "poopie suits" at the base swimming pool for a practice sea-survival session. Right to left, John Shinn, Hank Parsons, Rudy Anderson, Don Reynolds, Wilbur Regero, Sam Dickens, Walt McCarthy, Will Dickey, and the survival instructor (name unknown).

our military history." LaVerne H. Griffin retired from the US Air Force in the rank of colonel and was a presenter at the February 23, 2001, Early Cold War Overflights Symposium at the Defense Intelligence Agency in Washington, DC.

By 1956, the 67th Tactical Reconnaissance Wing had relocated to Yokota Air Base, near Tokyo, and the 11th and 12th TRS reequipped from the RF-80 and RF-86 to the brand-new RB-66B, C, and W photo, electronic, and weather reconnaissance aircraft. The 67th Tactical Reconnaissance Wing's mission had changed as well from overflights of North Korea, Communist China, and the Soviet Union to flying PARPRO surveillance missions with the RB-66C electronic reconnaissance aircraft along the borders of the USSR, North Korea, and Communist China. Yokota Air Base would continue to serve as a reconnaissance base for the US Air Force throughout the Cold War years, and in the early and mid-1960s I flew several reconnaissance missions out of Yokota from the Gulf of Tonkin to the Sea of Okhotsk when assigned to the 343rd SRS of the 55th Strategic Reconnaissance Wing, home-based at Forbes Air Force Base, Topeka, Kansas. For some of our reconnaissance missions, the Sea of Japan proved to be a very hostile environment.

REMEMBERING MAJOR RUDOLPH "RUDY" ANDERSON (1953–1955)

After Rudy was shot down, we got the word that Kennedy had warned Castro and
Khrushchev that if another reconnaissance airplane was shot down, we would
stage an all-out bombing attack against these installations. The rumor was he was
prepared to nuke the island. If we heard that rumor, figure the Cubans did too.
Ben Rich and Leo Janos, *Skunk Works*

"The Korean War began on June 25, 1950, when I was a senior at the University of Iowa. Although General Douglas MacArthur declared that United Nations troops would be home by Christmas, after the Chinese Communists entered the conflict in November it soon became apparent that the war would be long. I enlisted in the US Air Force the following year and passed the cadet pilot exams. A year later I was ordered to report to Marana Air Base, Arizona, for basic training flying the North American T-6 trainer. Advanced training followed at Williams Air Force Base, near Tempe, Arizona, and then on to instrument training at Moody AFB, Valdosta, Georgia—which was the best course I ever attended in my entire life. Reconnaissance training at Shaw AFB, near Sumter, South Carolina, finished my training cycle, and I found myself heading to Korea to a reconnaissance squadron. Finally, in November 1953 I flew on a C-54, packed to the gills, from Travis AFB, California, to Hickam AFB, Hawaii—twelve hours of misery. I thought that if one of the engines coughed, we'd all go down. The next stop was Wake Island and, finally, Tokyo, Japan." Robert J. "Jerry" Depew was worn out by the time he got there. One final hop took him to Kimpo Air Base, near Seoul, Korea, to the 15th TRS. Hostilities had ceased after the armistice that July, and Jerry wondered what kind of reconnaissance he could possibly fly with the war at a standstill.

"Korea was an ugly, mountainous, bitter-cold land where we lived six to a tent. At that time, the South Koreans were at least fifty years behind Japan on anything you'd like to think of. They had almost no motor vehicles, and I saw

December 1953—houseboy Kim, Jimmy Black, and Jerry Depew. To get out of this environment, Jerry flew as much as he could.

no paved roads. They plowed their fields with oxen, and we had to shower with our mouths closed because the water wasn't purified. Seoul had been devastated during the war, and there were very few structures over one story still standing. I left base only once when I went to the front lines to celebrate New Year's Eve with my former college roommate, an infantry lieutenant. I wore my air force uniform and his outfit thought I had flown all the air strikes they called in during the war. Since I never told them otherwise, they bought me drinks all night long—something I regretted the next morning. To cope with Korea and its challenges, I concentrated on honing my flying skills and, for the first time in my life, learned to appreciate reading books. Our squadron was equipped with RF-80As and RF-86As. Some of our flying was on a voluntary basis, so I volunteered every day. By the time four months had passed, I was one of the top pilots in flying hours each month.

"One day in March 1954 I was ordered to fly a mission along the west coast of North Korea in an RF-86F; it had no guns, unlike the A-model I had flown in the past. Seven F-86 fighters from the 4th Fighter Interceptor Wing, located across the field from us at Kimpo, were to serve as escorts. Why I was picked, one of the newest arrivals, a second lieutenant with minimum RF-86 time, was a puzzle to me. I attended the briefing and off we went, or sort of. Two of the fighter escorts never made it off the ground, [and] two more aborted in the air, leaving three escorts and one shutterbug to finish the mission. Poor weather in the target area made us turn back. I never said anything about the aborts, but I questioned the fighter squadron's maintenance. The balance of my subsequent missions I flew together with one other RF-86F, without escorts. Our motto was, 'We kill 'um with fillum.' On April 1, 1954, the 15th TRS transferred from Kimpo to Komaki Air Base, Japan. It extended my time from twelve to twenty-one months, but it got me out of South Korea and into a more civilized and actually fascinating country. Our transfer to Komaki was due to the arrival of RF-86F-30 Haymakers, not allowed to be based in South Korea under the terms of the armistice. The same rule applied to any other aircraft not based in South Korea at the time of the armistice. In Japan, we lived in Quonset huts in the town of Nagoya, about fifteen miles south of the air base. There was an officers' club downtown where the food was great. We were one of three small military units around Nagoya, so the town was not overrun with Americans. The Japanese were friendly, even though their city had been 85 percent destroyed during the war.

"The new RF-86Fs were dynamite ships. They had about ten hours on the airframe, and they even smelled new. Shortly after our squadron transferred to Japan, the operations officer, LaVerne Griffin, asked me if I would like to become a part of a special team of five or six pilots to fly classified photo reconnaissance missions in the Far East. I accepted immediately. The National Security Agency had apparently already investigated my background, and shortly thereafter I received a top-secret security clearance. I was told that the JCS selected our targets and that President Eisenhower personally approved all overflights of the Soviet Union. In the months that followed, I flew four classified missions over three Communist countries. I like to think that I flew more missions over more countries than anyone else, although none of us discussed these missions and I can't be sure. We flew far enough north requiring us to wear "poopie suits," one-piece waterproof suits designed to withstand the cold waters long enough to allow inflation of and ability to climb into a life raft. The suits went on over a quilted liner and were very difficult to get into. In addition to the poopie suits, we wore g-suits and a Mae West life preserver, a backpack parachute, a hard helmet, and oxygen mask.

"The service ceiling of the F-86 was about 42,000 feet. When we reached 54,000 feet with the RF-86, handling the plane became very touchy. It was almost like riding the edge of a stall. The aircraft also assumed a distinct nose-up attitude, which we corrected by cracking the wing flaps by about one and one-half inches. We had no viewfinder, like other recce aircraft, and the only way to be certain of our position in reference to the target was to stack the plane 90 degrees on one side and then 90 degrees on the other in order to

Jerry Depew, Ted Gesling, and Max Morris going through their morning rituals—make do with what you have.

be able to see the target and ensure that we were coming right over it. This maneuver, though, could slice away a lot of our precious altitude in a hurry.

"I flew my first mission on May 1, 1954. The target was Dairen in the People's Republic of China. Dairen, renamed Luta by the Communists after 1949, was a large port city. The camera focal length and our altitude allowed us to cover the entire target area including airfields, submarine pens, and so on. The distance of the target ruled out staging the mission out of Japan. To evade the UN inspectors, we took off at 0400 in the morning and an hour later landed at Kunsan Air Base, on the west coast of South Korea; refilled our oxygen and fuel tanks; and quickly took off again. My wingman was First Lieutenant Rudy Anderson from Greenville, South Carolina, a Clemson graduate and one of our best pilots in the squadron. His responsibility was to be my backup in case I had a camera malfunction, or one of my drop tanks didn't drop. In addition, it was his responsibility to warn me of any MiGs, should they appear, although this information was of dubious value since we didn't have any guns. We maintained radio silence from takeoff to touchdown and flew with about one mile separation. Much of our mission was over water. There were air-sea rescue aircraft, nicknamed Dumbos, on station during our overwater segment, but I had zero confidence they would ever find me should I go down.

Jerry Depew, center, with Fred Jeremias to his left and Hank Parsons on his right, in front of his RF-86F Haymaker, after flying his final mission before going home in July 1955.

"Following our take-off from Kunsan, we leveled off at 35,000 feet and burned off the fuel in the 200-gallon external tanks, then dropped them. We then climbed up to 43,000 feet to burn off and drop the two 120-gallon tanks. All jettisoned perfectly, and we slowly climbed up to 54,000 feet. Things were very quiet and very lonely. I kept a close watch on the instruments, scanned the air for enemy fighters, and eagerly looked forward to locating Dairen, take our photos, and then get the hell out of there. Finally, we sighted land ahead. We came in to the right of our target, corrected our heading, and turned on the cameras. The cameras were equipped with an intervalometer, which automatically took pictures at the proper intervals, compensating for our speed over the ground [and] ensuring properly spaced pictures for the use of the photo interpreter. Dairen was in the clear, and we did a wide 180-degree turn to the left in order to photograph Port Arthur. We saw no evidence of being detected, such as fighters. On our return, we put our aircraft into a shallow descent, picked up air speed, and made a quick return to Kunsan. The maintenance crew quickly refitted us with two 120-gallon wing tanks, and off we went to Yokota Air Base, near Tokyo, where they removed the film for analysis.

"The combination of wearing a poopie suit all day long, and drinking very little, combined with the stress of flying at great altitude, caused me to lose seven pounds. The following day, Rudy and I went to FEAF headquarters in Tokyo. This was the only time I ever got to see the film from any of my missions, going over the pictures with the photo interpreters who were pointing

HEADQUARTERS U. S. AIR FORCE
DIRECTORATE OF INTELLIGENCE
COLLECTION OPERATIONS DIVISIO
RECONNAISSANCE BRANCH
PHOTO INTELLIGENCE SECTION

TOP SECRET

WIND FALL

Cover sheet for pilot's Sensitive Intelligence (SENSINT) briefing folder describing the mission he was scheduled to fly, the target, and related flight information. A pilot's knowledge of the program was restricted to the particular flights he was involved in. In my experience flying PARPRO missions in the 55th SRW, the same rules applied. WIND FALL meant the product was shared with the CIA.

out to us what they could identify. During the film viewing, one of the colonels present said, 'Jesus Christ, look at all the submarines.' I asked him to point them out, and we counted fifteen. I don't know if the US Navy knew of Communist China's sizable submarine force, but until that moment I am sure the US Air Force didn't have a clue. That afternoon Rudy and I returned to Nagoya. No one asked where we had been. All I, and others, knew was that a couple of ships would disappear for a couple of days and the pilots came back smiling. Who could ask for more? I flew three additional overflight missions in 1955. One was of the Soviet Union and the other two were over North Korea.

"After being reassigned to Larson Air Force Base in Washington State, I decided to leave the air force. Here, at the Early Cold War Overflights Symposium, I had the great privilege to again meet George Best, Jimmy Black, Sam Dickens, Larry Garrison, and LaVerne Griffin to exchange experiences we couldn't talk about when we were flying with the 15th Tactical Reconnaissance Squadron. I wish to remember and acknowledge my wingman during my 1954 overflights, Major Rudolph "Rudy" Anderson Jr., United States Air Force, who at age thirty-five lost his life over Cuba when his U-2 reconnaissance aircraft was shot down by a surface-to-air missile during the 1962 Cuban Missile Crisis. He was one of the very best."

Jerry Depew was not the only one to fly with Rudy Anderson on these super-secret, deep-penetration reconnaissance flights; Jimmy Black was another. "I was born in York County, South Carolina, in 1927. I went to school in York, a small town of about three thousand about thirty miles south of Charlotte. After graduating from high school, I attended Clemson University for two semesters. It was 1944 and I decided to enlist in the navy, about three months before my eighteenth birthday. I took the written tests to get into flight training, which I passed, but I only had two semesters of college; the navy required four. So they sent me to Saint Mary's College in Winona, Minnesota. There was a small airport near the school. Since I was now making fifty dollars a month, I decided to see if I was cut out for flying. When the weather was nice I started taking flying lessons in a J-3 Cub with a 40-horsepower engine, flying off a grass strip. They also had an Aeronca Champ, but my preference was the Cub, for you really had to pay attention to make a good landing in the Champ. The Cub would almost land itself if you pointed it at the runway and pulled off the power. V-J Day came in the middle of August, and the navy was kind enough to let me finish the term before sending me to Great Lakes Naval Station for reassignment. I ended up at Treasure Island, California, to serve on a seagoing tug in San Francisco Bay. When my time was up I returned to Clemson University, graduating in January 1950. I still wanted to fly, and when the Korean War started that June I inquired about getting into the air force. I filled out the paperwork and never heard back from them. About a year later, in 1951, I went back to see the air force recruiter, inquiring about my status. It turned out, they had lost my paperwork at the Air Force Personnel Center. So I again filled out the forms, and this time around I got an assignment as an aviation cadet to Bainbridge, Georgia, class 53-B. I reported to Bainbridge on February 2, 1952. Flew the T-6 at Bainbridge, then was transferred to Laredo, Texas, for three months of flight training in the T-28, followed by three months in the T-33 jet trainer. Upon graduation I was commissioned a second lieutenant in the US Air Force. I was twenty-six years old.

"Prior to graduating from flight training, I had a conversation with one of my instructor pilots, and I told him that I wanted to be a fighter pilot. Said he, 'If you go into fighters, you'll be Blue Four, tail-end Charlie, for four or five months.' Meaning that the most junior person will fly the tail end of a four-airplane flight for that long or longer. He suggested I consider flying reconnaissance. After I learned that reconnaissance training was conducted at Shaw Air Force Base, about ninety miles from my home, I decided reconnaissance was for me. I first went to Moody AFB, Valdosta, Georgia, to instrument school, then to Shaw for RF-80 photo-reconnaissance training. The western part of Virginia, eastern Tennessee, and Kentucky simulated North Korea. They would send us up there with only a surface chart, using time and

Jimmy Black on his Honda in front of his Quonset hut at Komaki Air Base, Japan, August 1954.

distance, no radio, to go find somebody's bridge, somebody else's dam, and take pictures. And you had to watch out where you were going because they would send out an instructor ahead of time, and if he got a picture of you, or your tail number, that meant that you were 'shot down' for that day. This was pretty realistic training as far as I was concerned. Once I finished Shaw I was assigned to the 15th Tactical Reconnaissance Squadron at Kimpo Air Base, K-14, near Seoul, South Korea.

"I got there in mid-October 1953, and as a junior pilot I was assigned to fly RF-80s, the ship I trained in at Shaw. We had three RF-86A Honey Buckets. Those were flown only by pilots who had gone through F-86 training at Nellis Air Force Base in Nevada. We slept six to a tent in the winter cold in what was then a primitive, backward land. Four months later, we received twenty-four new RF-86Fs, Haymakers, with a hardened wing that could carry four drop tanks. We transferred to Komaki Air Base in Japan, near Nagoya, and I finally got to fly the RF-86F. When I got to Komaki in January 1954, some of the older pilots had already started flying secret overflight missions. They were referred to as 'spook missions' because nobody told anybody anything about them. They just disappeared with several airplanes, and a day or so later they would reappear with big grins on their faces. Security about these overflights was extremely tight. I finally got to fly one of those 'spook missions' in early March 1955. Rudy Anderson was the appointed flight leader of a three-aircraft flight. Fred Nichols was number two, and I was tail-end Charlie, number three.

"We flew from Komaki to Kadena Air Base, Okinawa, where we spent the night. Rudy Anderson briefed us on our route and the targets we would be photographing. To get into China, we used jet navigation charts—but for the target area, the targets were outlined for us on detailed surface charts. We took off from Okinawa around ten o'clock in the morning to get to our target area at noon. We were using full power, maximum EGT, and cruise climb, carrying four tanks, two 120-gallon tanks, and two 200-gallon tanks. We used the fuel from the 200-gallon tanks first and punched them off. As we burned off fuel and got lighter, we got as high as 50,800 feet. We flew parallel to each other with about 2,000 feet separation, Anderson in the middle, Nichols on the left, and I on the right. We flew in a northwesterly direction, coming in over the bay south of Shanghai, Hangchow on our left. Nanjing was the second target area where we turned right over the Yangtze River, coming back over Shanghai. I saw Rudy punch off his 120-gallon tanks just as we passed over Shanghai. He had not briefed us on that, so I punched off my tanks as well. We encountered no other aircraft and pulled no contrails. We arrived safely back on Okinawa right after lunch, around two o'clock. Our total flying time was three hours and forty minutes. We only stopped in Okinawa long enough to install two 120-gallon drop tanks, replacing the ones we punched off over China, refuel, go to the bathroom, and grab a quick sandwich. Then we flew to Yokota Air Base, FEAF headquarters, where the film was downloaded, developed, and analyzed. Lieutenant General Earl Partridge sent word that he wanted to see us. We were a little apprehensive because we thought maybe we made a mistake somewhere along the line. But as it turned out, all he wanted to do was tell us, 'Well done.' We had a conversation with him in his office. It was an honor to meet him. Needless to say, this was all pretty heady stuff for a first lieutenant.

"That was my only overflight mission. I stayed on until June 1955, when I was transferred to Moses Lake, Washington, flying SAC RF-84Fs for two years. I kept my eyes open for something better, and two years later, in 1957, I joined the 4080th Strategic Reconnaissance Wing at Laughlin Air Force Base, Del Rio, Texas. I flew U-2s with the 4080th for six years. The base was a good choice for our operation—it had two parallel runways and a minimal amount of nonmilitary air traffic. I checked out in the U-2 in July 1957 and flew it altogether for 1,040 hours. While at Laughlin we got some Cessna 310s, which we used as chase planes when checking out new pilots. We lost a couple of airplanes and pilots because they attempted to make too steep a turn from the base leg to final approach. If you made too steep a turn, because of wet wings, you would get a heavy wing and you just couldn't lift it up again. So we gave our new pilots a flight in the 310 and showed them the preferred ground track they should follow so they wouldn't get themselves in a box turning on final. The U-2 wasn't all that strange an aircraft—it had more lift, more power, less maneuverability, and more endurance than anything I had flown before. It was a good, straightforward airplane with a number of limitations, though, which, if ignored, would kill you. For instance, the older Pratt and Whitney J-57-P-37 engine, which we flew initially, would flame out for no apparent reason other than the engine tolerances were less than that demanded at high altitude. Sometime you would go for several weeks without a flameout, and then have a couple on one flight. The most difficult part of flying the U-2 was to make a good landing. It was a tail-dragger, and in order to make a decent landing I had to come across the threshold at three to five feet and ten knots above the stall speed. The threshold speed varied according to the amount of fuel carried." Like the B-47, the U-2 had a tandem main gear and outriggers to keep the wings from dragging on takeoff, called Pogos. The outriggers dropped off upon takeoff for the U-2, and retracted for the B-47. Landing on the front main gear, "you get a bounce, from which you may never recover, because you will always be 180 degrees out of synchronization.

"I flew a couple of reconnaissance missions while I was in SAC. They were called SFERICS, using weather reconnaissance as a cover story. We did air sampling on 'sniffer' missions out of a number of places, but the SFERICS missions were focused on picking up Russian radars. We flew about twenty to thirty miles off the coast of Siberia, in a straight line. That's a very dark place in the middle of the night in the far north in October."

Lieutenant Colonel James A. Black retired from the United States Air Force after a challenging reconnaissance career. He flew the RF-80, RF-84, RF-86A, RF-86F, and the U-2 reconnaissance aircraft, and was present for the Early Cold War Overflights Symposium held in February 2001 at Headquarters Defense Intelligence Agency, Washington, DC. Colonel Black's overflight recollections were made in September 1999 with R. Cargill Hall as part of the Oral History Program at the National Reconnaissance Office, Chantilly, Virginia.

THE LAST HURRAH OF THE "WILD BUNCH" (1954–1955)

I found that on every dive from 55,000 feet the airplane would pitch up at about Mach 0.95. The heavy buffeting at Mach 0.92 did not surprise me, but with even both hands on the control stick pushing forward I could not get the airplane to stay in a dive. The defector pilot told me that the MiG-15 had a tendency to spin out of accelerated, even one-G stalls, and often it did not recover from the spin. I did the stall tests of both one-G and accelerated stalls. The airplane gave virtually no stall warning and it demonstrated a nasty characteristic of snap-rolling from accelerated stalls.
—**Major General "Tom" Collins,** in Kenneth Chilstrom and Penn Leary, *Test Flying at Old Wright Field*

"I was assigned as an instructor at the US Military Academy at West Point," recalled Colonel Robert E. Morrison while participating in the Early Cold War Overflights Symposium in 2001. "When the Korean War broke out, I went to Personnel to request a flying assignment in Korea. They said I was too old for fighters, but would be happy to put me into night fighters or reconnaissance. I wanted no part of night fighters and accepted a reconnaissance assignment. I attended the usual courses—instrument school, reconnaissance school, survival training, and finally transition training into the F-86 at Nellis Air Force Base. After all this was done, in December 1954, off I went to South Korea to take over as commander of the 15th Tactical Reconnaissance Squadron. By the time I got there, of course, the war was over for all practical purposes. I arrived at the squadron at Kimpo Air Base, just as it was moving to Komaki, near Nagoya, Japan. I quickly learned that I was to be involved in a secret program. What program? We'll tell you when the time comes. I quickly realized that I had inherited this Mad Generation of motorcycle-riding aviators who were involved in this secret program that I still didn't know anything about.

"My pilots were the Mad Generation, not the X Generation or anything else, but the Mad Generation. Their bible was *Mad* magazine. 'What, me worry?' That was their mantra. They were the absolute wildest bunch of people I've ever seen, but they also were excellent pilots—and being their commander was the best job I ever had in my life. I assumed command of the squadron at Komaki Air Base in late March 1954, just as LaVerne Griffin and his associates were tasked to fly a set of three missions over Vladivostok. One of the pilots was Jerry Depew, who later flew a couple of missions with me as my wing- man. At the time we were undergoing a modification on our aircraft, changing our radios from VHF—Victor How Fox—to UHF—Uncle How Fox. One day, Jerry got into his speedy little RF-80 Shooting Star and headed for Yokota Air Base. He called in and requested Approach Control. The controller replied, 'Roger Rat-Race Three Two, do you have Uncle How Fox onboard?' With- out hesitation Jerry replied to the controller, 'Wait until I check my manifest.' Everybody on the air who overheard this conversation just broke up.

"After George Saylor and LaVerne Griffin, our operations officer, were reassigned, I chose Lieutenant Bill McLaren as my squadron operations offi- cer. I liked the way Bill worked with people, and he had a little more flying time than others, but he was just still a first lieutenant. I inherited a recently arrived captain who thought he should be the operations officer. I flew with him once and afterward told him, 'You are not going to fly again unless you have an instructor pilot with you.' He was that bad a flyer. The group com- mander didn't like my decision, and before you knew it he had me on the phone. 'I want that captain as your operations officer.' At that very moment I heard a loud BOOM out on the flight line. I put down the phone and raced out to the flight line. The captain in question, who was preparing for a flight, had just raised the ejection seat handle and blown himself out of the airplane. I returned to the office and picked up the phone. The group commander was still there and I said to him, 'Sir, if you don't mind, I am going to keep Bill McLaren as my operations officer. The captain just blew himself out of an airplane and I think he is AOCP—Out of Commission for Parts—for a while.

"Between March 1954 and February 1955, the 15th TRS flew a total of nine missions over Communist China and the Soviet Union. One disadvantage of running an organization like the 15th TRS was that nobody could talk about the unit or what it was doing. I reported to two different commanders. FEAF gave the overflight orders. I also reported to a group commander and a wing commander who commanded the 67th TRW, which we were a part of. Nei- ther of them knew what we were doing. They were not cleared. Soon after my arrival, I was summoned to Headquarters FEAF by Brigadier General Ben- jamin O. Davis. There, I was briefed by him on the overflight mission in the presence of Lieutenant General Earl E. Partridge, the FEAF commander. They were the people who provided the overflight instructions. Needless to say, I had trouble always meeting orders for airplanes for conventional reconnais- sance missions laid on by my wing commander, who was not informed. While receiving letters of commendation from General Partridge, I also garnered three of my worst fitness reports of my entire career as an air force officer from my wing commander—who knew nothing about our secret overflights.

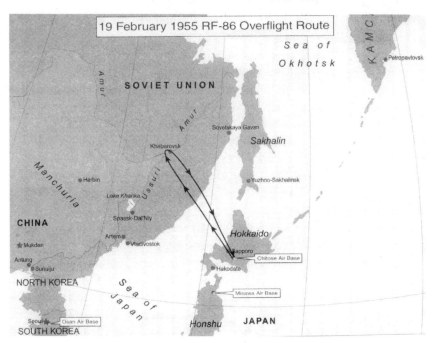

Colonel Robert E. Morrison's overflight route of Khabarovsk in February 1955.

Except for the Vladivostok missions, we were always briefed in Tokyo at Headquarters FEAF. Every mission was flown in complete radio silence. Our first two missions were flown over Sakhalin Island. On one of those missions, I recall, we were just nonchalantly flying along, when we encountered some MiG fighters at the same altitude as ours, coming directly at us. We saw each other almost simultaneously, as we flew through each other's formation. They were just as surprised as we were. After that we overflew Port Arthur. I flew as Bill Bissett's wingman for that mission, and he flew as my wingman on the next. I am sure we got some good pictures on the first flight, because they sent us back a second time to get even more. Later I participated in an overflight of Shanghai on November 20, 1954. The squadron flew another Shanghai mission in early 1955. For these flights we staged out of Kadena Air Base on Okinawa, overflew Shanghai, and returned to Yokota after first refueling at Kadena.

"One morning at Kadena there was a horrible fog, really very bad. We were checking out our airplanes on the runway when all of a sudden there was this deafening chuk—chuk—chuk noise. We looked up and there was a helicopter right overhead, barely visible in the fog. Bill McLaren, who was with me at the time, looked in the helicopter's direction and said in a normal voice, pointing in the direction of Base Operations, 'Base Ops is that way.' And the helicopter goes chuk—chuk—chuk and flies in that direction to the Base Ops hut. We had quite a laugh.

"Our last run during my tenure was to Khabarovsk, three and a half hours flying time, round trip, from Chitose Air Base on Hokkaido. My wingman had to abort because he had some mechanical issues to deal with as we were coasting in. I called, as I was supposed to in the event of an abort, and said, 'Red leader going in.' At the time I had red hair, thus the nickname 'Red.' I didn't receive a recall message, so I just kept on going. The weather was bad and I was in the clouds. I was over the Amur River with no target in sight. I had, however, a radio compass; Bird Dog, and I homed in on the local radio station, turned right, and headed for Khabarovsk. The standard procedure at the time was to punch off our 200-gallon tanks when we emptied them, and that is what I did. I kept on climbing to my mission altitude to about 48,000 feet. As I approached Khabarovsk, the 120-gallon tanks ran dry and I tried to punch them off. Only one of them dropped. I kept right on doing what I was supposed to—take pictures, roll to the right to take a look, roll to the left, then level out and take pictures. On the second roll, the 120-gallon tank that had hung up dropped right over Khabarovsk. When I got back, General Partridge asked me about the hung tank and dropping it over Khabarovsk. I told him that it probably was a maintenance issue. We didn't have any hangars for maintenance indoors. My troops lived in tents and had to perform all of their maintenance outdoors. Within two weeks, we had Butler hangars, brought in from Yokota."

In 1955, Colonel Morrison was reassigned to the United States and the 15th TRS transferred to Yokota Air Base, the location of the 67th TRW, and flew additional overflights in 1956. "In retrospect," notes Colonel Morrison, "we were a special group."

Major General Roger K. Rhodarmer, when serving as a young captain on the Air Staff in the Pentagon, was right in the middle of the overflight business as a "legman," the low-ranking guy who passed on messages, relayed orders, and made sure everything was working smoothly. Dropping a wing tank over Khabarovsk guaranteed a diplomatic protest. Recalls Rhodarmer, "Whenever an overflight was going, General [Frank Kendall] Everest [Jr.], US Air Force deputy chief of staff operations, wanted to know about it at the Pentagon, and quickly, because something might happen during the flight. If needed, he could send someone to advise the State Department guys because they were already being stomped on by the Soviet and Communist Chinese governments about overflights. The State Department man would brief Secretary of State [John Foster] Dulles. On one or two occasions we actually went into Dulles's office. He was very straightforward about the protests and publicly preferred to wash them off as propaganda. But the information we provided made it easy for him to downplay any incident so it would not become a big international flap. Remember, the Soviets never really wanted their people to know that we were flying over their country without getting shot down. So there was a kind of mutual agreement not to publicize the overflights.

"The most surprising thing about the overflights," recalled General Rhodarmer at the Early Cold War Overflights Symposium, "was the Soviets' ability to spot and track our aircraft at altitude. The RF-86s were flying at 50,000 feet. We listened in on the Soviet air defense network, so we had a feel for just how good they were. We sent up a C-47, or another aircraft, to loiter offshore with very sensitive electronic equipment to pick up when our guys' overflights were first detected and tracked. When did the Soviet air defense system come up? What frequency were they on? On one mission, the aircraft offshore recalled a pilot because MiGs were already airborne and waiting for him." That latter case involved an RB-45C over China, presented in an earlier section of this book. As for radar tracking? The Russians were very good at it, and their long-range search radars were excellent.

THE SHORT-LIVED RB-57A "HEART THROB" PROGRAM (1955–1956)

Captain Gerald E. LaVerne was flying an NRB-57D at 50,000 feet plus, in the winter of
1963 over Wright-Patterson AFB. LaVerne incurred an engine flameout. The resulting
abrupt yaw flamed out the other. The wings and engines both parted from the airframe.
He rode it down, on aircraft oxygen, until reaching a lower altitude before ejecting.

—**James E. Bauer,** in Kenneth Chilstrom and Penn Leary, *Test Flying at Old Wright Field*

While the RF-86 aircraft assigned to the 67th TRW were in the process of
phasing out, and before the RB-66 replacements arrived at Yokota Air Base, in
1956, the RB-57A-1 made its appearance in 1955, albeit for an extremely short
period of time. The program code name was "Heart Throb"—it's anyone's guess
how someone picked such a warm and endearing name for a mission filled
with anything but that. The B-57 aircraft, which was never given an American
name, is a derivative of the British Canberra, which, receiving very high praise
from air intelligence liaison officers at the American embassy in London, and
on their recommendations, was promptly picked up by the Air Staff to satisfy
an urgent need for a medium bomber and night-capable reconnaissance aircraft. The Martin Aircraft Company in Baltimore, Maryland, received an order
for 404 aircraft of all types. The first flight of a production B-57 took place in
1953, days before the signing of the Korean armistice. The entire program was
nearly killed by a string of spectacular accidents. The B-57 was not easy to
fly. Prior to modification of its longitudinal control and stabilizer systems, the
B-57 was uncontrollable if one of its two engines failed on takeoff or landing.
By 1957, the end of the production run for the B/RB-57, 47 of a production
total of 403 aircraft had been destroyed in accidents. The program was nearly
canceled in 1955 because of engine compressor stalls and structural problems.
Cooler heads prevailed, and the needed time and funding was invested in the
aircraft to make it work. The RB-57As assigned to the Heart Throb program
were aircraft that had most of the kinks worked out of them.[33]

Patricia Lynn, an RB-57E aircraft, at Danang Air Base, South Vietnam, January 1964. The E-model was a former B-57B tow-target aircraft converted to the reconnaissance role. Moonglow was their call sign, flying night IR, infrared, reconnaissance missions. The aircraft was lost on October 25, 1968.

In June 1955, Captain Joseph A. Guthrie Jr. suddenly found himself as the project leader for a group of four modified RB-57A-1 aircraft going to Japan, and Captain William "Bill" Gafford was in charge of six more of these aircraft going to Europe. Heart Throb was the overall cover name for the project—the aircraft bound for Japan would be known as West Wind, while those bound for Europe were assigned the moniker Blue Car. Ten RB-57As had been converted to high-altitude reconnaissance configurations, initially known as Lightweight, then renamed Heart Throb. Under Heart Throb all equipment not absolutely essential for daylight photography was removed, and the plane's J65-BW-5 engines were replaced with higher-thrust J65-W-7 engines, and the crew was reduced from two to one. The RB-57A-1 was 5,500 pounds lighter than the original configuration, and all the necessary modifications were completed in August 1955. Six Heart Throb aircraft eventually were assigned to the 7499th Composite Squadron at Wiesbaden Air Base, Germany, and another four went to the 6007th Composite Squadron of the Far East Air Forces at Yokota Air Base, Japan.

Recalls then Captain Joseph Guthrie at the Early Cold War Overflights Symposium, "In the spring of 1955 I was stationed at Randolph Air Force Base near San Antonio, Texas, as a B-57B flight instructor. On a warm day in May my boss, Lieutenant Colonel Jesse J. 'Pappy' Craddock, commander of the 3515th Combat Crew Training Squadron, called me into his office. He advised me that I had been selected for a classified project which would include some travel in the United States and eventual assignment to Japan. I wasn't too thrilled about this news. I had just returned from a tour of duty in South

Korea and been at Randolph for only a year. Pappy assured me that it was a great opportunity for a young captain and I would love the assignment—besides, the decision had already been made. I had been selected and that was that. In early June 1955 I flew to Washington, DC, to learn about my assignment. A Lieutenant Colonel Roger Rhodarmer told me to proceed to the Martin Aircraft Company in Middle River, Maryland, to oversee the modification of four RB-57A aircraft. After the reconnaissance modifications were completed, I was to test fly the aircraft and then ferry them to Warner Robins Air Force Base in Georgia for inspection and repair as necessary. While that was going on, I was instructed to obtain personal equipment for myself and three other RB-57A pilots, including newly designed partial pressure suits. Finally, I was to get everyone qualified in the new pressure suits at the high-altitude chamber at Wright-Patterson Air Force Base, Dayton, Ohio. After all that was done, I was to deliver the aircraft, when ready, from Warner Robins Air Force Base to San Diego for transport to Japan on an aircraft carrier.

"I learned that I was to be the project leader for the four modified aircraft going to Japan, and a Captain William Gafford was in charge of six more of these aircraft going to Europe. Needless to say, it was a busy summer for a young captain, but a lot of fun. I did everything I was told to do by Lieutenant Colonel Rhodarmer at the Air Staff—except make arrangements for transporting the aircraft to Japan on an aircraft carrier. The more I thought about that, the less I liked the idea. It seemed like such an inglorious way to send US Air Force aircraft to Japan. I got in touch with some Martin Aircraft Company performance engineers to figure out if the aircraft could be flown to Japan. The major obstacle was the first leg of some 2,300 nautical miles from California to Hawaii. Subsequent B-57B flights to Japan would have a 3,000-pound ferry tank in the bomb bay, but our modified 'featherweight' RB-57A-1s had the bomb bay removed and skinned over to reduce weight, and did not have the capability to carry such a tank. To my delight, the Martin engineers informed me that I could make it with 2,000 pounds of fuel remaining under conditions of no serious headwinds. So I took an aircraft and flew it 2,300 miles. Sure enough, I had 2,000 pounds of fuel remaining when I landed. Off I went to see Colonel Rhodarmer in the Pentagon. He was on leave, so I turned to his associate for advice, Lieutenant Colonel Ralph Steakley. I showed him the performance data and the results of the test flight. He told me to forget about the US Navy and plan on flying the aircraft to Japan. When Colonel Rhodarmer returned from leave, he was less than overjoyed about my decision, and let me know it.

"The Military Air Transport Service, MATS, in later years renamed MAC, Military Airlift Command, renamed again as Air Mobility Command, its present name, was in charge of all long-distance ferry flights. Rhodarmer directed

Flying in a pressure suit is anything but fun—just getting the thing on took effort, and movement in it was restrictive. Many high-altitude flyers had to prebreathe 100 percent oxygen before flight. The Heart Throb pilots did not, but breathed pure oxygen inside the pressurized cockpit.

me to make arrangements with MATS at their headquarters at Andrews Air Force Base in Maryland. These people wanted no part of our deployment. After all, they had no aircraft that could get up to 50,000 feet and lead us across the Pacific. Besides, all we had in way of navigation gear was a radio compass, which was totally inadequate for long-distance flights such as ours. I went back to the good colonel for help, and he must have twisted some arms, because the Military Air Transport Service suddenly became agreeable to support our flight.

"On August 25, 1955, I departed Hamilton Air Force Base, near San Francisco, with Lou Picciano on my left wing and Jim Bryant and 'Pappy' Hines on the right. Five hours and fifty minutes later we arrived at Hickam Air Force Base in Hawaii. I had 1,800 pounds of fuel remaining and the aircraft with the least had 1,300 pounds. We proceeded across the Pacific stopping at Johnson Island, Kwajalein, and Guam, finally arriving at Yokota Air Base on September 4. Colonel Avery, the commander of the 6007th Reconnaissance Group, met us on arrival. He seemed glad to see us, at least until he learned that none of us had any reconnaissance experience. He immediately set up an in-house school, and we spent the next two months learning how to take pictures from aircraft. Our RB-57As were equipped with two K-38, 36-inch focal length cameras that shot diagonally across the aircraft, and a 6-inch focal length T-11 mapping camera that shot straight down. In addition, the aircraft had been equipped with a viewfinder that permitted the pilot to look down through the nose, which made positioning the aircraft much easier. In mid-November we were declared 'as ready as we would ever be.' Captain Bryant outranked me, but since I had done all the dog work getting the aircraft ready, he did not exercise his rank and graciously agreed to let me fly the first mission. The mission was planned to be flown from Chitose Air Base on the northernmost Japanese island of Hokkaido. Jim Bryant served as my backup, and only the two of us were briefed. This was standard operating procedure for all over-flight missions. That way, if something untoward happened, you would know little about the overall program. We flew two days ahead of the mission to Chitose to make preparations for the flight, to be flown in total radio silence.

"I was to fly north from Chitose along the eastern side of Sakhalin Island far enough out to sea and at a hundred feet altitude to avoid radar detection. I would then continue to a point abreast of the northern portion of Sakhalin, where I would jettison the tip tanks and initiate a climb to maximum attain-able altitude. At some point of the climb I had to initiate a 180-degree turn so as to arrive over the northern tip of the island heading south at 55,000 feet. Then I would fly down the entire length of the island. Once I got over Hok-kaido I was allowed to break radio silence to land at Chitose. There I would refuel, then take off again for Yokota, where the film would be downloaded and analyzed.

"The day of the mission, November 26, 1955, the weather was excellent. We gathered early for the briefing. We had a controlled takeoff time, so it was imperative I got dressed and strapped into the aircraft in time. I went to the aircraft, did a walk-around inspection, then back inside to get suited up. That was quite a task. I put on a pressure suit, an air vent suit, a padded suit, a water survival suit, and a Mae West life preserver. I now resembled the Pillsbury Doughboy and moved with the dexterity and appearance of a robot. It made me wonder if I could still fly the aircraft. Worrying about making the takeoff time, I got dressed way too early. It did not take long for me to get very hot inside the pressure suit, so I stepped outside into the frigid Hokkaido air to cool off. Finally, it was time for me to go. With all the equipment I was wear-ing it took a technician to help stuff me into my seat. Then he spent some time getting my parachute buckled and everything hooked up before check-ing everything out thoroughly. For the first time in my life I wished I was somewhere else. But the feeling didn't last long. As soon as I got the engines started I was raring to go. We had one of our own men in the control tower, and as soon as he saw I was ready to taxi he told the controller to issue taxi instructions. Two minutes before takeoff I was cleared on the runway, then

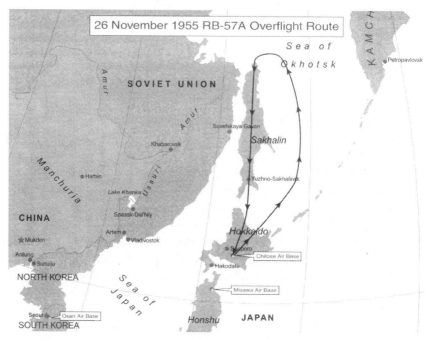

November 26, 1955, overflight of Sakhalin Island by Colonel, then Captain, Joseph A. Guthrie Jr. in an RB-57A-1.

cleared for takeoff. Exactly on time I rolled down the runway, lifted off, and took up my first heading.

"I was soon over the ocean east of Sakhalin, flying 100 feet above the water. Before long I ran into some low clouds and found myself flying completely on instruments. I was flying at 350 knots indicated, making for a sporty ride over the ocean. I decided that a little more altitude was desirable before I ended up in the drink, so I climbed an additional 200 feet and held that altitude for the rest of the way north. I could not see anything and piloted completely by dead reckoning. At the appropriate time I punched off the tip tanks and initiated my climb to 55,000 feet.

"I had worried that the mission would be a washout because of the weather. But as I gained altitude I could see that the entire island was completely cloud free. Everything looked great until I saw that I was too far east to photograph one of the airfields. Not knowing better, I made a 360-degree turn and picked it up. As a result, I got every target assigned. There were many targets on Sakhalin, and, as best as I could see through the viewfinder, there were plenty of MiG fighters on them. There also was no doubt that the Soviets knew I was there. We had a cockpit warning device that told us when we were being tracked by radar. I could discriminate between airborne and ground radars by the tone of the audio warning—a high piercing tone meant airborne radar, and trouble. I picked up airborne radar warnings, but when I looked around, changing headings when I could, I saw nothing. There wasn't much I could do but head south. In frustration, I turned the warning device off. It was good to see Hokkaido Island slip under the nose, and I broke radio silence and called Chitose for landing instructions. I made an uneventful landing and logged four hours and forty minutes. After a quick turnaround and a change into a normal flight suit, I joined Captain Bryant on a return flight to Yokota, landing just before dark. The next day, Colonel Avery debriefed us. I got a lecture about all the bad things that can happen to a reconnaissance pilot making 360-degree turns. He told me in no uncertain terms that it was 'one pass and haul ass.' For penance, I was sent back to reconnaissance school for another week.

"A day or two later, Colonel Avery told me that we had to go to Tokyo to brief General Lyman L. Lemnitzer, the commander in chief of the Far East Command. I thought Colonel Avery was going to give the briefing; he informed me that the general wanted the briefing given by the pilot who flew the mission. I practiced in front of the colonel and the group staff until I was sick of the mission. Finally, we left for Tokyo. I was a captain, and a new one at that, and had never seen so many stars assembled in my life. I kept thinking, how do I get out of this mess with my skin and captain's bars still in place? General Lemnitzer soon put me at ease. I [was just getting] started when General [Roger Maxwell] Ramey interrupted me at least three times with questions. Finally, General Lemnitzer raised his hand and said, 'General, why don't we let the officer finish his briefing, and then you can ask all the questions you want.' From then on it was a piece of cake. I remain eternally grateful to General Lemnitzer.

"As far as the airborne threat was concerned, I do not believe anyone in our group had any serious concerns about fighters, or any trouble from ground-based defenses. The only serious in-flight problem occurred on one of our air aborts later in 1956. Jim Bryant was the pilot. He was to fly on the deck, as I did, then climb to altitude and get rid of the tip tanks. The right tank hung up, yawing the aircraft violently to the right with a subsequent snap and spin. Jim broke the spin, but in the recovery exceeded the Mach number and pitched up in a stall and violent spin. Again Jim recovered, but he had to shut down the right engine because of turbine damage. The generators from both engines quit working, and he had to rely on battery power. In addition, during all the thrashing around in the cockpit during the spins, Jim broke an armrest and started the ejection sequence. Despite all this, he brought the aircraft back and made a smooth single-engine landing. We secured the ejection seat so Jim could get out of the aircraft safely. The next morning, when Jim opened his front door, he found a case of scotch whiskey on the doorstep from the Martin Company with a note attached, 'Thanks for a job well done!' The RB-57A-1 Heart Throb operated in Asia for less than a year. During that time we flew four overflights before the SENSINT program ended in late 1956."

Captain Robert E. Hines Sr., nicknamed Pappy, was one of the pilots who flew Heart Throb with Joe Guthrie. "In June 1953 I was assigned to the 1738th Ferrying Squadron in Long Beach, California. At that time, the Martin Company built a version of the British Canberra aircraft, many of them needed to be ferried to Warner Robins Air Force Base near Macon, Georgia, for additional modifications—B-57A, -B and -C models. Although the three models of the B-57 were similar in many ways, there were important differences such as the larger canopy on the B-57A and the dive boards on the B-57B and C models. In early 1955 it was whispered around the Martin Company plant in Middle River, near Baltimore, Maryland, that a lightweight version of the RB-57A would be employed in a special US Air Force reconnaissance project. I volunteered for the Heart Throb program, and before I knew it I found myself at Edwards Air Force Base in California involved in the final engineering test flights of the RB-57A-1. The Heart Throb version of the RB-57A depended on a 10-pound charge of black powder to start rotation of the engine turbines, making engine start a commanding process. The huge pall of black smoke that resulted caused considerable comment. No one had ever seen so much smoke on the flight line except as a result of an aircraft accident or fire. With a 104-foot wingspan, and without any airspeed drag controls, tight formation flying in the RB-57A-1 was quite a bit more demanding than flying an F-86. Aside from the problem of trying to read the instruments while watching adjacent aircraft, the wing design added another problem. The A-model did not have dive boards like the later B and C models. Instead, it relied on 4-inch-long spoilers to provide airspeed control. Even in a gentle glide, activating the spoilers gave the same sensation as applying brakes while driving on an icy road. Another RB-57A anomaly was that the 104-foot wing had a wing root of about four feet which allowed extremely low wing loading. The wing was located high up on the fuselage, giving nearly uninterrupted airflow across the entire wing, which provided great stability. The high altitudes we flew at required wearing a partial pressure suit with a helmet anchored by a quarter inch of braided steel cable. Wearing all of this equipment added stress to a mission of up to seven hours in duration. We all had to adjust to the tender and touchy flying techniques of the RB-57A-1.

"Finally the day arrived for us to depart for Yokota, Japan. After a close fighter formation takeoff from Hamilton Air Force Base, California, and a very long flight across the Pacific Ocean, Mauna Kea on the island of Hawaii came into view. Although we were still several hundred miles out, land was

Typical B/RB-57 engine starting process. The 10-pound black powder charge made the aircraft appear to be on fire, and anyone not familiar with the aircraft and its peculiar starting mechanism would indeed be startled if witnessing the process for the first time.

a welcome sight. Three days later we took off for Kwajalein in the Marshall Islands. The flight was uneventful until we neared Kwaj, where a huge thunderhead, which topped out at 45,000 feet, sat squarely over the entire island. My assigned position was on our lead's right; I was number 4. The bouncing around during our descent through the fully developed thunderstorm caused me to suffer acute spatial disorientation. The sense of impending disaster affected my radio transmissions to the flight leader. His and my transmissions were of course monitored in flight operations at Kwajalein. Although we pilots did not find anything amusing about this episode, the ground control personnel, mostly navy types, seemed to have been greatly amused by our radio chatter and wanted to know who number 4 was. To this day I have nightmares of that flight and the disorientation I suffered.

"We refueled and got ready for takeoff the following day. As I tried to start my number one engine—the starter blew. A blown starter required an engine change. It was the group's consensus that the other three aircraft should continue, and I would remain behind to resolve my problem. It took three days to fly in a spare engine from Hickam Air Force Base, Hawaii. Fortunately it came on its own hydraulic frame, which permitted precise placement in the engine nacelle. There was only one US Navy mechanic, a three-striper, on the island with limited training on reciprocating engines. The two of us lowered the damaged engine onto a GI mattress and had an aircraft tug pull it away.

Two RB-57A-1s over Japan in 1956, trying color schemes for camouflage. Joe Guthrie was one of the pilots. The black aircraft has two J65-7s installed, raising thrust from 7,200 to 7,800 pounds per engine.

All of the aircraft TOs, technical orders, fortunately were on board my aircraft, so the two of us went by the numbers and did each task in proper sequence. In a few hours my US Navy mechanic and I had things ready for a test flight. I arbitrarily decided that an hour's flight time over the island was sufficient. The flight to Yokota was uneventful, except for the beautiful coral reefs I could see below and a distant waterspout.

"There had been no time to develop a training course for Heart Throb pilots, so we developed our own. For the first couple of months we spent most of our time getting familiar with aircraft systems, especially our photographic suite. We also arranged for some F-86Ds stationed at Yokota to fly intercepts on our aircraft so we could correctly interpret our nose and tail radar warnings. After a period of concentrated training, we certified ourselves as mission ready. I only flew one mission over Manchuria. Over Vladivostok a MiG locked onto me, staying with me for about thirty-five miles out over the Sea of Japan. I thought this might be my final day on earth. Finally, my 'hunter friend' broke off his chase. I knew he couldn't get up to my altitude, but certainly he could fire an air-to-air missile if he could stay locked on long enough. My mission did reveal the first MiG-19 aircraft deployed in the Vladivostok area. Shortly after this flight, the Strategic Air Command, in November 1956, deployed six RB-57D aircraft to Yokota. I was tasked to give a theater briefing to the newly arrived SAC pilots. At the end of my briefing, there was not one question. Unbelievable, I thought. We had so many questions when we arrived, it seemed unreal that these guys didn't have one question for me. The CinC SAC, General LeMay, was at Yokota Air Base at the time, and after completion of the first SAC overflight mission in early December personally decorated each of his pilots with the Distinguished Flying Cross. Instead of flying solo missions, SAC launched all six aircraft at once. Three feigned a mission and turned around before crossing into Soviet territory; the other three penetrated, causing the Soviet air defense system to be activated. A serious behind-the-scenes diplomatic ruckus followed this SAC effort—there would be no more overflights. I was out of a job again.

"In December 1956, we still had four functional RB-57A-1 reconnaissance aircraft sitting on the flight line at Yokota—doing nothing," recalled Robert "Pappy" Hines at the symposium. "I had an idea. Why not give the aircraft to the Chinese Nationalists and let them continue flying reconnaissance over Communist China? I presented my idea to my superiors, who tasked me to come up with a concept of operation. It then went up the chain of command, to the very top, and it was approved. When eventually my operations officer revealed all this to me, I suggested they designate a colonel as project officer. I, as a captain, was the chosen one. I argued a captain didn't have enough horsepower. To no avail. With the dedicated assistance of then Captain Louis Picciano, five noncommissioned officers, and one technical representative from the Glenn Martin Company, we had a new foreign reconnaissance team ready for action in six months. With that project completed, I was reassigned to Wright-Patterson Air Force Base, where I remained until my retirement in 1964." "Pappy" Hines, as he was affectionately known to his fellow aviators, retired as a major from the US Air Force and participated in the 2001 Early Cold War Overflights Symposium at DIA Headquarters in Washington, DC.

Captain Louis Picciano, one of "Pappy" Hines's fellow RB-57A flyers, accompanied the transfer of the RB-57As to the Nationalist Chinese. "We often took the Chinese pilots out over Iwo Jima," he recalled, "and all the other different islands surrounding Okinawa, to do dead reckoning flights just like they were going to do on an actual mission." The RB-57A-1 was a single-seat aircraft, so for instructive purposes two aircraft had to be launched. "During this time we moved our families to Taiwan. The Nationalist Chinese pilots flew two or three successful overflights over mainland China. In 1958 one of the RB-57As was shot down. This incident ended RB-57A overflights of Red China. It was evident that such missions were no longer going to go unchallenged.

The MiG-19 was capable of engaging our aircraft at operating altitude. With MiG-19s deployed in the Soviet Far East and in China as well, it looked like the RB-57A-1 was just about done in Asia."

Cargill Hall, Emeritus Chief Historian of the National Reconnaissance Office, and good friend, notes that as a result of that mass overflight by SAC RB-57D aircraft over the Soviet Union on December 18, 1956, an agitated President Dwight D. Eisenhower ordered a cessation of all American overflights of denied territory. Although the president would authorize CIA U-2 overflights to begin again in 1957, the air force SENSINT Program ended with Eisenhower's December edict. Eisenhower may have shut down the SENSINT Program, but technology was as much of a player in that decision as that multiaircraft SAC overflight in the Vladivostok region. The first flight of the Lockheed U-2 high-altitude reconnaissance aircraft took place on August 4, 1955, a fact that President Eisenhower was very much aware of and a development that he had high hopes for. In 1957, the Space Age began when the Soviets launched Sputnik-1 into earth orbit. A moment of panic ensued for America's military when the Vanguard rocket that was to take America into space exploded on its launchpad—a moment for Dr. Wernher von Braun to come on stage and begin to set things right.

As for the European Heart Throb contingent. Six of the ten RB-57As converted to RB-57A-1 Heart Throb aircraft arrived at Rhein-Main Air Base, Frankfurt, Germany, on August 23, 1955. The pilots Captains Ralph Findlay, William Gafford, Robert Holladay, Kenneth Johnson, Robert Thorne, and Gerald Cooke were the initial selectees. Within months of his arrival, Ralph Findlay transferred to the 10th TRW, RB-66s, at Spangdahlem Air Base and was replaced by Major Bert Grigsby. They went through the same training at Wright-Patterson Air Force Base, Ohio, as did the Heart Throb contingent that went to Yokota Air Base. They flew a limited number of missions against Eastern Bloc countries such as Czechoslovakia, Hungary, Yugoslavia, and as far as western Romania and the former East Prussia, now a Soviet possession. Their last overflight was in August 1956, after which they flew numerous photo reconnaissance missions over western Europe. Recalled Major General Gerry E. Cooke, then a captain, "We took pictures of everything in Europe from the New Hebrides off Scotland's coast, to Gotland Island off the southeast coast of Sweden, to Turkey, Saudi Arabia, North Africa, to Morocco. We deployed to many places and trained constantly. At one time we flew four aircraft into Bandırma, Turkey, a primitive place, where we flew off grass strips. This was a new experience for me in this aircraft. The Heart Throb bird did well on grass. Ground support needs were minimal if pilots were not in a pressure suit. All we needed was a box of starter cartridges, a case of engine oil, and a screwdriver—and some bottled oxygen. One sortie in the winter of 1956 to 1957

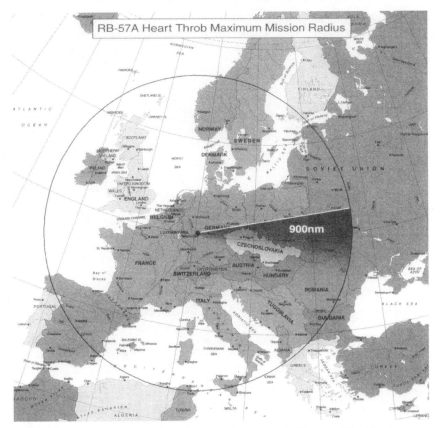

RB-57A-1 Heart Throb maximum mission radius for the six aircraft flying out of Frankfurt in 1956.

took me to Gardermoen, Norway, where the snow was about ten feet deep except on the runway and in the revetments.

"In 1958, the Black Knight RB-57D version of the RB-57 began to arrive at the 7407th Support Squadron at Frankfurt Air Base, Germany, from Laughlin Air Force Base, Texas. It was a swept extended-wing version of the Canberra with two extra jets on pylons beneath each wing. It was the model just before the big wing RB/WB-57F. To me," recalled General Cooke, "the 'D' airplane was unimpressive. It lacked the grace of the basic, clean Canberra. Furthermore, U-2s had arrived in theater, first in England and then at Wiesbaden in 1956, before moving to Giebelstadt, and soon thereafter to Incirlik Air Base in Turkey. Since the 7407th Support Squadron frequently operated from Adana on temporary duty, some of us were briefly involved in the orientation of the U-2 flyers. Although impressed with the U-2's performance, I could muster no feeling for this operation. The civilian intelligence control, combined with using 'demilitarized' air

The early version of the U-2 high-altitude reconnaissance aircraft was a clean looking, lightweight aircraft; in years to come, it was to grow in size, weight, and complexity to the point where the later versions in fact are quite different airplanes. Tail #56-6696 was the first U-2 delivered to the 4080th SRW at Laughlin Air Force Base, Texas, on June 11, 1957. The aircraft pictured here was #13 of the first batch of twenty U-2s built for the air force and flown by the 4080th.

force fighter pilots who were receiving salaries almost seven times our own, produced mixed feelings. With my Heart Throb experience behind me, I would not have been comfortable in this kind of operation and thought it a strange setup. I never envied those in the program, although their salaries were head turning. Subsequent events confirmed the accuracy of my misgivings, and General LeMay's early scorn of the program. The air force subsequently turned the U-2 to salutary use during the Cuban Missile Crisis in 1962."

In summary, Major General Cooke concluded at the Early Cold War Overflights Symposium in 2001, "The RB-57A Heart Throb was a great airplane and a joy to fly. In subsequent flying assignments I was never again to experience such measure of pilot freedom to decide and act, and to exercise personal judgment about flying and operational matters, as I did in Heart Throb. I believe we represented the tail end of the kind of military flying that began in World War I, and last existed in the 1950s. We were given objectives and responsibilities—and entrusted to deliver. I believe we did deliver."

Looking back at his experiences as a young captain in the Heart Throb program, General Cooke at the Early Cold War Overflights Symposium noted,

"Most of us in the Heart Throb environment found ourselves for the first time in a Top Secret, need-to-know, Compartmented, national-level controlled security apparatus. Up to this time I had never heard of any security clearance category above Top Secret. I do not remember having a Top Secret security clearance prior to this assignment. Yet, not once do I recall pilots discussing a classified overflight mission with each other or anyone else in our squadron or in social situations. Our subsequent assignments scattered us throughout the air force. We had no opportunity to share our common experiences. We also had no squadron reunions. We were never released to talk about these experiences until now. Security also became a family responsibility. Our spouses undoubtedly knew, in general terms, what we were up to. In those days they just simply did not talk about 'Dad's job.' All military things were secret as far as they were concerned. My wife never knew where I flew in the Heart Throb program until the summer of 2000 when we were informed that the Heart Throb missions had been declassified."

THE RB-57A-1 HEART THROB: A CHALLENGING PLANE TO FLY (1955–1956)

Ike was very cautious, but he was so intent to gain information on Soviet missile development that he approved a joint CIA/RAF operation in 1955. A stripped down Canberra flew at 55,000 feet, and photographed the secret test facility at Kapustin Yar. The Canberra was hit by ground fire and barely made it back to base. Years later, the CIA concluded that the operation had indeed been compromised by Kim Philby, who was a mole for the KGB.
—Ben Rich and Leo Janos, *Skunk Works*

Louis J. Picciano Jr. was one of a small group of RB-57A-1 flyers, including Joe Guthrie, Jim Bryant, and "Pappy" Hines, based at Yokota Air Base, Japan, a perennial reconnaissance hub for the US Air Force, a base from which in later years I flew many PARPRO missions in RB-47H reconnaissance aircraft. The RB-57A-1 Heart Throb was a modification of the B-57A, requiring 110 major modifications of the original British Canberra bomber to turn it into an RB-57A-1—and that didn't mean that all of its peculiarities had been discovered or fixed. Lou Picciano and his fellow aviators rose to the challenge, but at times it was a close thing as each and every one of the four discovered.

"I became involved in the reconnaissance business before I even knew what the word meant," recalled Lou Picciano in 2001 at the Early Cold War Overflights Symposium at DIA Headquarters in Washington DC. "I was just a few years out of the aviation cadet program in 1951, assigned to a ferrying squadron in Amarillo, Texas, flying C-119s around the world. I had a good squadron commander who ask for volunteers to ferry jet-powered B-57s. I was sent to San Antonio for five rides in the T-33 jet trainer to see if I was 'adaptable for jets.' When I tested well, I was sent to Shaw Air Force Base in South Carolina. Bill Gafford, who eventually led the Heart Throb contingent to Europe, was my B-57B instructor. It took several months to check out in the aircraft because of a low in commission rate. I finally finished and ended up

115

A Royal Air Force Canberra Mark 2, one of two Canberras delivered to the Martin company, bearing USAF insignia, left Northern Ireland on February 20, 1951, for Gander, Newfoundland, and landed in Baltimore on February 21. This was the first jet aircraft to complete an unrefueled flight across the Atlantic Ocean. On March 2, 1951, the air staff directed production of the B-57, eventually building a total of 403 of all models.[34]

back in Amarillo ferrying B/RB-57s from the Martin Company Middle River plant in Maryland to Robins Air Force Base in Georgia.

"One day while at the Martin plant I ran into Bill Gafford again. 'What are you doing up here?' I asked him. 'Aren't you supposed to be down at Shaw?' He was evasive and said he couldn't talk about it. I asked him if he would be interested in me joining his unit, whatever it was they were doing. He said, 'Yes.' Then told me that his unit would move to Europe and I might enjoy the assignment. I asked him to drop my name in the hat. Two weeks later I received orders to go to Wright-Patterson Air Force Base in Ohio, where I met Bill Gafford and Joe Guthrie. Gafford told me that there had been a mix-up and he couldn't take me with him to Europe; instead, he said, Guthrie and I would be going to Japan. At Wright-Patterson we were measured for our partial pressure suits before departing again for Robins Air Force Base to pick up four sleek-looking RB-57A-1s. I still did not know what sort of a mission I had volunteered for. As I inspected the aircraft I could see they had no bomb bays, but they had little windows underneath. Probably for cameras, I figured. We flew all four to Hamilton Air Force Base in California, where we sat for quite some time waiting for favorable winds. Our names were painted on the airplanes. I was a lieutenant at the time, the other three were captains. You could see our names on the aircraft from a long way off.

"On August 25, 1955, we took off from Hamilton for Hawaii, then on to Johnson Island. I was Guthrie's wingman, and next to me was another pilot, 'Pappy' Hines. Pappy was on Jim Bryant's wing to the right of Guthrie. After we landed at Johnson Air Base, Guthrie told me he wanted me on his right wing in a formation takeoff. I was stunned. Because I had not flown in formation since training as an aviation cadet. I had never made a formation takeoff. While Jim Bryant and Joe Guthrie planned the next leg of our flight to Kwajalein and Guam, Pappy and I sat in the corner smoking. I think I had two cigarettes in my mouth at once. Nervously I asked Pappy, 'Can you give me any tips on a formation takeoff?' 'Once your power gets stabilized,' he replied, 'make small throttle movements and stay close to Joel. You absolutely do not want to go off the right side of the runway and roll up in a fireball.' I quickly put another cigarette in my mouth. I only had eight hundred hours flying time, total. Didn't feel I was really up to snuff for this maneuver. As it turned out, the formation takeoff went great.

"After Pappy arrived at Yokota Air Base after his engine change in Kwajalein, we realized that none of us knew anything about reconnaissance. So we began ground school training. I still remember the formula: focal length over altitude equals scale. Once we had that information, we had to compute how much film it would take to cover the target. It was a good school and taught us most of the tricks of the trade. While still learning the nuts and bolts of aerial reconnaissance, Joe Guthrie would kick us out onto the tarmac to fly our planes. Every couple of weeks we would have to struggle into our suits and fly a mission we had worked out in reconnaissance school. I remember the mission Joe Guthrie flew to Sakhalin Island where he made a 360-degree turn. The group commander said, 'Get that guy back to reconnaissance school. You don't make 360s.' What did we know?

"Everything was going well and I began to think this duty was going to be a piece of cake. Then things turned sour. I loved the RB-57A-1 Heart Throb airplane, but it was a one-way romance. The aircraft was tricky to fly and prone to strange behavior in flight. On one occasion, the left engine just quit on me. No problem. I came in on one engine and landed, hoping this was not a bad omen. Then Jim Bryant went out on his overflight mission, and one of his tip tanks failed to jettison and lodged up against the vent mast. When that happened, his airplane pitched up and stalled. When the cockpit armrest came out, it triggered the ejection sequence. Jim tried to put the pin in but couldn't do it. He was sitting on a hot seat. All the violent movement sheered off some engine compressor blades, so that engine was gone and useless. Jim Bryant managed to deal with all of his problems, but it didn't look good for us. The next time I went up I couldn't get the landing gear to retract. I had three green lights, indicating the gear was down and locked. After burning some fuel I landed, rolled about 400 feet, then heard a 'clunk, clunk, clunk' as all three wheels retracted into the undercarriage. 'You should have seen the sparks,' one wide-eyed mechanic told me. I was beginning to wonder about this airplane.

"Joe Guthrie took my RB-57A-1 into the hangar, and he and Jim Bryant put it on jacks to examine the undercarriage. They were able to duplicate the problem I experienced in the air. When they picked up the airplane on the runway, they dropped and bent it a little bit. Now we had to fly it to Tachikawa, about ten miles away, where there was a repair depot. Joe Guthrie and Jim Bryant patched the plane up the best they could, and Joe flew it, gear and flaps down, to Tachikawa. There it stayed for four months until we got it back. I continued to have difficulties with this airplane. I was flying to Johnson Air Base, put the gear down, put the flaps down, and 'boom' straight down I went to about 1,000 feet. All of a sudden the aircraft recovered and flew normally. This airplane featured a flap-and-yoke-connected operation, I learned. When the flaps went down, the airplane tended to pitch up, then the yoke automatically moved forward to pitch it down. When the signal went to the yoke to move forward, the flaps did not come down right away, explaining my startling loss of altitude on approach to Johnson. I knew this airplane was out to get me.

"Joe Guthrie flew the first overflight mission. Jim Bryant flew the next one, followed by Pappy Hines. It was my turn with Joe Guthrie as my backup. Sometime that October I took off and immediately tested my cameras. There was no green light on the six-inch camera. I swapped the bulbs—that wasn't the problem. I came back and called the tower, the signal for Joe to take off. The problem turned out to be a sheered camera film drive shaft. Somebody up there didn't want me to fly that mission.

"Our overflight operations began to wind down, but for a reason we would never have suspected possible at the time. We had a young lieutenant named Ray Ramsey stationed with us, a little bitty guy who flew the RF-86. On one training flight over Japan, soon after he had finished his mission, he decided to see how high he could get the RF-86 to fly over Yokota Air Base. He kept going up, and up, and up to above 50,000 feet. He happened to look up and to his great surprise there was an aircraft flying over him to the east, toward Tokyo, at an even higher altitude. Alarmed, he immediately went into a dive and landed. He reported to Colonel Kaufman, our squadron commander, that he had seen a strange-looking airplane flying above him. Kaufman called Colonel Avery at Group Headquarters and reported the sighting. Avery in turn called 5th Air Force, and Ramsey was ordered to report immediately for interrogation. So, Ray did as he was told, and they showed him pictures of various Russian aircraft. Finally, they showed Lieutenant Ramsey a picture of

Mig-19C Farmer, reproduced by the PRC under license from the USSR, flown from the PRC by a defector to the ROCAF, Taiwan. Picture taken by Dr. Richard Hallion in 2010 while lecturing at the ROCAF Academy.

a MiG-19, and he immediately recognized it. With the MiG-19 in the Russian inventory, they had the ability to intercept any of our reconnaissance aircraft over their airspace. This was not possible with the MiG-15 or MiG-17 fighters. The MiG-19 deployment to the Far East shut us down." And of course the same was true in Europe, where the MiG-19 was deployed even earlier, before its deployment to the Pacific region of the USSR.

A P2V-7 NEPTUNE SURVIVING THE
CZECHOSLOVAK BORDER (1956)

During flight training, two-plus years in VP-23, and almost two years on the staff of Fleet Air Wing
Three, I flew first a PB4Y-2, then P2V-2, -3, -5, -5F, -6, and–7. They were a dream to fly after the -5
became a -5F and then a -7, both with jets, in addition to the Wright R-3350, a terrible engine.

—Lieutenant Commander Joe Grace

"I was born in 1928, and I always wanted to fly," recalls Joseph "Joe" Grace. "I
built lots of model planes as a kid, flew them and hung them from the ceiling
in my room. I grew up in Tonowanda, New York. Just south of town there was
a mile-square airfield of grass. One hangar, several Piper and Taylor Cubs.
An operator offered 'See Niagara Falls for $1.50.' Two friends and I saved our
dimes until we each had fifty cents, then rode our bikes out to the field. We
didn't have to climb very high before we could see the falls, about ten miles
down the river. We weren't so much impressed by the falls, but were thrilled to
fly. In 1947 I received an appointment to the US Naval Academy in Annapolis,
Maryland. Once I reported to the academy we received indoctrination flights
in N3Ns—a beautiful biplane on floats.

"On graduation from the Naval Academy in 1951 I was assigned as a ship's
company officer on the training carrier USS *Monterey* (CV-26) at Pensacola,
Florida. After one year, in 1952, I was finally entered into flight training. I managed to hold my own and not wash out, although many did. About a year after
I started flight training it was time for our basic carrier qualification on the
Monterey. We flew out to the carrier in a flight of six. I flew a beautiful ROGER
pass on my first approach—only to have the LSO wave me off, instead of giving me a 'cut.' My second approach was the same—another 'foul deck wave-
off.' The deck was not fouled. After the third wave-off in a row, I was getting
mad. Finally, on my fourth approach, I got a 'cut' from the LSO permitting me
to land. As the deck crew was freeing my tailhook from the arresting gear wire,
the ship's air boss announced on the radio and on the ship's intercom: 'This

P2V-7 Neptune antisubmarine aircraft assigned to Patrol Squadron 23, VP-23, at Brunswick, Maine, while deployed to Keflavik, Iceland. Patrol plane commander, LTJG Joe Grace.

ship's 57,000th landing has just been made by Lieutenant JG Joe Grace, former ship's officer.' They set me up. There was cake that night in the wardroom. We flew SNJs in training; the air force called them AT-6s.

"After completion of flight training in 1953, I requested an assignment to Patrol Squadron 23 at Brunswick, Maine. I was serving as navigator on a crew of eight by 1954. We had a squadron officers party one Friday night, had a good time and went to bed early. At 0200 hours Sunday, our duty officer received a call, not from our boss, not from his boss, Fleet Air Wing Atlantic, or our operational boss, Commander Eastern Sea Frontier in New York, but from the duty navy captain at the Pentagon—'Get your squadron in the air tomorrow morning. Fly to the municipal airport at San Juan, Puerto Rico, and find us a Russian ship running guns into Guatemala to start a revolution.' We had two planes down for major checks planned for Monday morning. The night check crew came in and had them ready to go by 0700. The recall worked like a charm. Each of us got his call, and called three others, packed a bag, and were out at the air station by 0700. Soon thereafter we had twelve planes in the air, in formation and flew VFR, visual flight rules, just offshore to San Juan.

"Our crew, Lieutenant JG Bourke, pilot, Ed Cumie, copilot, and I as the ship's navigator, were flying just offshore of the Dominican Republic, then very unfriendly to the United States under the dictatorship of General [Rafael] Trujillo. We had been briefed to stay outside their three-mile limit. The capital city, Ciudad Trujillo, could be seen just a few miles up the river from the coast. There, we spotted our quarry tied up to a pier in the city. We sent a FLASH contact report to Commander Caribbean Sea Frontier. There was no revolution in Guatemala that year.

A P2V-7 Neptune Surviving the Czechoslovak Border (1956)

Joe Grace's crew in front of their P2V-7 Neptune antisubmarine aircraft at Keflavik, Iceland, 1956. Standing, left to right: Aviation Radioman 2nd Class Brand; AD1 Joe Amaviska, plane captain; LTJG Art Detonnancourt, copilot; LTJG Joe Grace, patrol plane commander; AT3 Harry Harrison, radar operator; AT3 Nash, ECM operator; and Ensign Paul Sorenson, navigator. Kneeling, left to right: AO3 Meinoc, aviation ordnanceman; and AM3 Haulk, 2nd mechanic. The photo was taken by AO1 Wiebe, gunner, member of the crew.

"A couple of years later in 1956 I had made PPC, patrol plane commander, and had my own crew. While deployed to Keflavik, Iceland, we had a week-long deployment flying reconnaissance around northern Europe with a brand-new P2V-7 Neptune, with jets nonetheless. Wow. I remember flying into Fürstenfeldbruck Air Base near Munich. I shot three GCA approaches, but was still in the soup each time. I didn't dare break minimums as a LTJG, lieutenant junior grade—first lieutenant in the army and air force—because our skipper, Commander Harvey Hop, had broken minimums to land just the week before and had been put on report by the air force. So we headed for our alternate, Frankfurt Air Base, adjacent to the Frankfurt civil airport.

"The airway out of Munich ran right alongside the Czechoslovak/East German border. We hadn't been briefed to expect any trouble from the Russians, but they must have overheard our radio transmissions and knew we were not in familiar surroundings. I had put the navigator, Paul Sorenson, in the left seat and gone back to the aft station to have a cup of coffee with our gunner. When I came forward, Art [Detonnancourt], my copilot, was flying the plane heading for a radio beacon on the airway. I don't have any idea why I looked at the bird-dog needle, but thank God I did. It kept trying to swing off to starboard, and Art was chasing it. I told him to ignore it and just fly the heading. In less than five minutes, the needle was sticking straight out to starboard, to the right, into Czechoslovakia. I am sure they were waiting for us there, less than five miles away. We had all heard of the VP-5 PB4Y-2 that had been shot down over the Baltic Sea in April 1950, but nothing since. So we came close to being just another incident in the Cold War. The next day we flew from Frankfurt back down to Fürstenfeldbruck; the weather was much better this time around. Took a train to the Third Army rest camp in Garmisch for a wonderful, but shorter-than-planned stay."

It was a routine practice for the Russians and their satellites during the Cold War years to interfere with aerial navigation aids, such as radio beacons, to lure American aircraft, passing near their borders, over their territory—then shoot them down. It happened to a luckless American F-84 fighter as early as 1953, being shot down by a Czech MiG-15. Meaconing, as the practice of bending radio beams was referred to, was a frequent experience for MATS/MAC transport aircrews who flew to diverse places around the world. It was also the practice for American aircrews to be briefed on Soviet meaconing activities and to be cautioned, if at all possible, to avoid using radio aids that could be easily compromised. As in the case of the P2V Neptune commanded by LTJG Grace, such interference often was rather obvious, but it could also be subtle, drawing an aircraft off course through the use of a number of small, incremental changes to a radio navigational aid. The losses of a C-118 transport over Armenia in June 1958, and an RC-130 reconnaissance aircraft that same September, showed how vulnerable aircraft could be if relying on radio aids for navigation near Soviet-controlled territory. In the case of the RC-130, which was on a border surveillance flight, its shootdown by waiting MiG-17 fighters resulted in the loss of its entire crew of seventeen. For aircraft assigned to the Strategic Air Command, the RC-130 downed by the Russians was assigned to the National Security Agency, NSA, tactical radio navigation aids were never used for navigation purposes. Tactical navigation aids such as radio beacons or Loran were deemed unreliable and would not be available in wartime anyway, so it made no sense for SAC crews to use them during peacetime. All SAC navigators used either radar, celestial, the stars and the sun, or grid navigation in the Arctic regions, and if none of that was available, they flew time and distance—dead reckoning. On reconnaissance missions over the Arctic, radar returns often were distorted because of ice formation along shorelines, while the sun and stars were not always available due to cloud cover, so dead reckoning was used as a fallback position more often as not. It is indeed a credit to SAC reconnaissance navigators that they consistently kept their aircraft on track regardless of time of day or adverse weather conditions.

FRANZ JOSEF LAND (1952)

There had been dozens of American attempts during the early 1950s to gather important Russian
radar and electronic communications by flying provocatively up against the Soviet coastline.
Several of these reconnaissance aircraft were shot down either by Soviet jets or ground fire. Most
of the crews disappeared off the scope and were presumed to have been sent to Siberia or killed.
—Ben Rich and Leo Janos, *Skunk Works*

The Franz Josef Archipelago is a group of nearly two hundred islands adjacent
to the Barents Sea, above 80 degrees north latitude, northeast of Spitzbergen,
Norway. A cold, rocky place if there ever was one. In the early 1960s, I recall
flying by that desolate place in an RB-47H electronic reconnaissance aircraft
on our way to the Kola Peninsula and Novaya Zemlya. All the action we
encountered was always on the Kola Peninsula—very little on Novaya Zemlya, which was called Banana Island by us because of its shape. I recall intercepting a lone early-generation Knife Rest early warning radar coming up
when we flew by Franz Josef. It must have been the high point for the Russian
crew for the week to have seen any activity at all. But in September 1952 there
was not even that lone Knife Rest radar site active in Franz Josef Land. There
was nothing there but lots of ice and rocks. However, planners with a vivid
imagination at Headquarters Strategic Air Command in Omaha, Nebraska,
just wanted to make sure the Russians hadn't somehow sneaked up to Franz
Josef Land, hacked an air base in secret out of ice and stone, and based some
of their TU-4 bombers, copies of our World War II–vintage B-29s, on this
godforsaken place—so they scheduled a reconnaissance mission. There were
no RB-47s available in 1952; RF-86s didn't have the legs and were busy anyway fighting the war in Korea. The RB-45C, however, was a SAC-owned asset
and could have been used—but wasn't. For one reason or another, the selection fell on a piston-powered and propeller-driven RB-50E aircraft, which was
not really known for its reliability. The aircraft and crew was assigned to the
38th Strategic Reconnaissance Squadron of the 55th Strategic Reconnaissance
Wing—at this period of time based at Ramey Air Force Base, Puerto Rico.

The normal crew complement for the RB-50E was ten, but for this unique mission an additional navigator and photographer were added. Major Roy E. Kaden was the aircraft commander, and he would need all the good judgment he could muster to ensure the safe return of his aircraft and crew. Very early in the mission briefings, he was given to understand that in case of aircraft malfunction, there was no rescue capability available. In other words, Major Kaden and his crew were on their own.

R. Cargill Hall, an air force historian and former chief historian at the National Reconnaissance Office, writes in the *Early Cold War Overflights Symposium Proceedings*, "In July 1952 a request was submitted to high-level government and military officials for approval of a photographic and electronic reconnaissance overflight of Franz Joseph Land. The purpose of the mission was to determine whether the Soviets were building airfields on Franz Joseph Land [to accommodate TU-4 bombers] and if they had installed any supporting radar facilities. At what level this request was initiated is unknown, but owing to its high degree of political sensitivity and proximate timing with Presidential approved eastern Siberian Overflights, we believe only the President could have approved it. I presume that this information was deemed critical not only for U.S. defense planning, but also for war planning that included plotting the course of American bomber streams over the high Arctic into central and European Russia. The Franz Joseph Land islands were astride the flight path that some of our bomber streams would take."

Of all the Cold War overflight missions that I have reviewed, plus my own experience flying over a hundred PARPRO peripheral reconnaissance missions, this one I find truly strange and unusual—and I find it difficult to believe that the president of the United States would have felt compelled to approve it. In fact, President Truman had serious reservations approving limited Siberian overflights across from Alaska by brand-new B-47s. It is much more likely that approval was derived from other overflight requests granted about this time, such as the authorization for three RB-45Cs flying deep into Russia under the British flag. It gets even stranger in my estimation that the aircrew was not briefed or debriefed after mission completion at SAC headquarters in Omaha, which was the practice, but at a subordinate major air command, and was scheduled to fly the mission out of Thule Air Base, a very inhospitable environment, instead of flying out of the United Kingdom, a much safer approach all around. One should keep in mind also, for the Soviets to establish a functional air base in an inhospitable environment such as that found in Franz Josef Land without arousing the suspicions of their Norwegian and Swedish neighbors would have been nearly impossible. This is one overflight mission that should never have been flown, and certainly not using an RB-50 aircraft with a crew of twelve, with no rescue support at any point of its flight. No matter the what and the how, these were American airmen who followed orders and did what they were told to do to the best of their ability.

Recalls then Major Roy E. Kaden, the aircraft commander, "In April through early August of 1952, the 38th Reconnaissance Squadron, the squadron I flew with, was on a routine deployment in the United Kingdom flying out of RAF Sculthorpe and RAF Upper Heyford. We flew electronic and photographic PARPRO missions over the Baltic Sea, no closer than forty miles to the Soviet border. Such missions lasted from twelve to fifteen hours. We also flew the Berlin air corridors and along other areas of interest near the periphery of East Bloc states. In July 1952, intelligence personnel assigned to United States Air Forces headquarters in London requested the 38th SRS provide a navigator and flight engineer to determine the feasibility of flying a reconnaissance mission out of England over Franz Josef Land. After evaluation of all requirements, the conclusion was reached by all involved in the study that the requirement could not be met with confidence using an RB-50 aircraft flying out of England because of the distance involved. The 38th SRS thus returned to Ramey Air Force Base, Puerto Rico, its home base—soon to move to Forbes Air Force Base in Topeka, Kansas. On August 13, 1952, the 55th SRW directed the 38th SRS to provide one aircraft and crew to fly a special Top Secret photographic and electronic reconnaissance mission out of Thule Air Base, Greenland. My squadron commander asked me if my crew would volunteer for this assignment. Of course I said 'Yes.' We had flown together for some time and flew the same aircraft for the past three years, an RB-50E, tail number 47-130, which we had named *High and Lonesome*. Additionally, we had one of the few aircraft that had a K-30 100-inch focal length oblique camera installed, used for high-definition photography of targets from a considerable distance. On August 28, 1952, we were confident that our aircraft was ready, and two days later we received our temporary duty orders—which did not specify a destination or purpose.

"I received verbal instructions to report with my crew to Headquarters 2nd Air Force at Barksdale Air Force Base, Louisiana. In accordance with instructions, our crew chief and squadron intelligence officer were to accompany us on our aircraft to Barksdale. Our maintenance support team was to fly on a C-97 aircraft provided by the Military Air Transport Service, MATS, directly to Thule Air Base. We made a night flight to Barksdale and on September 2 were ready for our briefing. The SAC briefing team presented the photographic and electronic intercept objectives to be accomplished on an overflight of the Franz Josef Land archipelago. We were briefed to obtain photography at a flight altitude of 20,000 feet. To the flight crew, the briefed mission requirements were nothing more than a routine reconnaissance sortie. What made the requirements exceptional were the hazards of the high Arctic operational environment, and that we would be almost 1,500 miles from Thule with no place to land in the event of an emergency. It became apparent that briefing personnel could tell us very little about what to expect. They had no information relative to the environmental hazards of the islands because their charts were based on nineteenth-century information. There was not even positive assurance that the location of the archipelago itself was accurately depicted on the charts. Knowing that we would be violating Soviet territory, we were interested in the possibility of encountering Soviet fighters. The Soviets had shot down an RB-29 a few months before, we were well aware of the risks involved.[35] We asked about the possibility of a rescue operation. The SAC officers replied honestly—rescue would be impossible. I then asked about a navy submarine contact, surveillance, or pickup. They said, 'Forget it.' Ditching in Arctic waters was not an option in my book. Following the briefing, there was no question in my mind that if we had a problem, we were on our own.

"Weather over the archipelago was a controlling factor from the photographic standpoint. We were briefed to contact SAC personnel when we arrived at Thule Air Base, and their weather forecasters would attempt to forecast the best conditions for our mission. We took off for the air base at Goose Bay, Labrador, serviced the aircraft, and on September 4 made an early-morning takeoff for Thule. I informed Headquarters SAC that we were in place awaiting an execution order. Everyone was issued the essential Arctic clothing and assigned quarters in a building that resembled a cold storage box. Thule Air Base, on which construction had begun in May 1951, featured rudimentary facilities. While waiting for a break in the weather over Franz Josef Land we decided that the outside ramp was not a suitable place to park our aircraft if we were to maintain it in a constant state of readiness. A solitary black-colored hangar had recently been erected, and I decided that this was the place for our aircraft. The base commander thought otherwise. He had no knowledge of our project. I suggested he call SAC headquarters. He soon advised me that hangar space was available after all. President Truman's approval of the overflight of Wrangel Island and eastern Siberia and search for air bases was secured on August 2, 1952. My flight crew and support team was assembled a few days later to prepare for the Franz Josef Land mission. Neither planning nor after-action records have been found. Why we were briefed and debriefed at Headquarters Second Air Force in Louisiana rather than SAC headquarters in Omaha remains an open question. Many more questions regarding our mission remain unanswered, and perhaps will never be answered. In any event, on September 8, 1952, we received orders to execute the mission. We planned the overflights so that the sun would be over the islands when we arrived to give us best possible light conditions for the photography. This dictated a takeoff in predawn darkness. I filed a 'round robin' flight plan with

Thule Air Base housing. Even everyday human necessities became a problem in an environment of minus 40 degree temperatures. Here shown a human waste removal truck trying to keep toilets functional—they didn't always succeed.

base operations for a flight time of fifteen hours. Our alternative, in the event Thule was socked in on our return, was the air base at Sondrestrom Fjord, some 750 miles south of Thule.

"The next morning we started engines, received the light signal for taxi clearance, and moved into position at the head of the runway. While performing the pre-takeoff checklist, the flight engineer informed me that we had no control over the number two engine propeller. John Goolsbee observed electrical arcing near the propeller governor junction box. I canceled the flight for that day. We taxied back to the ramp and shut everything down. With the aircraft in the hangar, we proceeded with the repair of the malfunction. During the engine run-up, a fuel leak was discovered in a right wing fuel cell. The tank was defueled and repaired with much difficulty and refueled. On September 10, I advised SAC headquarters that the aircraft was in commission and we were ready to go. On September 16, we received word to proceed the following day. That morning the base was enveloped in dense fog. After starting engines and preparing to taxi, the fog became so thick that I could not see the runway centerline. I could only see one light at either side of the runway. On lining up on the centerline, I set my gyrocompass to the runway heading. Sergeant Goolsbee made an engine run-up check, and I advanced the throttles to full power and began my takeoff roll into the fog. Lift-off was smooth, and we leveled off at 18,000 feet. Shortly after level-off, we began fuel transfer from the

700-gallon pylon fuel tanks mounted beneath each outboard wing panel. The right tank would not feed. We had a booster pump failure. Quick calculation indicated that even without the 700 or so gallons of that tank we would be able to complete the mission.

"Navigation in the Arctic requires a totally different approach to navigation in the lower latitudes. The magnetic compass is useless because of errors induced by the magnetic pole. A gyro compass also degrades near the pole, as does a fluxgate compass. Grid navigation is what we had to fall back on, a system devised by the Strategic Air Command for its bomber crews who would have to operate in those high latitudes. All three of my navigators were intensely involved in keeping us on track. Radar was good as long as we were over land, but our charts were of course of questionable accuracy. One navigator maintained a dead reckoning plot, while also shooting the sun. Another would plot the sunlines to determine an accurate line of position [and] compute wind direction, velocity, and ground speed. After leaving the northeast coast of Greenland, we faced some thousand miles of Arctic Ocean. The accuracy of navigation from this point depended entirely upon the accuracy of sun observations, the dead reckoning plot, and the navigator's computation of wind direction and velocity. At this time, we test-fired our guns. They worked.

"About six hours into the flight our navigator told us that we were near Franz Josef Land. Major Heiman, our radar navigator, saw some of the islands creep up on his scope. Earl Schureman, the electronic countermeasures observer, advised that his search for electronic radar signals produced nothing. Flying over a lower overcast cloud deck, it was obvious that photography from our planned altitude was impossible. The SAC weather forecast was a complete bust. I made a decision and descended down to about 2,500 feet to give our mission the best shot at success. The visibility at this lower altitude was surprisingly good. I reduced airspeed to about 180 knots. At that altitude and airspeed, photography with our camera installations was not practical. So this part of the mission became mostly one of visual observation as we passed the islands. In our flight at 2,500 to 3,000 feet over numerous large and small islands, we did not see anything that would indicate a Soviet presence. We had been flying over the islands for a considerable length of time when someone over the intercom yelled, 'Let's get the hell out of here.' I had no desire to stretch our luck, and agreed.

"The navigators provided a heading for our return to Thule, and I started climbing back to 18,000 feet. After leveling off, I alerted the gunners and had them fire their guns. Firing the guns fulfilled a SAC combat crew training requirement, and I had no intention of taking any live rounds back to Thule anyway. On approach to Thule I descended to 8,000 feet, having maintained radio silence throughout the mission. Remembering what the weather was

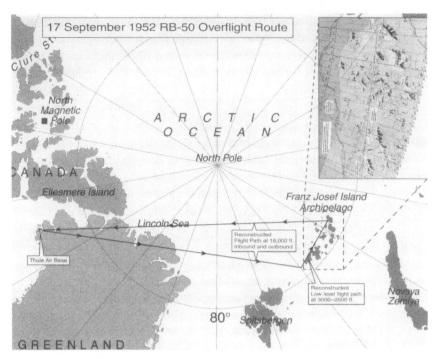

September 17, 1952, overflight route of RB-50 *High and Lonesome* of Franz Josef Land by Major Roy E. Kaden and crew.

The RB-50E reconnaissance version of the B-50 bomber was flown by the 55th Strategic Reconnaissance Wing in the early 1950s. A total of six RB-29/50 reconnaissance aircraft were shot down by Russian fighters—the last as late as September 1956 over the Sea of Japan.[36]

like fourteen hours earlier, I had no assurance that things had improved. I broke radio silence, and the tower advised that the weather was above minimums. It was a relief to know that the GCA was operating. I trimmed the aircraft to compensate for the nearly 4,500 pounds of fuel remaining in the right pylon tank. Our landing was normal, turning over the aircraft to our waiting ground crew. I advised SAC headquarters of mission completion. On September 22, we returned to Barksdale Air Force Base. Intelligence personnel collected all of our film, logs of whatever kind, tape recordings, and so on. We could report with assurance that we detected no Soviet military presence whatsoever.

"After the debriefing at Barksdale, we were left without a shred of evidence that we had ever flown over Franz Josef Land. Our orders gave no location or ultimate destination. All directions and instructions were given verbally. Some weeks later, the record of our flying time arrived in the form of a memo that included points of takeoff and landing, as well as our round robin flight from Thule. In all of my flying experience, nothing impressed me as much as the low-level flight over those forbidding, desolate, ice-covered islands. All of us on that mission knew then that we had seen an utterly fantastic land, a land that few people in the world will ever see."

TEAMWORK: P2V AND RB-50E (1952)

A Forbes AFB RB-50 from the 38th SRS on temporary Alaskan duty was attacked by two MiG-15 jet fighters 25 miles off the Kamchatka Peninsula on March 18, 1953. T/Sgt Jesse L. Prim peered through his sights and pulled the trigger that sent six guns into action in the top turrets of the RB-50, the Laboring Lady. Prim said the Soviet jet was coming in fast and flames and smoke from his guns were plainly visible. I don't think I hit him. He broke off his attack when I fired.

—**Bruce Bailey,** *We See All*

Commander Richard A. Koch in 1952 was the copilot on a P2V Neptune antisubmarine aircraft assigned to Patrol Squadron VP-931, then flying out of Kodiak, Alaska. VP-931 flew a variety of twin-engine Neptune P2V-2, P2V-3, and P2V-3W aircraft on sea surveillance, antisubmarine, and electronic reconnaissance missions over the Bering Sea and the Bering Strait between Alaska and Siberia. "From late 1951 until late 1952," recalled Commander Koch at the Early Cold War Overflights Symposium, "my squadron operated out of both Kodiak and Adak, Alaska. In the latter part of 1951, Intelligence indicated that Soviet TU-4 long-range bombers were moving into air bases in northern Siberia. Such a buildup, if true, presented a threat to Alaska and the west coast of the United States. Part of my squadron's mission involved flying the Bering Sea on passive electronic reconnaissance missions. We had new receivers and direction-finding equipment installed in our P2V-3W aircraft, which allowed us to intercept and locate any Soviet search radars in nearby Siberia.

"In March 1952, a meeting was convened by the commander, Fleet Air Alaska, at the naval air station on Kodiak Island to plan the eastern Siberia operation. This meeting involved both my crew, piloted by Commander James H. Todd, and air force personnel. The aircraft involved in this reconnaissance mission were our specially modified P2V-3W, an air force RB-50E photo reconnaissance aircraft, and a rescue boat–equipped B-17. At the meeting, we established our routes to be flown, communication and emergency procedures, and the operating dates. The P2V-3W, RB-50E, and B-17 rescue aircraft assembled on Shemya Island in the Aleutians. All three crews met on

All missions flown by the P2V-3W and the RB-50E were flown from Shemya Air Force Station on Shemya Island, shown above, at the very end of the Aleutian chain of islands. Shemya, renamed Erickson AFS, in future years would become a key operating base for the 55th SRW to monitor Soviet ICBM/nuclear tests.

April 1, 1952, to address altitudes to be flown, the location of the B-17 rescue aircraft, and the radio frequencies we intended to monitor. The following day, on April 2, we flew our first mission. No radio contact was made throughout the operation, even during takeoff and landing. The three aircraft maintained visual contact until the B-17 departed for its offshore track over international waters, where either the RB-50 or P2V were to go in case of an emergency. The RB-50 flew at 15,500 feet altitude, with the P2V-3W slightly lower, at 15,000 feet.

"Flying north over the Soviet coastline, we proceeded to intercept and track Soviet radars in the vicinity of Rukavichka on the lower Kamchatka Peninsula. Using our direction-finding equipment, we homed in on the Russian radar and overflew it and the nearby airfields, taking radar photography, while the RB-50E photographed the radar sites and airfields. The RB-50 took overlapping time-coded photographs, and our radar intercepts were also time coded so that the lines of intercept could be overlaid on the photographs taken by the RB-50 to precisely locate the radar site. With two or more lines of intercept, the position of the radar site could be located with great accuracy.

"Our joint reconnaissance flights were scheduled to be flown between April 2, 1952, and the end of June. The total effort involved three increments,

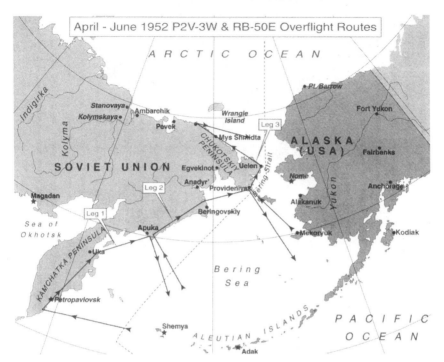

P2V-3W and RB-50E overflight routes, April–June 1952.

referred to as Leg 1, Leg 2, and Leg 3, to be flown in a total of nine or ten missions by each aircraft involved. The legs involved overflights of Soviet coastal areas. To the best of my recollection, the first leg to be flown along the coast and over the Kamchatka Peninsula proceeded from Rukavichka, directly to Kamchalskly Poluostrov, then on to the vicinity of Ostrov Karaginskly and Kavacha. The second leg, or segment, commenced at Kavacha and proceeded to Beringovskly to Kivak. And the third segment commenced at Kivak, then to Uelen and finally to Val'Karay southwest of Wrangel Island, Ostrov Vrange-lya, in the Chukchi Sea. Because of weather conditions, two or three missions were flown to complete each increment, or leg.

"Upon departing Wrangel Island on a later mission, the RB-50 separated from us and proceeded back to Fairbanks, Alaska, for refueling. Maintaining radio silence, penetrating the Air Defense Identification Zone, ADIZ, we were intercepted as an intruder by air force F-94 fighters and escorted to Ladd Air Force Base near Fairbanks, landing in complete radio silence. After parking near base operations, we were confronted by gun-waving military police, had to throw our identity cards onto the tarmac, and were confined aboard our aircraft for some time until someone could be found at higher headquarters to vouch for us.

An RB-50E of the 55th SRW at Eielson Air Force Base, near Fairbanks, Alaska. Ladd Air Force Base, also near Fairbanks, was turned over to the US Army in 1961 and renamed Fort Wainwright. The 55th Wing tail insignia was a *V* in a rectangle when assigned to the 2nd Air Force; it changed to a circle when the wing transferred to the 15th Air Force in 1952. In the mid-1950s, such unit tail designators were dropped.

"The same RB-50E flew on each of the missions, its crew, like our own, being the only one in its squadron cleared for them. On two occasions, MiG-15 aircraft intercepted our P2V-3W and the RB-50E—once over the Bering Sea near Saint Lawrence Island and once over Soviet territory. The Russian fighters flew next to us for a time and, although creating immense tension for the aircrews, did not take any hostile action—probably because we were flying parallel to the coast and not on a course heading directly into Siberia." Just months later, Russian MiG jet fighters were much less charitable toward American overflights, or even peripheral reconnaissance missions flown over international waters. An RB-29 of the 91st SRS flying a PARPRO mission was shot down on October 7, 1952, by Russian fighters near the Kurile Islands with the loss of eight airmen.[37] And on July 29, 1953, an RB-50E flying out of Yokota Air Base, Japan, on another peripheral reconnaissance mission was shot down over the Sea of Japan by a MiG-15 jet. Of the crew of sixteen, only the copilot, Captain John E. Roche, survived.[38] The Cold War wasn't very cold for American reconnaissance crews flying dated World War II–vintage aircraft in a world of jet fighters.

"One amusing incident occurred on the first mission. Our flight path took us south of the Komandorski Islands, west-northwest of Attu, at the end of the Aleutian chain of islands. The US Coast Guard ship *Sugar*, stationed many miles southwest of Attu, on the flight path between the Aleutians and Japan, detected our clandestine flight. They called for over thirty minutes to inform us that we were off course and not heading toward Japan, but westward toward the Soviet Union. This was done on unguarded frequencies that could have been monitored by the Russians, which probably gave them notice of our approach. The last of these missions, which completed the three legs of our planned track, was flown on June 29, 1952, and I returned to the United States on July 13. The electronic and photographic data collected was forwarded to Washington, DC, and other places unknown to us. It is very likely that the intelligence we collected in our joint overflights that spring was used in planning the subsequent overflights into Siberia from the area of Wrangel Island by two B-47Bs on October 15, 1952."

COME THE B/RB-47 STRATOJET (1952)

On the morning of July 19, 1948, high-level air force brass visiting Seattle had virtually no
interest in the XB-47. Even though they would be flying over Moses Lake that afternoon
in their B-17 on their return to Dayton, they were so disinterested in the XB-47 that they
were unwilling to spend even a few extra minutes stopping at Moses Lake to see it.
Boeing president, Bill Allen, was finally able to convince them to stop just briefly. Major
General Wolfe, on a twenty-six-minute demonstration flight in the XB-47, followed by a
spectacular four-minute flight using eighteen JATO rockets, was so impressed that within
ten days Boeing had an informal order for ten B-47As to jump-start production.
—**Mark Natola,** Boeing B-47 Stratojet

The B-47 jet bomber was part of a design competition in 1944. It featured, like
all the other contenders, straight wings. Nothing out of the ordinary about
these planes, except that they didn't have propellers. George Schairer, the
senior Boeing design engineer for the B-47 program, heard of an opportunity to accompany Dr. Theodore von Karman, General Hap Arnold's technical adviser, in April 1945 on a mission to Germany, to review German jet and
rocket aircraft developments. He jumped at the opportunity and learned of
the benefits derived from sweeping an aircraft's wing backward by 35 degrees,
plus other insights that benefited the development of the B/RB-47.[39] Just a bit
over two years later, the XB-47 made its maiden flight on December 17, 1947,
from Boeing Field in Seattle, Washington. Nearly four years later, on October
23, 1951, Colonel Michael McCoy, the commander of the 306th Bomb Wing,
flew the first operational B-47 bomber from the Boeing Airplane Company
plant in Wichita, Kansas, to MacDill Air Force Base near Tampa, Florida. This
B-47, serial number 50-008, was christened *The Real McCoy*, the first of a total
of 2,042 B-47s built. The B-47 took the US Air Force into the jet age, but at a
cost. Over a period of seventeen years, the aircraft's service life from 1951 to
1967, a total of 203 aircraft were destroyed with heavy loss of life.

In the late 1940s, the Russians had begun to exercise their growing TU-4
Bull bomber fleet and deployed them on exercises at northern bases, posing

An RB-47H electronic reconnaissance aircraft of the 55th SRW at Yokota Air Base, Japan, 1967.
I got my last fight in #4302 in May 1967, flying offshore along the Russian coastline out of Yokota
Air Base over the Sea of Japan and the Sea of Okhotsk.

a potential threat to the United States. In December 1950, President Truman authorized the first overflight of Soviet territory to determine with certainty what the Russians actually had deployed at Dickson Island in the Kara Sea, at Mys Shmidta on the Chukchi Sea, and at Providuniya on the Chukotskiy Peninsula, just across the Bering Strait from Alaska. The fourth B-47 coming down the Boeing production line in Wichita, Kansas, was yanked off the line, B-47A 49-2645, one of ten A-models built, and modified to carry appropriate cameras for an overflight of eastern Siberia. Headquarters SAC picked Colonel Richard C. Neely, the primary B-47 test pilot, to command this mission. Neely and his crew flew the modified B-47 bomber to Eielson Air Force Base near Fairbanks, Alaska. On August 8, 1951, some say it was August 15, while the crew was awaiting weather conditions to improve and authorization to proceed with the mission, the aircraft caught fire on the ramp during refueling. General LeMay was livid, and the accident set back the planned overflight of Russian air bases in Siberia for a year until additional aircraft could be modified to fly such a mission.

On July 5, 1952, the Air Staff directed the Strategic Air Command to modify two B-47 bombers for special photo reconnaissance missions if so requested by the National Command Authority, the president. That August, President Truman approved a second overflight scenario reaching from Ambarchik to Provideniya. SAC then gave direction to deploy the two modified B-47s to Eielson Air Force Base, near Fairbanks, Alaska. The B-47 at that point in time was the most sophisticated aircraft of its day, both as a nuclear bomber and as a photo/electronic surveillance aircraft.[40]

The KC-97 aerial refueling tanker was incompatible with the B-47 jet it frequently refueled. The aircrews made it work. Once the KC-135 jet tanker replaced the KC-97, it was a match made in heaven.

The year 1952 must have driven the Russian military crazy and sowed serious doubt in the competence of its air defense commanders. On April 17 of that year, three RB-45C reconnaissance aircraft penetrated deeply into the European part of the Soviet Union—and returned home without ever being seriously challenged by either ground or air defenses. Then, that September, a lone RB-50 overflew Franz Josef Land in the high Arctic, and that October, not known to the Soviets of course, two RB-47B bombers, the most modern aircraft yet fielded by their adversary, the United States of America, were going to overfly eastern Siberia, right across the Bering Strait from Alaska. Recalls Colonel Donald E. Hillman, "In 1952 I was the vice commander of the 306th Bomb Wing at MacDill Air Force Base, Florida, the only B-47 equipped wing at the time. In late July or early August, Major General Frank Armstrong, 6th Air Division commander, also based at MacDill, asked me to accompany him to SAC headquarters at Offutt Air Force Base in Omaha, Nebraska. There, the commander of SAC, General Curtis E. LeMay, briefed us personally. Intelligence reports from several sources, he said, indicated that the USSR was constructing a number of air bases in Siberia from which attacks against the United States could be staged. In the interest of national security, LeMay said, it was deemed necessary to verify these reports with aerial photography, if possible. I was to lead a flight of two B-47Bs over the Soviet territory in question. The mission itself was identified only as Project 52 AFR-18. Assigned the highest security classification, only a very small circle of LeMay's staff knew about it. The project called for two B-47Bs to stage out of Eielson Air Force Base in Alaska. Back at MacDill, I began planning details for the flight,

A MiG-15 fighter on display at the New England Air Museum, Hartford, Connecticut. A stubby little fighter with lots of design flaws, nevertheless it was a terrible adversary for American conventionally powered reconnaissance aircraft such as the RB-29/RB-50.

spending long hours in my office behind locked doors. Two B-47Bs had been modified with special radar and photographic cameras installed in the bomb bay. My copilot, Major Lester Gunter, recalled at the time that all B-47s had been grounded because of a number of fatal accidents. But we were directed to continue training, underscoring the urgency of the mission. Two KC-97 tankers from the 36th Air Refueling Squadron were designated to transport men and equipment to Eielson and to refuel our two B-47s just as we left Alaskan territory on the outbound leg of the mission.

"The four mission aircraft, two B-47s and two KC-97s, departed MacDill on September 21, 1952, and we flew our first leg as far as Rapid City, South Dakota. There, we conducted some additional training flights. The B-47 was still a novelty, and for that reason, the wing commander at Rapid City Air Force Base, Brigadier General Richard E. Ellsworth (Rapid City Air Force Base would in time be named after General Ellsworth) asked for a ride on one of our local training flights. We strapped him into the copilot's seat, and my copilot, Ed Gunter, rode in the aisle. We started down the runway, gathering speed. I glanced down at the instruments and saw to my horror that the flaps were fully retracted. Somehow, we had missed that vital check. Without flaps, we would not get off the ground, and it would all end in a disastrous fireball when we ran off the end of the runway at 200 knots. A ground abort was no longer feasible. I pulled down the flap handle and watched the flap indicator creep slowly downward. Somehow, we made it, but I was looking at grass when our B-47 reached flying speed. Almost every military pilot experiences a close call of one sort or another in his flying career—I never forgot that one. Project 52 AFR-18, and the lives of its primary crew, nearly ended in Rapid City, South Dakota.

"On Sunday, September 28, 1952," recalled Colonel Hillman, "we flew our B-47Bs from Rapid City to Eielson Air Force Base. Clear weather now became the determining factor for mission launch, for only these conditions would ensure the success of visual photography. Mine was designated as the primary aircraft, and Colonel Patrick D. Fleming was the pilot of the backup aircraft. The handpicked aircrew consisted of Majors Ed Gunters, flying as my copilot, and Edward 'Shakey' Timmins as my navigator. Colonel Fleming's copilot was Major Lloyd 'Shorty' Fields, and Major William 'Red' Reilly was his navigator. The mission we were to fly would stage out of Eielson, flying in a northwesterly direction. Then we were to refuel from one of our KC-97 refueling tankers before leaving the Alaskan Arctic. We would then fly westward off the north coast of Wrangel Island to the East Siberian Sea. There, the second aircraft would turn back and overfly and photograph Wrangel Island, then orbit in a racetrack pattern over the Chukchi Sea and serve as a communication relay. My aircraft would swing to the southwest until we made landfall in northern Siberia between Ambarchik and Stanovaya, turn due south for a while, then swing east toward the Bering Strait, flying a zigzag pattern that would take me over several air bases. I would finally exit Soviet territory over the Chukotskiy Peninsula and turn northeast for the run home to Fairbanks, Alaska. Air Force Intelligence had briefed us that we could expect reaction from a MiG-15 regiment stationed in the overflight area and possible antiaircraft fire. Our defenses relied on surprise, our aircraft's speed and high altitude, electronic countermeasures, and the 20mm cannons installed in the tail of our B-47s.

"Finally, on the evening of October 14, weather forecasts called for favorable weather, and we got the thumbs up from General Armstrong for the next day. Armstrong had the authority to approve or deny the start of the mission based on weather predictions. On Wednesday morning, October 15, after sunrise, Project 52 AFR-18 began with the departure of the two KC-97 refueling tankers. One hour later, Pat Fleming and I followed them into the air in our B-47s. We refueled over Point Barrow, Alaska, and took on full loads of fuel. We proceeded with the mission as briefed. Fleming returned to the Chukchi Sea and took up a racetrack pattern as the mission backup aircraft. I turned southwest toward the Soviet coast. We made landfall close to noon, swung south for a short period, then turned east and flew back toward Alaska—through the heart of Siberia. In this fashion, we hoped to disguise our presence and appear to Soviet ground controllers as if we were a friendly, though unidentified, aircraft approaching from the western USSR. The weather, which had been clear throughout the flight, changed as we crossed the coast into Siberia. We turned

October 15, 1952, B-47B overflight routes. Colonel Donald Hillman, pilot; Major Lester Gunter, copilot; and Major Edward Timmins, radar navigator of the primary aircraft. Colonel Patrick Fleming was the pilot of the backup aircraft; his copilot was Major Lloyd Fields, and the radar navigator was Major William Reilly.

on the cameras. Beneath us, scattered clouds appeared, and occasional ground haze obscured photography.

"By now, we had burned off enough fuel to climb above 40,000 feet at about 480 knots true. We had finished covering two of our five targets, taking radar and visual photography, when warning receivers aboard our aircraft indicated that we were being tracked. I advised Ed Gunter, my copilot, to get our 20mm tail guns ready in case we encountered MiG-15s, which we knew were stationed in the area. Soon Ed advised me that he had MiG-15s in sight, climbing desperately to intercept us. I broke radio silence and notified Pat Fleming, still orbiting over the Chukchi Sea, of our position and situation. Gunter kept his eyes on the Russian fighters, but they had scrambled too late and couldn't make it up to our altitude. However, there were other MiG-15 bases ahead of us, and we still had to overfly Providenyia, the MiG regimental headquarters. We completed photographing the three remaining targets without encountering any more MiGs. We continued east, coasting out of Russian

A MiG-17 making too close a pass on an RB-47H electronic reconnaissance aircraft of the 55th SRW. It is indeed a miracle that no midair collisions occurred.

territory over the Chukotskiy Peninsula, landing at Eielson Air Force Base well after dark. Pat Fleming's aircraft came in a few minutes later. The mission lasted for over seven hours, flying 3,500 miles, 800 of which was over Russian territory. Immediately after landing, technicians took our film for development and shipment to Washington. As for the Russians—we later learned that the regional commander had been sacked, and that a second regiment of MiG fighters was to be moved into the area. We returned to the warmer climate of MacDill Air Force Base, Florida, the next day. Until the records were declassified some forty years later, we remained under restrictions which prevented us from discussing any aspect of this most secret mission."

Colonel Patrick D. Fleming, the handpicked pilot to participate in Project 52 AFR-18, was no ordinary American airman. A 1941 graduate of the US Naval Academy, he served as a naval aviator during World War II in the Pacific aboard the USS *Ticonderoga* and the USS *Hancock*, downing a total of nineteen Japanese aircraft. After first serving as a test pilot at NAS Patuxent River, he then resigned his commission and joined the Army Air Forces in September 1947, just days before the establishment of the US Air Force. Colonel Fleming continued his service as a test pilot at Wright-Patterson and Edwards Air Force Bases, with subsequent assignment to the first B-47 bomb wing at MacDill Air Force Base in Tampa, which led to his call to participate in Project 52 AFR-18. While serving as deputy commander of the 98th Bomb Wing at Castle Air Force Base, California, the first wing flying the B-52, he died on a mundane training mission. Fire damaged his parachute, which failed to open properly. It was the first Stratofortress crash, on February 16, 1956. Colonel Fleming, age thirty-eight, was the holder of the Navy Cross, the second-highest military award for valor, the Silver Star, and the Distinguished Flying Cross. He was an airman's airman and a great loss to the nation.

CHALLENGING THE RUSSIAN BEAR (1954)

"When I saw the flashes of fire from the nose of the fighters," recalled Captain Carl Holt, "I knew
it would not be a 'milk run.' I had trouble to get the tail guns to fire and since I was in a reverse
seat position I could not eject in case of a direct hit. Also, the radar firing screen would not
work so I felt a little like Wyatt Earp, looking out the back end of the canopy and firing at will."
—Mark Natola, Boeing B-47 Stratojet

The year 1953 was one of those Cold War years that challenged both the American and the Soviet political systems. Dwight D. Eisenhower, the man who had led both the invasion of North Africa and the landing in Normandy, leading Allied troops to the Elbe River to end the war for America in Europe, assumed office that January. Only weeks later, on March 5, Joseph Stalin died, setting off a scramble for his succession among the chosen few. Although the Soviets chose a new premier, Georgy Malenkov, purges and the struggle for succession weren't over and continued. On May 1, 1954, the Soviets flew what appeared to be one hundred new M-4 Bison and TU-16 Badger strategic jet bombers over Moscow. Western observers were stunned, and in Washington the debate led to what would become the so-called bomber gap. In retrospect, it is hard to believe that such a gap could exist in the minds of Washington politicians and senior military officers. The Strategic Air Command in 1954 fielded 795 of its awesome new B-47 nuclear bombers, and production for hundreds more was in full swing. Yet in Washington the bomber gap appeared real, and soon, General Curtis E. LeMay, the cigar-chomping commander of SAC, had to find out what was really going on. Where were these phantom bombers, if they were aimed at the United States, most likely they would be based somewhere on or near the Kola Peninsula and northern Siberia. The only way to be sure was to overfly the place and see what showed up.

On March 21, 1946, the Strategic Air Command was established under the command of General George C. Kenney, with its headquarters at Bolling Field on the Potomac River. That October, the command relocated to Andrews Field in Maryland, to occupy more spacious quarters. Carl "Tooey"

Spaatz, the commanding general of the Army Air Forces, tasked the command to be prepared to conduct long-range offensive operations in any part of the world either independently or in cooperation with land and naval forces; to conduct maximum-range reconnaissance over land or sea; to provide combat units capable of intense and sustained combat operations employing the latest and most advanced weapons; and to maintain and train units and personnel for the maintenance of strategic forces in all parts of the world. SAC was a mishmash of bomber, fighter, and transport groups in a deplorable state of readiness when Lieutenant General Curtis E. LeMay took over in October 1948, leaving his post as CinC USAFE at the beginning of the Berlin airlift. Almost immediately after his arrival, LeMay ran a maximum simulated bombing effort against Wright-Patterson Air Force Base near Dayton, Ohio, with the small bomber force then at his disposal. He wanted to see how bad it really was. "Not one airplane finished that mission as briefed. Not one." Not only that, during an inspection of a SAC mess, LeMay found low quality even there. "Let any reader think of the many bad messes he must have encountered during World War II, and apply that to SAC in 1948–49, and he'll know what is meant. The s-on-s was there alright, and it wasn't even good s-on-s. Steaks obviously came from the nearest shoe repair shop; potatoes had been cooked in the laundry; the spaghetti and macaroni might have interested an entomologist or a herpetologist, but not any hungry customers."[41]

By the time General LeMay moved to the Pentagon in 1957, SAC had been turned into an air force within an air force and was the envy of those who were not part of it. He built SAC in the image of the 8th Air Force, where he had first earned his spurs, but it was many times more lethal than the old 8th. I recall when I first joined the Strategic Air Command, I was issued all the flying gear that I needed to do my job. Within just a little over three years of active service, just getting used to being a first lieutenant, I received a spot promotion, temporary obviously, to captain, for being on a Select aircrew. Every six months we had to be recertified as Select or lose our promotions to someone better than us. Flying reconnaissance out of Eielson Air Force Base in Alaska, I ate in a mess hall that had a SAC section to it. When I went into the mess for the first time, I lined up in the regular section—I was in my flight gear getting ready for a mission. A cook said to me, "Sir, you are a SAC crew member, correct?" I said, "Yes." He responded, "We serve you SAC guys over on the other side," pointing to a section that had a sign saying "SAC Crews Only." I could order nearly anything I wanted—T-bone steak cooked the way I wanted it. In return, I spent more time away from home while flying with the 55th SRW than I spent at my home base. And when I was home I spent little time with my family, completing a seemingly endless series of training missions and ground-training assignments. In LeMay's air force you either cut the mustard or you got thrown out—to wing commanders that fate frequently happened sooner than they ever thought possible. At its peak in the late 1950s and early 1960s, SAC was a force of nearly two thousand B-47, B-52, and B-58 jet bombers, supported by a large fleet of KC-97 and KC-135 tankers, the latter being a jet aircraft and totally compatible with the bombers it refueled. The refueling tankers allowed the bombers to strike anywhere in the world.

In late 1949, after flying the Berlin airlift, Colonel Harold R. "Hal" Austin, then a captain, was assigned to the 324th SRS of the 91st SRW at Barksdale Air Force Base, Louisiana. In the summer of 1950, Hal was selected to transition into the RB-45C reconnaissance aircraft. He picked up a brand-new aircraft from the factory in Long Beach, California, and began the task of learning to fly a jet airplane. Hal Austin had no checklist, no technical data, and no company technical representative with pilot qualifications who could answer his many questions. "Every one of us," Hal recalled when I interviewed him, "had to try and see how high we could get in the airplane—49,500 feet is the highest I got. The day I got up to 49,500 feet, when I pulled the power back, the airplane hardly slowed down. It had no speed brakes. I pushed the nose down, which put me in a high-speed buffet, and of course when I pulled back I was in a stall. I was right between buffet and stall as I tried to get down—that's how we discovered 'coffin corner.' It took me thirty minutes to get down to 40,000 feet.

"The RB-45C was powered by the early model J-47 engine, which in later years proved to be quite reliable on the B-47. But that engine was less than reliable when we were flying it in early 1951. The engine had to be pulled every twenty-five hours of flying time for a complete overhaul. The cockpit of the RB-45C was laid out like that on a fighter aircraft. The visibility was excellent. The air-refueling receptacle was behind the canopy, so the airplane ended up right under the tanker and didn't feel the prop wash as much as one did in the newer B-47, with its receptacle in front of the canopy. By 1952, we had resolved most of our engine problems. We didn't fix them, mind you, we just learned how to manage the engines. All that aside, it was a great pilot's airplane."

Air force pilots fly whatever airplane they are given. In a period of one year, the 91st SRW lost eight of thirty-three B-45 aircraft assigned, 24 percent of the force. In most cases, all aboard the doomed aircraft perished. This was the sort of attrition that flying units experienced in combat in Korea and later in Vietnam. But this was peacetime flying in the early 1950s. Austin coped with day-to-day stress by focusing on those aspects of the airplane that gave him pleasure, and the RB-45C was a pleasure to fly when compared to any piston-engine powered aircraft of the day.

Men such as Hal Austin were trained to fly anywhere, anytime, and prevail, no questions asked. Hal's turn came on May 8, 1954. By 1949, Austin had

RB-45 APPROACH SPEEDS
GEAR AND FULL FLAPS

GROSS WEIGHT	FINAL APPROACH	OVER THE FENCE	STALL
60,000	140	130	105
70,000	150	140	115
80,000	160	150	125
90,000	170	160	135
100,000	180	170	140
106,000	190	180	150

RB-45C approach/stall speed chart, displayed in the squadron mission planning area, with gear down and full flaps. The aircraft's empty weight was 50,687 pounds; takeoff weight with a full fuel load was 110,721 pounds. The planes used J47-7 to -15 engines with 5,000 pounds of thrust.

become a charter member of the newly formed and rapidly expanding Strategic Air Command flying the RB-45C reconnaissance aircraft, first out of Barksdale AFB, Louisiana, and later out of Lockbourne AFB, Ohio. In those early years, Hal frequently deployed to England. "Flying was a thrill in the nearly empty skies of postwar Europe," Austin wistfully recalled. "I never made more than two or three radio calls on an entire mission. In between those two or three calls I flew at whatever altitude I chose. One of my jobs was photo mapping the Rhine River basin and Spain. What a way to see Europe. In 1953, I transitioned from the RB-45C to the RB-47E. It was a sleek aircraft with swept-back wings, a raised cockpit which provided fighter-like visibility, and lots of speed. I loved flying the B-47. It was an aircraft of advanced design which eliminated many of the troublesome shortcomings of the RB-45C."

In April 1954, Crew S-51, a select aircrew, of the 91st SRW, consisted of Captain Harold Austin, his copilot Captain Carl Holt, and Major Vance Heavilin, the radar navigator who sat in the nose of the aircraft and had to eject downward in an emergency. However, this was a great improvement over the RB-45C, which provided no ejection seat at all for the navigator. Hal's crew deployed with seven other RB-47E crews that March from Lockbourne to RAF Fairford, near Oxford, England. Fairford was a Battle of Britain base, many of which were used by SAC bombers deployed to England on Reflex. Reflex deployed squadrons of B-47 bombers to bases in Morocco, Spain, and England for periods of three weeks at a time, where the crews sat "alert" for two weeks, and the remaining time was spent on R&R, rest and recreation. C-54 transports were made available to the bomber crews when on R&R to take them anywhere in Europe where they might want to spend their time relaxing. A nice reward for sitting for two weeks in a bunker waiting to respond

RB-47E reconnaissance aircraft refueling from a KC-97 tanker. The KC-97 tanker squadrons were usually part of a wing, providing support to their own B/RB-47 aircraft. That relationship, of the men knowing each other, would save the life of Hal Austin's crew on an upcoming over-flight mission.

to the sound of a klaxon. We reconnaissance crew members, time permitting, took advantage of the program and flew on these R&R flights as well; popular destinations being Denmark, the ski areas of Germany and Austria, London, and Spain, for those not pulling Reflex duty in England or Spain. In later years, I flew out of RAF Brize Norton, another Battle of Britain base.

Hal Austin and his crew spent a couple of weeks familiarizing themselves with the local area by flying short training flights. There was enough off time for the crews to enjoy the nearby historical sites near Oxford, and of course London. The Columbia Officers' Mess, donated during the war by a patriotic and generous Englishman, fronted Bayswater Road across from Hyde Park. Speaker's Corner was within walking distance, as were many of London's noteworthy tourist attractions. There was no better, certainly no cheaper, place for aircrews to stay in London, and Hal and his crew took full advantage of the opportunity. The 55th Wing reconnaissance crews came through England so frequently that for long periods we had a suite of rooms reserved at the Columbia Club just for us. Fairford's March weather was exceptionally bad in 1954, and the eight RB-47E photo reconnaissance aircraft were recalled to Lockbourne after only two weeks. During that period, however, they flew long-range reconnaissance training missions as far north as Spitsbergen, high above the Arctic Circle. Hal Austin and his crew, accompanied by five other

RB-47s, returned to Fairford that April and again were directed to plan a flight to Spitsbergen.

On May 6, 1954, only days after the Russian's May Day Parade in Moscow and the overflights of what appeared to be more than a hundred Bison and Badger jet bombers, Austin's aircraft and the five other RB-47 aircraft took off in the early-morning hours for their distant target. The countryside reverberated from the throaty roar of powerful jet engines until all six B-47s had faded into the morning mist, leaving behind a shroud of black smoke, covering the base, caused by the water-alcohol injection into their engines to gain an additional 1,000 pounds of thrust per engine. Slower KC-97 tankers had departed earlier that night to meet them at a prearranged rendezvous point off the coast of Norway. That evening at the local pub, some older Englishmen confessed that they thought World War III had started when they heard the Yank airplanes taking off.

The six RB-47Es were outfitted with the same camera suite as their RB-45C predecessor. They flew in loose trail formation, called Station Keeping, on a great circle route north out of England. Past the Faroes, over open ocean, the bombers refueled from their waiting KC-97 tankers and continued northward between Ian Mayen and Bear Islands until reaching their target area. When they turned their cameras on, the navigators noted in their logs that they were at 80 degrees north latitude, where the ice never melts. They were only miles from Franz Josef Land and just a few minutes' flying time east of their target, Spitsbergen. The small crew of the lone Soviet Knife Rest early-warning radar on Franz Josef Land must have come to life when the American RB-47s showed up on their radar screens. The 3,500-mile flight took nearly nine hours of flying in an ejection seat, a seat not built for personal comfort but for saving lives in an emergency. On returning to Fairford, the crews slid down the aluminum access ladders from their cramped cockpits, feeling every bone in their bodies, or so it seemed. Time for a good stretch, a hot shower, and a "yard-of-ale" at the officers' mess. But maintenance logs and numerous chores had to be completed before the flyers could leave the smell of JP4 jet fuel behind them. Austin and his crew didn't know that the feint they had just flown over Spitsbergen, and the one earlier in March, were major rehearsals for a mission Austin and his crew were slated to fly two days later, on May 8. They also did not know that three RB-45Cs, manned by British aircrews, had flown a night reconnaissance mission deep into the western Soviet Union only ten days earlier. Russian air defense commanders had been fired as a result of not shooting down those planes, and in case of another overflight the Russians could be expected to pull out all stops.

"In the early morning hours of May 8, Carl, Vance, and I had an ample breakfast at the club. We stopped by the in-flight kitchen on our way to the secure briefing area to pick up three box lunches and two thermos bottles filled with hot coffee. It was going to be just one more training mission," Austin thought. "We intended to pick up our charts and then go out to the aircraft for preflight, have a short cigarette break, and get ready to launch. As we entered the secure briefing facility, we were met by our wing commander, Colonel Joe Preston. 'What does he want?' I thought. The colonel turned to me and said, 'Please follow me.' 'Yes, sir,' I replied. We followed Colonel Preston into a classified briefing room built for target study for bomber crews, providing security from sophisticated listening devices. Colonel Preston held the door for us as we entered the room, which was definitely out of the ordinary. He closed the door behind us and left. In the briefing room were two colonels from SAC Headquarters at Offutt Air Force Base, Nebraska. The colonels had no smiles on their faces and immediately got down to business. One of them, a navigator, handed Heavilin a strip map. We looked it over and saw where our flight was to take us—over the Kola Peninsula past Murmansk, southeast to Archangel'sk, then southwest before turning west across Finland and Sweden back to Fairford. We were stunned, to put it mildly.

"'Please sit down gentlemen,' said the second colonel. He wore pilot wings. Neither of the colonels wore a name tag on their blue Class-A uniforms. 'I will give you your mission brief, weather, intelligence. You will photograph nine airfields as annotated on your maps.' Later, I learned that the purpose of the mission was to determine if the Soviets had deployed their new Bison bombers to any of these airfields. 'You will launch in a stream of six aircraft, just as you did on the sixth. Three aircraft will fly the Spitsbergen route. You and two others will proceed to your turning point one hundred miles north of Murmansk. You, Captain Austin, are number three. The other two will turn back at that point. You will proceed on your preplanned mission. The entire mission from taxi to exit from the hostile area will be flown in complete radio silence—no tower calls, no reporting back when reaching altitude, no radio contact with the tankers, no radio calls if anyone has to abort. Radio silence is essential to the success of this mission.'

"Then the pilot colonel reviewed the weather at the altitudes we were supposed to fly, the camera turn-on points noted on the strip maps, and he briefed us on expected opposition. 'Only MiG-15s,' he said. 'They can't reach you at 40,000 feet. No contrails are expected to form in the areas you will be passing over.' That information was important to us if we didn't want to streak across the sky looking like a Times Square ad. 'You'll be flying through a clear airmass. The weather couldn't be better for this mission.' The briefing over, Heavilin started to annotate his chart. 'Don't do that,' directed the navigator colonel. 'Everything you need to know is on those charts.' The two SAC colonels measured their words carefully, only saying what needed saying. They

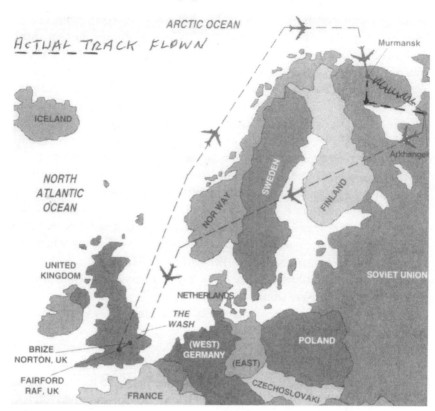

RB-47E overflight route on May 8, 1954. Map courtesy of Harold Austin.

answered no questions and offered no additional comments. On the way out, one of the colonels reemphasized the need for absolute security before and after we returned from our mission. We could not discuss any aspect of the mission outside a cleared area, we were given to understand, nor with anyone not having a need to know. No talk about the mission, period.

"Colonel Preston met us as we exited the building and drove us to our aircraft. An aircrew was already there, just finishing preflight. From the looks of it, they were none too happy to have been asked to do our job. As they slid down the ladder from the crew compartment, the pilot said to me, 'The aircraft is cocked'—a bomber term—and he, his copilot, and his navigator walked to their crew car without saying another word and drove off. We climbed into the aircraft and strapped into our seats. Everyone of us was quiet, I recall, tending to our own thoughts."

Major Heavilin noted that his map had been annotated with radar offset points, such as lakes and other natural and manmade features, that would

A B-47E bomber taking off from RAF Bruntingthorpe. The engine exhaust from a group of B-47s taking off in quick succession would cover the runway area in a black cloud of smoke. The J-47 engine powered the B-45, B-47, and F-86, and was the best there was at the time.

show well on the radar scope. Austin was number six in line, last for takeoff. "I taxied after number five moved out. Number one lined up at the end of the runway, set his brakes, and ran up his engines. The other five aircraft sat in line on the taxiway, waiting to take their turn on the active. When number one received the green light from the tower, he released his brakes, and the aircraft slowly moved down the runway. The other RB-47Es launched at two-minute intervals, buffeted by the violent jet wash from the preceding aircraft. When I took the active, a trail of black smoke from the exhaust from the other five pointed the way for me."

Takeoff data computations were in front of Austin and Holt, strapped to their thighs. They were a team, no longer individuals. Prompts and responses were automatic. As the copilot Holt called the checklist:

"Throttles."

"Open. All instruments checked," Austin responded. Austin slowly moved the throttles to 100 percent. The exhaust gas temperatures (EGTs) were within limits, he noted, glancing down the row of gauges on his instrument panel. Fuel flow was stabilized.

"Steering ratio selector lever."

"Takeoff and land."

"Start, six lights out." Austin released the brakes of the shuddering aircraft, which began its slow roll down the 12,000-foot concrete runway. Carl Holt quickly turned left and right and checked the engines. He saw black smoke coming from all six and reported to Austin, "Engines and wings checked."

They continued their takeoff roll. When the aircraft reached 70 knots, Holt called out, "70 now."

Heavilin responded, "Hack."

Fourteen seconds later, their acceleration good, Heavilin called out, "S-One now." Decision speed—their last chance to ground abort. Austin's eyes were on their EGT gauges, compass, and airspeed indicator. Temperatures looked good. Speed looked good. They continued their takeoff roll. He held the aircraft down. It wanted to climb because of ground effect before it had sufficient airspeed to sustain flight—a novice trap that had cost lives. Austin could feel the plane grasping for its element. At the 7,500-foot marker, the 180,000-pound aircraft strained to rise, and Austin let it go.

"Unstick," Austin called. The nose rose slightly, and the aircraft began its long climb heavenward. Climb speed was looking good, Austin noted mentally.

"Landing gear," Austin called, and Holt placed the gear lever in the up position. They were at 185 knots indicated and gaining speed.

"Flaps." Holt put the flap lever in the up position and kept his hand on it, simultaneously watching the airspeed. They were at 210 knots at 20 percent flaps, and he continued flap retraction. The aircraft's nose started to pitch down, but Hal had already cranked in nose-up trim and smoothed out the predictable perturbation.

"Climb speed," Holt called.

"Climb power set." Hal set it to 375 knots indicated. They continued with their checklist as they climbed straight ahead to 34,000 feet. Their mission didn't officially exist. They had filed no flight plan, which was nothing new to understanding British air traffic controllers.

Holt continued to check that the HF radio was on, the APS-54 radar warning receiver was set to the nose/tail position, the chaff dispensers were on, and the Identification Friend or Foe (IFF) transponder was on standby. He called, "Altimeters."

"Set, Pilot."

"Set Nav."

They reset their altimeters to 29.92 inches of mercury. When they passed over open water, Holt tested his guns. They fired. "I guess it's a go," Holt said over the intercom. Hal clicked his mike button twice on the control column in response. A little more than one hour into their flight, the navigator picked up the tankers on his radar at the briefed air-refueling orbit and gave Hal a heading and altitude. The tanker pilot saw Hal approaching from above

An RB-47 reconnaissance aircraft in the process of refueling. This takes some serious flying by the pilot. The distance between the two aircraft is the length of the refueling boom.

and departed the orbit for his refueling track. At the two-mile point, Hal pulled back on the throttles to decrease his rate of closure. They were 500 feet below the tanker and slowly eased in behind the KC-97 Stratocruiser, its four engines churning at maximum power in a slight descent. Hal looked up at the tanker looming ahead and above and moved into the observation position. He watched for light direction from the boom operator—two amber, one green, two red lights on the belly of the KC-97. He saw the forward amber light come on, urging him to move in closer. He moved in slowly. The green light illuminated, and he held his contact position. He could see the boom operator in the tanker flying his boom toward the open refueling receptacle located right in front of Hal's cockpit window. The aircraft pitched in the wake of the turbulence generated by the KC-97.

"Contact," Hal muttered into the mike implanted in his oxygen mask. Normally, he would have said it out in the open over the radio. Not this day. The green light illuminated on the air refueling panel, and Austin and Holt knew they had a good contact. The tanker transferred fuel into the empty tanks of the receiver at the rate of 4,000 pounds a minute until all of the RB-47s internal fuel tanks were filled, causing an automatic pressure disconnect. Hal dropped away from the tanker, saluted the boom operator, and initiated a climb to 34,000 feet to rejoin his two companion aircraft. Three lone RB-47s, high above the cold Atlantic waters. Soon, someone would pick them up on his radar. Time passed slowly, or so it seemed. The aircraft was on autopilot and flew itself. Not much for any of them to do but listen to the static on the HF radio for a possible recall. No recall came. The three aircraft flying in a trail formation turned east toward the Barents Sea. Hal, Carl, and Vance got out their box lunches and ate their ham and turkey sandwiches and hard-boiled eggs, drank their cold milk, and put their apples aside to be eaten later, if there was time. They had coffee. They were at 40,000 feet.

"How much further to the turn?" Hall asked his navigator.

"Oh, four minutes and thirty seconds, I'd say," Vance responded. They put on their oxygen masks, tight. Their compartment was pressurized to 14,000 feet. Should they get hit and lose pressurization, anything loose would be flying into their faces, so they made sure that everything was tied down, buttoned, zipped, or out of the way. "On my command, turn to a heading of 180." Hal clicked his mike button in response to the navigator's direction. "Turn now," the navigator called out to Hal. The big aircraft turned surprisingly easily toward the Kola Peninsula, the Soviet Union. The other two RB-47s who had preceded them made their 180-degree turns to the left, away from land, and headed home. "We coasted in over the Kola Peninsula at 40,000 feet at twelve o'clock noon Greenwich mean time," said Hal Austin, looking down at the floor when I interviewed him in his comfortable California home. His voice was terse, his facial muscles tight. "We were about 4,000 feet above our optimum altitude for our weight. Our first targets were two large airfields near Murmansk. The navigator turned on his radar cameras at the coast-in point and started the three K-17 large area visual cameras in the bomb bay. The weather was clear as a bell. You could see forever. Perfect picture-taking weather."

Carl Holt also remembered that moment well. He looked back from his position behind the pilot, and what he saw did not make his heart jump for joy. "We started to generate contrails like six white arrows pointing to our airplane. As we passed over our first target, I could see the fighters down below circling up to meet us, and I knew it would only be a matter of time before they reached our altitude."

"About the time we finished photographing the second airfield near Murmansk," Austin continued, "we were joined by a flight of three Russian MiG-15s. I don't know whether or not they were armed. I don't believe they were. They kept their distance and stayed about half a mile off our wing. About twenty-five minutes later, another flight of six MiGs showed up. Those, too, were MiG 15s, appeared to be unarmed, and kept their distance. I guess they confirmed that we were the bad guys. A few minutes after their arrival, another two flights of three each arrived behind us with obvious intent to try to shoot us down. By this time we had photographed five of our assigned

MiG-17 in North Vietnamese colors displayed in front of the 8th Air Force Museum in Pooler, Georgia. The MiG had a combat ceiling of 54,000 feet and carried one 37 mm and two 23 mm cannons.

target airfields and were turning over Kandalaksa east toward Archangel'sk and our last four targets. We had been over Soviet territory for an hour. We had been briefed that the MiG-15 would not be able to do any damage to us at 40,000 feet with our airspeed at 440 knots. Well, you can imagine what we called those Intelligence weenies when the first MiG-17, not a MiG-15, made a firing pass at us from the left rear and we saw cannon tracer shells going above and below our aircraft. And the MiG was still moving out rather smartly as he passed under us in front. 'Enough of this 40,000 feet stuff,' I thought. I pushed the RB-47 over, descending a couple thousand feet and picking up about 20 knots indicated airspeed in the process."

Carl Holt recalled, "When I saw the flashes of fire from the nose of the fighter, I knew it would not be a milk run. I had trouble to get the tail guns to fire, and since I was in a reverse seat position, I could not eject if we were hit. Also, the radar firing screen would not work, because the MiGs stayed out of the RB-47's radar envelope, so I felt a little like Wyatt Earp, looking out the back end of the canopy and firing at will. I did not hit any of their fighters, but kept them away from a direct rear firing pass. They could only make passes from either side at a greater than 45-degree angle to stay outside the area covered by our guns."

"The second MiG-17," Hal Austin recalled, "made his firing pass, and I don't care who knows, it was scary to see tracers go over and under our aircraft. This guy had almost come up our tailpipes. Carl Holt turned around to operate our tail guns after the first MiG fired at us. It was typical for the two remote-controlled 20mm cannons not to fire. I told Holt he'd better kick them or something, because if our guns didn't fire, the next SOB would come directly up our tailpipes. Fortunately, when the third MiG started its pass, our guns burped for a couple of seconds. General LeMay didn't believe in tracers for our guns, but the Russian pilots must have seen something, because the third guy broke off his attack, and the next flight of six MiG-17s which joined us later stayed about 30 to 40 degrees to the side, outside the effective envelope of our guns. Of course the MiGs didn't know that our guns wouldn't fire again.

"The fourth MiG of the second group finally made a lucky hit as I was in a turn, through the top of our left wing, about eight feet from the fuselage, through the retracted wing flap. The shell exploded into the fuselage in the area of the forward main fuel tank, right behind our crew compartment, knocking out our intercom. We felt a good 'whap' as the shell exploded, and of course all three of us were a bit anxious—scared is a better word—but we continued on our mission as briefed. Basically, because of habit. I firmly believe that's what good, tough, LeMay-type SAC training did for his combat crews. Later, we also discovered the shell had hit our UHF radio. It would no longer channelize, meaning it was stuck on channel 13, our command post frequency, which we had on the set at the time."

"After we were hit in the left wing and fuselage," recalled Carl Holt, "one MiG tried to ram us by sideslipping his fighter into our aircraft. On one ramming pass, he stalled out right under our aircraft, and our vertical camera took one of the first closeup pictures of the new MiG-17."

"By then we had covered our last photo target," Austin continued, "and turned due west toward Finland to get the hell out of there. The six MiGs which dogged us since Archangel'sk must have run short of fuel. They left. Six others appeared to take their place, two of whom initiated firing passes but didn't hit anything. After those two made their unsuccessful passes, the third came up on our right side, close enough to shake hands, and sat there for two or three minutes. As we departed the area south of Helsinki, Finland, he gave us a salute and then turned back toward the Soviet Union. We proceeded to cross neutral Sweden, then Norway. Over the North Sea, we headed south-southwest, looking for our tanker. But our excitement for this mission wasn't over by any means. An airborne standby KC-97 tanker was holding for us about fifty miles from Stavanger, Norway. We really weren't sure how the damage to our left wing and fuselage would affect fuel consumption. Initially, it didn't look bad. As we came into UHF radio range of the tanker, I heard him calling in the blind on command post common, the only frequency we had available on our radio. He came in garbled. His transmission was breaking up. We were running about thirty minutes behind schedule, and I heard the tanker pilot say that he was leaving his orbit at the scheduled time. I tried frantically to acknowledge his call, but when I later spoke to him, he said he never heard me. Of course they had not been briefed about our mission, but they were aware that six RB-47s went through refueling areas that morning and that only five had returned. Usually they were smart enough to figure out the situation.

"As we coasted out of Norway, it was obvious to me that we had fallen behind the fuel curve. I climbed to 43,000 feet and throttled back to maximum-range cruise. I thought we could get back to a base in England, not necessarily Fairford. We knew there was a tanker on strip alert at RAF Mildenhall awaiting our call. Carl Holt had spent much of the time since the last MiGs departed sitting in the aisle below me, acting as the intercom between me and the navigator. You don't realize how handy the intercom is until you don't have one. Holt was monitoring our fuel consumption and beginning to panic as we reached a point about 150 miles from the Wash. Carl wasn't afraid for himself. He was worried about losing our film. He said to me, 'All this effort was for nothing if we have to bail out of the airplane and have no film for Intelligence to process.' He was right. At one hundred miles off the Wash, I started calling for the strip tanker from Mildenhall to launch. Jim Rigley, the tanker pilot, later said to me, 'I heard a word or two of your transmission, enough to recognize your voice.' He was one of our tanker guys from Lockbourne. We all knew each other. He attempted to get permission to launch. The tower wouldn't give permission because the RAF had an emergency of some sort working at nearby RAF Brize Norton. Rigley announced that he was launching, and he did. When he returned to base, the local American commander, a colonel, threatened him with court-martial, and British air traffic control gave him a violation. Both situations were later fixed by General LeMay.

"In all my nine years of flying up to that time, I was never more thrilled to see another airplane in the air than I was to see that beautiful KC-97 tanker. As soon as I saw Rigley's airplane, I headed straight for him. We as a crew already decided to land at Brize Norton and were in the process of letting down when I spotted Rigley. At the same time, Holt looked at our gas gauges from the aisle below me and yelled, 'We're going to run out of gas.' The gauges were analog gauges and usually moved a little if there was still fuel remaining in a tank. None of the gauges moved, and Holt was sure we were about to flame out." As for the B-47's glide ratio? It wasn't a glider. When the power was pulled back or the engines quit because of a lack of fuel, the aircraft would drop out of the sky like a rock. "In the meantime, Rigley had his crew looking upward, searching for a glimpse of us. They caught a glint which they thought was our airplane rapidly descending toward them. Rigley leveled off at 3,000 feet, heading south, toward land. He was positioned perfectly to allow me to use an old RB-45 refueling maneuver. Since we had no way to slow that aircraft down other than pulling back on the throttles, we came up from behind the tanker, flew below him, and then got on his tail in a climbing turn. This bled off the airspeed in the RB-45. The old maneuver worked perfectly. When I pulled up behind the lumbering KC-97, its engines were giving all they could to keep us from stalling. The boomer skillfully flew his boom into our refueling receptacle.

"'Contact,' Holt called out to me. 'We are taking on fuel. All gauges show empty.'

"'Tell me when we have 12,000 pounds, Carl.'

"'Now,' Holt called out at the top of his lungs, still sitting below me in the aisle.

"I punched the boom loose, gave the boom operator a salute, and headed for Fairford. I got down to 500 feet and buzzed the control tower. They gave us a green light to land. When we reached the ramp and brought the aircraft to a stop, the crew chief was the first up the ladder. He saw the damage we sustained. 'What kind of seagull did you hit, sir?' he shouted at me. I smiled back at him. I couldn't give him a straight answer. Colonel Preston met us at the aircraft. We jumped into his staff car, and he took us to our quarters, where we took a quick shower and changed into Class A blues. Then he drove us to London, and we met with the US ambassador to Great Britain at his home. The ambassador greeted us cordially and offered us a drink. Then he whispered, 'Let's go outside. I think my house is bugged.' The next morning, my crew flew back to Lockbourne. I took another guy's RB-47E to get back, since mine obviously needed repairs. We arrived at Lockbourne in the afternoon, and the following morning we took a B-25 base flight aircraft and flew to Offutt: Headquarters SAC at Omaha, Nebraska. The commander in chief himself, General Curtis E. LeMay, attended our mission debriefing. We met in a room in the old Douglas aircraft plant because the new SAC headquarters building was still under construction. It was a three-hour meeting. The first question the general asked was, 'How come they didn't shoot you down?'

"'I guess they didn't have the guts,' was my answer. There was no doubt in my mind that the MiG-17 pilots could have shot us down if they had been willing to come right up our tail pipes. General LeMay responded, 'There are probably several openings today in command positions there, since you were not shot down.'" Carl Holt also reflected on the occasion. "Having flown combat in World War II and later been recalled during the Korean War, I thought we were in a Cold War with Russia, not a hot one.'" All the Cold War shootdowns had been kept secret. "During our debriefing I said to General LeMay innocently, 'Sir, they were trying to shoot us down!' Smoking his usual long cigar, the general paused, leaned back in his chair, and said, 'What did you

Colonel Hal Austin in 1999, when I interviewed him, holding the entry point section, cut out from his damaged aircraft by Maintenance, of a 23 mm cannon shell fired by a Russian MiG-17. Austin is the Face of Courage.

think they would do? Give you an ice cream cone?' His aides smiled. I was serious. I didn't smile."

Three months after the debriefing of Crew S-51 at Offutt Air Force Base, General LeMay visited Lockbourne, where he was met by the wing commander. After the usual saluting back and forth, the general came right to the point of his visit. He wanted to meet with Captains Austin and Holt, and Major Heavilin. When they arrived, he asked the wing commander to leave. General LeMay decorated each member of Crew S-51 with two Distinguished Flying Crosses, in lieu of the Silver Star, for their reconnaissance flight over the Soviet Union. According to Austin, the general apologized, saying: "The award of the Silver Star had to be approved in Washington, which could cause two problems: first, they'd get the thing screwed up, and, second, I'd have to explain this mission to too damned many people who don't need to know." Hal asked if they could see their photography. The answer was "No." But to the question, "How did we do?," the general answered, "You got all targets."

Colonel Austin's epic May 8, 1954, overflight of the Kola Peninsula accomplished at least two things. First and foremost, it assured the American military and political leadership that the Soviet Union had not massed its new jet bombers at potential staging bases on the Kola Peninsula. The second, although unintended, result was to again point out reconnaissance aircraft's vulnerability to shootdown. The RB-47 could not fly high enough to escape the MiG-17's cannon fire, and even more capable aircraft would soon follow. An alternative solution had to be found. The higher-flying U-2 reconnaissance plane was an interim solution itself, and by 1960, technology caught up with it, too, when SA-2 surface-to-air missiles demonstrated that they could reach its 70,000-foot-plus operating altitude. Earth-orbiting satellites, as well as the remarkable SR-71, eventually provided the necessary solutions. But in 1954 it took the courage of men like Hal Austin, Carl Holt, and Vance Heavilin to fly over the Soviet Union to provide the United States with the critical information it needed to defend itself.

Colonel Harold R. Austin went West in February 2018 to join his fellow flyers at a place where he'd see all the fellows who'd flown West before, and they call out his name, as he comes through the door. For this is the place where true flyers come, when their journey is over, and the war has been won. Farewell to an American hero, and a friend.

SLICK CHICK RF-100As (1955–1956)

The F-100 is remembered with respect and some affection by a generation of aviators. Its good features were viceless handling, a robust airframe and reliable systems. Between 1956 and 1970 more than 500 F-100Ds were lost in accidents, out of a total build of 2,294 Super Sabres.
—**Jim Winchester,** American Military Aircraft

Major General Roger K. Rhodarmer recalled at the 2001 Early Cold War Overflights Symposium how he got into the reconnaissance business. "In the summer of 1941, I got my private pilot's license, and then came Pearl Harbor. Shortly afterward I received a letter from my local draft board. Within three weeks I was in the army at Camp Croft, South Carolina, eventually ending up in San Antonio, Texas, as an aviation cadet. I trained in twin-engine aircraft and after commissioning as a second lieutenant entered advanced training in Martin B-26 medium bombers. In May 1943, I am in North Africa looking at the Germans. I said to myself, 'I'm not old enough yet, I'm only twenty-one years old. I'm not ready for this.' I was assigned to the 319th Bomb Group and stayed with them for the rest of the war. We flew bombing missions in North Africa, southern France, Austria, and all through the Alps. Then in 1945 they packed us up and brought us back to the United States, reequipped us with A-26s, and sent the 319th to the Pacific Theater of Operations. We took one hundred brand-new Douglas A-26s and flew them from Savannah, Georgia, to Okinawa. I only flew five or six low-level bombing and strafing missions before the Japanese surrendered in September 1945. I then ended up at Wright Field, Dayton, Ohio.

"At Wright Field, I learned they were looking for experienced A-26 people to participate in a 'special project.' I checked into it and learned that it was something in Europe. I didn't know what the project was but I wanted to go back to Europe, so I volunteered. In April 1946, I was assigned to the 10th Reconnaissance Group at Fürth Airfield. Of course I wondered what the hell I am doing in a recon outfit. I'm supposed to be an A-26 pilot, and there weren't any A-26s anywhere on that base. The group commander told me that some

A-26s were on the way, and in a hangar across the field an A-26 was being modified with a camera installed in its nose. A very skillful guy cut a hole in the nose of the A-26 that you could barely see, and that became the eye for a forward-looking camera. That's how the project got its name—Birdseye. And because all of our operations involved flying and taking pictures at very low levels, it was called 'dicing.' The reason for equipping A-26s with cameras was to avoid violating the Four Power Agreement, which prohibited reconnaissance aircraft from flying in the Berlin air corridors connecting Berlin with the British and American Zones of Occupation. I flew eighty to ninety hours a month and covered targets in western Europe—industrial sites, bridges, tunnels, that sort of thing. We flew as low as we could go. I actually got pictures of railroad tunnels where you could see both ends of the tunnel. I don't know who was in charge of the operation, but whoever it was had plenty of clout. I once took low-level photos of the Vatican, which upset a US representative assigned to the Vatican. I was ordered to report to a general about this. He called the State Department. After the call, he told me, 'OK, go back and do your business.' Birdseye ended in late 1946, and I returned to the United States.

"I reported to the 363rd Reconnaissance Squadron at Langley Air Force Base, Virginia. I didn't stay long. In October 1947, I went to England in a pilot exchange program, then served as instructor pilot at Shaw Air Force Base, South Carolina, upon my return to the United States, training reconnaissance pilots in the RF-80. All of our pilots went directly from that school to the war in Korea. I finally went to Korea in April 1953 and served as commander of the 45th Reconnaissance Squadron flying RF-80s out of Kimpo Air Base, near Seoul. in March 1954, I reported for duty at the Pentagon to learn to be a staff officer—they referred to us as 'legmen.' I was assigned to the Reconnaissance Branch in Operations as a tactical reconnaissance officer. SAC ran the peripheral reconnaissance program, PARPRO, so I didn't have anything to do with that. I was in the building maybe six months, just long enough to find my way around, when I was told to go and report to Major General Kenneth B. Bergquist, the director of operations on the Air Staff. I was a lieutenant colonel and did not know what I had done so wrong that the director of operations wanted to see me. I reported as directed, and General Bergquist said to me, 'I want you to go up and see the boss.' I had no idea who he was talking about. The 'boss' turned out to be Lieutenant General Frank Everest, the deputy chief of staff operations, the right-hand man and personal friend of General Nathan F. Twining, the US Air Force chief of staff. So I went up to the general's office, saluted, and he barked, 'Sit down.' He was a rough-talking guy, very direct. He started speaking very fast, and the gist of what he said was, 'The Korean War is over. We're in a hell of a position with the Soviets, and these damn nuclear weapons and missiles and all the aircraft they got.

We're going to have to improve our knowledge of them. The way we are going to do this is to overfly and photograph parts of the Soviet Union. You are going to be my "legman" on this program—starting right now. We are going to have security you have never heard of before. And we are going to have some schemes, and the director of operations, director of plans, and the director of intelligence are each going to have a legman. We are going to have exceptional security, and we must have it or the whole project is going to self-destruct and create a major international incident. You are working with me on operational matters, that is, with aircraft which may or [may] not be flying.' He continued talking and telling me that the air force had already started acquisition of six new and modified supersonic F-100s for this overflight program, and I was to monitor their acquisition. He finished by saying, 'The State Department is giving us hell on this program. Remember, we cannot lose this. Don't write anything down.' I was knocked off base listening to this.

"This was more than target intelligence. The air force wanted to get data about the Soviet force structure and location of weapons, especially nuclear stuff. We knew when one of our aircraft was penetrating on an overflight how the Soviets were tracking it and what they were seeing on their radar scopes. In a short period, we collected this intelligence. But there were problems. The air force was also flying separate peripheral missions around the USSR and the PRC and had two of these aircraft shot down, one over the Baltic. You did not want these peripheral reconnaissance flights and our penetration flights mixed up. One program going on independently can aggravate things for the other without being aware of it. There was a guy over in State, a special assistant to Secretary of State John Foster Dulles, I had to touch base with whenever a request for an overflight came in. Such requests were validated by the air force, the JCS, then taken to State. Sometimes I went along and sat outside while they coordinated the mission. Our military overflight organization was really informal. There was just General Everest and the staff. General Bergquist told me, 'You are also my legman, but frankly I am going to step out of the way because you are working directly for General Everest.' Everest worked for General Nathan Twining, the chief of staff of the air force and also the chairman of the Joint Chiefs of Staff, JCS. I heard later that the overflights were being decided at the National Command Authority, president of the United States, but we did not know that at the time, nor did we ask or talk about it.

"My other job, when General Everest ordered it, was to go to the North American Aircraft Company and see what they were doing with the RF-100s. I was supposed to talk only to the head knocker, so I did. He told me they had six F-100s all blocked off and were mounting a camera lying down under the hood with a rocker on it with a mirror to allow it to look down at the earth. It

An F-100D Super Sabre. Note the refueling probe extending from under the right wing. A KB-29/50 or KC-97/135 aerial refueling tanker would extend a flexible hose that had a basket-like contraption attached to its end, and the receiver had to slowly fly his probe into that basket to get his fuel. It wasn't every pilot's piece of cake, and especially at night some just couldn't do it.

was remarkable. The aircraft was named Slick Chick, and I recruited the pilots for Slick Chick primarily from Shaw Air Force Base. They would come up to my little office in the Pentagon, and I would brief them on what they would be doing. I did this one at a time. Three aircraft would be going to Europe, and three to Asia. It so happened that the air force had been making great propaganda statements about their new supersonic fighter. The big claim was that they were air-refuelable and can go anywhere in the world. Well, these six airplanes weren't, and I told General Everett. 'How in the hell are we going to get them over there?' he said. I said, 'I think on an aircraft carrier, sir.' He said, 'You go tell that to General Twining.' It turned out General Twining had to go hat in hand to the US Navy to get a little place on an aircraft carrier to get the planes to Europe and Asia.

"Anyway, we used them in Europe first. The Slick Chicks flew primarily over the satellite countries because of their limited range. And it was a flap when they first went in. It was not the photography that was such a shock. When they did that first penetration, they encountered ten times more radars than we ever thought existed. And they went in at 50,000 feet at close to Mach 1.0, and the Soviets still picked them up easily and tracked them easily every bit of the way. That information came back to Washington, and the Joint Chiefs of Staff and everybody was shaken up to learn that the Soviet radars were that good. That was the first time we ever used a really high-performance airplane to punch in over there. So nobody cared about the pictures that resulted at the time because of the air defense radar network reaction that the penetration touched off."

Slick Chick was an attempt to acquire intelligence by means of overflight by a high-performance aircraft. The idea probably germinated in someone's mind remembering how successful the RF-86 was in Korea, and the new supersonic F-100 should, if anything, be even a better performer. Each aircraft would mount five cameras. The cameras would provide coverage from horizon to horizon. The primary cameras were two Fairchild K-38, 36-inch focal length cameras mounted in a split vertical configuration. To mount the cameras, North American removed the 20mm cannons and all ammunition bays. It was also necessary to mount the K-38 cameras horizontally and let them shoot through a mirror to achieve the desired viewing. A viewfinder was installed in the cockpit so the pilot could view the earth beneath him. The aircraft, like all fighters, had a limited fuel-storage capability. With two external tanks carried under the wings, the aircraft fuel capacity was 1,702 gallons, or 11,000 pounds. The two external tanks were designed for supersonic flight and were carried on nearly every flight. The plane's J-57 Pratt and Whitney engine produced 10,200 pounds of thrust at sea level at military power, and 16,000 pounds of thrust with the afterburner engaged. Using the afterburner, however, greatly diminished the range of the aircraft. In September–October 1954, Lieutenant Colonel Rhodarmer selected the Slick Chick project officers—Captain Cecil Rigsby was assigned to Europe, and Captain Ralph White to Asia.[42]

"We were told," recalled Colonel Rigsby at the Early Cold War Overflights Symposium, "to attend F-100A ground school at George Air Force Base, California, and we were to do our flying at nearby Edwards Air Force Base, the US Air Force's flight test center. One reason for our selection was that both of us had RF-86 pilot hours, and the RF-86 was considered the lead-in aircraft for the F-100. Once checked out, White and I were responsible for checkout and training of the other pilots. We were also briefed on the security aspects of our mission and issued blanket orders allowing us to travel to all necessary locations. I did not know then, and for many years afterward, that Slick Chick was just one component of an American overflight effort called the Sensitive Intelligence, SENSINT, Program. There was a short program delay when it was discovered that the rudder on the F-100A was too small to maintain directional stability at maximum speed. North American's chief test pilot, George S. Welch, was killed when his F-100A yawed to one side at maximum speed and broke apart. [Actually, it was the vertical stabilizer that was too

An early model F-100 with the short stabilizer on the right, like those flown by the Slick Chick pilots, one of which killed George Welch, North American's chief test pilot. On the left, a later model F-100A with the larger tail, which solved several of the F-100's shortcomings.

small, and George Welch died while demonstrating a flight-point at Mach 1.55 during a 7.33G pull-up.] We also learned that many F-100A models were lost, and their pilots killed, in what was called the 'Jesus Christ' maneuver. At low altitude, when the aircraft experienced turbulence, or the pilot went into afterburner, the nose of the airplane would begin an up-and-down movement, which increased in intensity until the pilot lost control. The solution was to let go of the stick when encountering such movement—the airplane would recover itself. North American solved both of those problems by installing a larger tail section and making the ultrasensitive elevator control nonlinear.

"Colonel Rhodarmer, meanwhile," continued Colonel Rigsby, "had selected the additional pilots and support personnel for our project. For flights in Europe, Rhodarmer selected Captains Bert E. Dowdy and Edgar H. Hill. Hill and I had served combat tours together in Korea flying the RF-86A. For Asia, Rhodarmer selected Captains Bond, White, and Moomaw. Once we finished ground school and checked out in the F-100A at Edwards, we all went to Palmdale to check out in the RF-100A. While there, we flew a few photographic exercises; however, since all of us were highly skilled in tactical reconnaissance, we concentrated on maximizing aircraft performance. We developed our own flight profiles with no external tanks, two tanks, or four tanks. The RF-100A did not respond well to four tanks. The airplane would yaw left to right, and the CG was such that the elevator control became very sensitive. The additional two 200-gallon tanks did extend the range of the airplane, but the increase in drag resulted in no significant gain. Because the RF-100A was not equipped with antiskid brakes, we concentrated on short-field landings with heavy braking. We wanted to know how much braking power we could use before a tire would skid or blow out. I had my crew chief watch my landings and tell me if he saw any smoke from my tires. The aircraft landed at 150 knots; the pilot then deployed the brake chute and used the brakes to come to a full stop. If the chute failed to open, or you landed on a short runway, maximum brake pressure was required. We learned early about landing the RF-100A and never had any problems, unlike our counterparts in the F-100 fighter units.

"Then we moved on to Wright-Patterson Air Force Base in Ohio, where we were fitted with partial pressure suits. Each of us was suited up to take a test flight in the pressure chamber. They took Captain Dowdy to 65,000 feet, and he promptly passed out. They took me only to 55,000 feet, but forgot about me and left me in the chamber for eight and a half hours. We bade good-bye to those going to Asia, and flew our three Slick Chick airplanes to Mobile, Alabama, where they were cocooned for shipment on a small aircraft carrier to Belfast, Northern Ireland. Upon arrival in early May 1955, our three aircraft were processed without any problems, and we took off for Bitburg Air Base in West Germany. Upon arrival in Belfast, I learned that Captain Dowdy had been promoted early to major, and now as the senior officer became the commander of our little group. We were assigned to the 7499th Support Group in Wiesbaden, and our squadron, the 7407th Support Squadron, was located further east at Rhein-Main Air Base in Frankfurt. The high-altitude RB-57D reconnaissance airplanes also were assigned to this unit. It was not practicable to locate our aircraft at Wiesbaden because it only had a short 5,000-foot runway. Frankfurt was also a commercial airport, and we would attract too much attention there. So Bitburg, with its F-86 fighters, was an excellent location for us. We were the first F-100s in Europe. The 36th Fighter Wing at Bitburg was slated to receive F-100s within a year, so our presence there attracted little attention. Captain Buzz Aldrin, the second man to walk on the moon, was a squadron operations officer at Bitburg.

"It took us a little while to settle in, but on June 1, 1955, we considered ourselves operationally ready and began regular flight training. In West Germany at this time there were no restrictions on supersonic flight. You could go supersonic at low or high altitude. A perfect training environment for us. We had been in Bitburg only a few days when in late May 1955 we were ordered to Headquarters USAFE in Wiesbaden. Lieutenant Colonel Robert Holbury, a longtime reconnaissance officer, briefed us on the security of our project. In no case were we to tell each other about any mission we flew, or even if we were planning or had flown a mission. We could make up any cover story we wanted, but were never to tell anyone, including our wives, about our overflight

Slick Chick RF-100A 53-1551 at Bitburg Air Base, West Germany, modified with the larger stabilizer. This plane was number five out of six built and is now on exhibit at the National Museum of the USAF at Wright-Patterson Air Force Base, Dayton, Ohio.

missions. This was essentially the same security briefing we had received from Colonel Rhodarmer in Washington. For each overflight mission, we would go to Wiesbaden for our preflight briefings including intelligence, weather, and so on. After a mission, the pilot was to proceed immediately to Headquarters USAFE at Lindsey Air Station in Wiesbaden for debriefing.

"At our first meeting in May we presented to Colonel Holbury possible RF-100A flight profiles. I could tell he was disappointed in the limited range of our aircraft. We made it clear to him that we would fly any profile he chose. Our speed advantage over the MiG-17 without afterburner amounted only to a few knots. Considering all factors, Holbury decided that our first mission would be flown at 50,000 feet at Mach 0.96. Should Soviet air defenses show any weakness, then other flight profiles might be feasible for future missions. Returning to Bitburg, we spent the remaining practice time we had flying at 50,000 feet using afterburner. At takeoff, the afterburner makes a loud bang and throws your head back against the headrest. But at 45,000 feet you can barely feel it, and at times it doesn't light. At this time, the people living near Bitburg experienced a lot of sonic booms.

"During the year in which we flew overflights, between 1955 and 1956, each of us flew two missions over the East European satellite countries. That's a total of six missions for our entire program. I flew my two missions out of Bitburg. The first was to Prague, where the primary targets were airfields. When

A MiG-17 fighter over North Vietnam as seen through the gun camera of Major Ralph Kuster's F-105 in 1967. Without afterburner, the RF-100A's speed advantage over the MiG-17 amounted to only a few knots.

I crossed the border, my aircraft was at 50,000 feet at Mach 0.95 or 0.96 in full military power and afterburner. As I approached my targets, I could see through the viewfinder of my vertical cameras a number of fighters scrambling to get airborne at one of the airfields, and other fighters circling over it. When I reversed direction after photographing all my targets, I had a great deal of company. The Russian fighters were going all out to match my speed and reach my altitude. One airplane managed to get in my eight o'clock position, but he was about 20,000 feet below me. I did not drop my external fuel tanks because I never felt threatened. The Russian fighters broke off when I reached the West German border. Lieutenant Colonel Holbury debriefed me and shared the photographic negatives of the flight. They were of excellent quality, and I could easily see the airborne fighters and those taking off. Intelligence experts at USAFE were pleased with the outcome of the mission.

"My second overflight targets were near Leipzig and Potsdam. I was less than fifty miles into East Germany when a flight of four MiGs, in finger-four

F-100A-1 #52-5760, the fifth production aircraft, in a 45-degree climb over Edwards Air Force Base, the US Air Force flight test center.

formation, came toward me at high speed. They passed only a few thousand feet below me. I had learned a long time ago in World War II and Korea, when you meet another airplane head-on, you are not likely to ever see it again. I covered all my targets and returned to the border without seeing another aircraft. I recovered at Bitburg and was flown to Wiesbaden. When I told Holbury about the four fighters, he was concerned. At Headquarters USAFE they had access to signals intelligence, which was immediately checked. The analysts concluded that my encounter with the Russian fighters was a chance encounter.

"Major Bert Dowdy later sent me an e-mail describing his two missions. The first he flew from Fürstenfeldbruck across Austria into Hungary. His second mission took him over Czechoslovakia flying out of Bitburg.

"One day in June 1956, when I was at one of the US Air Force hotels in Wiesbaden, I encountered a dozen or more civilians wearing black military shoes just like mine, accompanied by Colonel Fred McCoy, who was in uniform. McCoy had been in reconnaissance for many years, and we knew each other. I did not recognize a single reconnaissance pilot in that group in civilian attire, and McCoy disappeared before I could talk to him. Returning home that evening, the TV was showing pictures of a new high-altitude weather-sampling aircraft, the U-2. At the time I had no idea what was going on; however, after the arrival of the U-2, we Slick Chicks never received another overflight mission. Shortly afterward, I was promoted to major, and Major Dowdy assumed command of an RF-84 squadron in France. We continued to train for the next two years—but were never tasked again.

"We did lose one of our aircraft. Captain Hill was flying in the local area when his engine flamed out and would not restart. He elected to eject instead of trying a dead-stick landing. USAFE gave us another aircraft, an F-100C, so we could continue our training. We had other incidents. Major Dowdy's brake chute deployed at 50,000 feet in afterburner. The chute burned off before he could release it. I took my last RF-100A flight on June 27, 1958. Then we closed out our operation in Europe. Captain Hill transferred to B-47s, later to U-2s. Major Dowdy and I went off to Command and Staff College at Maxwell Air Force Base, Alabama. I heard later that our two remaining Slick Chick aircraft were transferred to another country in Asia for overflight purposes."

The F-100 was the mainstay of the tactical forces during the so called Cold War years, deployed both in Europe and Asia. The famed high-speed Misty FACs flying out of Danang Air Base, South Vietnam, flew F-100 two-seaters, built as trainers but employed in the Forward Air Controller role, and produced several US Air Force future chiefs of staff and major air command commanders. The two-seat F-100 was also the initial choice for the Wild Weasel mission to kill North Vietnamese SAM sites; however, it was soon replaced by the more survivable and lethal F-105.

PROJECT HOME RUN: RB-47S OVER SIBERIA (1956)

To this day, the SAC Thule missions remain one of the most incredible demonstrations
of professional aviation skill ever seen in any military organization at any time.
—**R. Cargill Hall,** "The Truth about Overflights"

The Cold War had some truly cold aspects to it, speaking from a climato-
logical perspective. Waged from air bases near or above the Arctic Circle, the
US long-range reconnaissance war against the Soviet Union was essential to
ensure national security. The two principal air bases from which the polar
reconnaissance missions were flown were Eielson Air Force Base near Fairbanks, Alaska, just above the Arctic Circle; and Thule Air Base, on Danish
Greenland, at approximately 78 degrees north latitude, on Baffin Bay. Both
man and machine were put to severe tests in winter. Flyers and maintenance
men who served in these inhospitable climes never forgot the conditions
under which they had to get aircraft ready to fly, especially at Thule. Cold
froze the inside of the nose when anyone stepped out of a vehicle or a building. Vehicle tires shattered like glass. Static electricity dogged nearly every
move made in the dry Arctic air. In temperatures below minus 40 degrees
Fahrenheit, the simplest function became difficult to execute. Closing a valve,
or opening a hatch—operations that under normal conditions required little
thought—became difficult to perform and were carefully planned. Aircraft
landing at Thule could close the airfield with ice fog for hours or even days at
a time. To maintain aircraft in such a hostile environment and to fly them routinely were challenges that required skill, perseverance, and a little bit of luck.
Cabin fever, combined with deep boredom, became another enemy. Given
enough time and the right circumstances, such conditions could drive a man
to the edge of his sanity.

At Thule, the 55th Strategic Reconnaissance Wing maintained Operating
Location 5, OL-5, in support of its standard PARPRO electronic reconnaissance flights. A comparable setup existed at Eielson Air Force Base in Alaska,
where the 55th SRW maintained OL-3. From these two locations, the 55th

SRW launched year-round electronic reconnaissance flights to maintain and update the Radar Order of Battle, ROB, maintained at SAC headquarters in Omaha, Nebraska. Life in the remote and hostile Arctic world was controlled by the environment. Each building at Thule was built like a cold storage vault, with large ice house–type doors and three-foot-thick walls perched on three-foot-high pillars. Many buildings had their own water supply, delivered by truck and pumped into freshwater tanks. Water used for washing was drained into an intermediate tank and then reused to flush toilets. The final waste was eventually pumped into a truck and shipped out. In the spring, snow and ice melted, including mounds of frozen human waste from truck spills and water that had accumulated as a result of the constant drip, drip, drip from access pipes. The ensuing putrid smell often pervaded the entire air base. Colonel Joseph "Joe" Gyulavics, an RB-47H pilot and close friend who flew out of Thule on several occasions, put it this way: "It was pretty gruesome living."

Water was a precious commodity and used sparingly when the winds were blowing. It wasn't that water was scarce; to the contrary, there was plenty available from a nearby freshwater lake. The problem was delivery. Water was delivered by truck. When the winds were blowing, or the base was closed by ice fog, the trucks could not operate, and each building had to make do with what water was available in its tanks. Showers were short. None of the routine luxuries of the lower forty-eight states applied at Thule. Going to the toilet was frequently a dreaded undertaking. Manual flap-valve pumps were used to pump wastewater into the toilet. The user then had to manually pump the waste into a tank. This required frequent opening and closing of the valves, and the pumps frequently backfired and splattered waste onto the individual. The only flush toilet in Thule was in the Officers' Club, which didn't open until three o'clock in the afternoon. Lieutenant Colonel Bruce Bailey, a 55th Wing Raven who flew out of Thule, recalled, "We sat around with our legs crossed, miserable, in pain, and unable to stand straight when the time came, waiting for the club to open—just to use that one, regular toilet."

Another Thule phenomenon was the suddenly arising winds, referred to as phases. The intensity of the Arctic winds was defined in terms of their velocity—Phase I, II, III, and IV. Phase IV winds were the most dangerous, threatening human life and requiring outdoor activity to come to an immediate halt. Phase II and III winds closed down flying operations, and Phase I winds resulted in a warning to aircrews attempting to land at Thule. In actuality, any phase usually resulted in the closing of the base and outdoor activity coming to a halt. It wasn't just the winds that closed the base but also the accompanying loss of visibility due to blowing snow, and the danger of freezing to death. The transition from lower to higher wind velocities could occur quickly. An effective warning system was devised by using the base radio station, KOLD,

Colonel Joseph Gyulavics, far left, and his crew of copilot, radar navigator, and three Ravens (the guys who sat in a capsule located in the former bomb bay and operated the electronic receivers and direction finders to locate Russian radar sites) in front of their RB-47H electronic reconnaissance aircraft. Silver King was a modification program that upgraded the electronics used by the Ravens. This crew photo was taken at Forbes Air Force Base four years after Project Home Run was flown.

which operated twenty-four hours a day. Everyone working outside carried a small, portable radio to receive warnings. Phase wind warnings and freeze notices were announced on KOLD. Warnings such as "Flesh will begin to freeze in forty-five seconds" were common. Warnings considered not only the outside air temperature but also the wind chill factor. In anticipation of the sudden occurrence of a phase, every building was stocked with water and emergency food. Once a phase hit, it was nearly impossible to go anywhere.

The final hazard at northern locations such as Thule was psychological. The dark season played with a man's mind. At 77 degrees north latitude, darkness was a significant factor. "Some people," noted Colonel Charles Phillips, "suffered severe psychological problems during the November–February period when near total darkness prevailed. On the shortest day of the year, December 21–22, if the weather was clear, I could see a glimmer of light to the south for a few minutes at noon. Otherwise it was dark around the clock." Colonel Gyulavics recalled, "We had slot machines in the Officers' Club which could

KOLD-TV and radio station at Thule Air Base, Greenland. A life saver for many caught outside by a suddenly arriving high-velocity wind storm.

keep people busy for hours. And there were free movies every night. But it got to where we didn't even bother to go to see a movie anymore. We adapted as best we could. A few came close to the edge, but I am not aware of anyone actually breaking under the stress of living at Thule."

Recalled Lieutenant Colonel Lloyd Fields at the 2001 Early Cold War Over-flights Symposium, "I always wanted to be a pilot. As a boy on a tobacco farm in Georgia I could see airplanes flying overhead and wondered what it would be like to fly one of those aerial machines. In high school I acted on my dream and went down to the army recruiting office to find out what it took to become a pilot. I learned I needed two years of college. Thereafter my goal was to get a college education and make my dream come true. During my second year in college in 1941, I signed up for a government-sponsored pilot training program. After thirty-five hours of flight time I received my private pilot's license. About the same time, an Army Air Corps recruiting team visited the campus, and I signed up. At age twenty, on July 12, 1941, I entered the Army Air Corps. Flight training took place at the usual places in Texas, and after I received my wings and was commissioned a second lieutenant I was assigned to the 305th Bomb Group, Heavy, at Salt Lake City, Utah. Equipped with B-17s, the group was commanded by a demanding Colonel Curtis E. LeMay. In 1943, the 305th Group participated in some of the roughest aerial combat then known to man over occupied Europe and Germany. After completing twenty-five combat missions, I returned to the United States to train B-17 crews scheduled to fly over Germany. At the end of the war I flew for a while for American Airlines until the summer of 1947, when I was offered a regular commission and returned to active duty. I was assigned to MacDill Air Force Base, Tampa, Florida, flying B-17s and B-29s equipped with special reconnaissance cameras. [Colonel Fields was assigned to the 55th Reconnaissance Group at MacDill, the same group that Colonel Marion 'Hack' Mixson was assigned to at that time.] We photomapped large parts of the United States and South America.

"In 1950 I began training to fly the new swept-wing six-engine B-47 bomber. Although I was assigned to the 367th Bombardment Squadron, again at Mac-Dill Air Force Base, because of my reconnaissance background I soon found myself involved in a top secret overflight mission in 1952, flying as the copilot of Colonel Patrick Fleming. On October 15, 1952, Colonel Don Hillman overflew the Chukotskiy Peninsula of Siberia. Colonel Fleming and I overflew Wrangel Island, then I served as Fleming's backup. Both of our aircraft were modified B-47B bombers. In late January 1956, I was stationed at Lockbourne Air Force Base, near Columbus, Ohio, flying RB-47E photo reconnaissance aircraft with the 10th Strategic Reconnaissance Squadron. I was summoned to the office of Colonel William J. Meng, the commander of the 26th SRW. I commanded the 10th SRS, and the wing as a whole was part of the 801st Air Division commanded by Brigadier General Hewitt T. Wheless. When I arrived in Colonel Meng's office, he asked me to be seated, then he asked the vice wing commander and his secretary to leave. After their departure, he advised me that General LeMay, the SAC commander, had directed him to select one RB-47E reconnaissance squadron of sixteen aircraft [fifteen squadron aircraft plus one spare] to perform a special mission. He added that our photo reconnaissance aircraft would be augmented by four RB-47H electronic reconnaissance aircraft from the 55th SRW at Forbes Air Force Base in Topeka, Kansas. All of the aircraft would proceed to Thule, Greenland. The special mission involved reconnaissance overflights of the Soviet Union—and the assignment would be voluntary. The question posed by Colonel Meng: 'Would you volunteer your squadron?' My response: 'I would be pleased to volunteer my squadron.' I had no doubt that Colonel Meng knew I would immediately volunteer and that I had participated in the overflight of Wrangel Island and the Chukotskiy Peninsula flown on October 15, 1952.

"Colonel Meng decided we needed to make a survey trip to Thule. Because I had flown the 1952 mission over Soviet territory, I basically knew what to expect. The code name assigned to this mission was Home Run. Its purpose was to conduct photo and electronic reconnaissance of the Soviet Arctic from Banana Island, as we referred to it because of its shape, Novaya Zemlya, to the

Bering Strait. We proceeded to Thule by way of Goose Bay, Labrador, in early February 1956. Thule Air Base is north of the magnetic North Pole and only about seven hundred nautical miles from the geographic North Pole. It is the northernmost operational air base on earth, located close to an Eskimo village of the same name. We arrived at Thule in midafternoon, but the place was cloaked in total darkness as the sun had set around November 15, the previous year, and was not scheduled to rise again until February 15, 1956, a few days after our arrival. When we landed, the temperature was minus 42 degrees, which is pretty cold for a Georgia boy who had never even seen a flake of snow until he was twenty-one years old.

"We found Thule to be a compact and efficient place, home to about 3,200 officers and airmen. On arrival, we received a briefing and orientation by the base commander. I made the mistake of asking why all the Arctic parkas had big numbers on the back and was told that some of the parkas had ended up being worn by female Eskimos. Base officials subsequently identified each GI parka with a serial number on the back, and if it went missing, you better had reported it stolen. We completed our initial survey and returned to Lockbourne in mid-February, training intensively for the next four weeks. On March 21, 1956, we arrived at Thule Air Base with sixteen RB-47Es and four RB-47Hs from the 55th SRW." Two of the 55th SRW crews came from the 38th SRS, and two came from the 343rd SRS, the squadron I later flew with for five years starting with the Cuban Missile Crisis in October 1962. All told, twenty RB-47 reconnaissance aircraft and twenty-seven KC-97 refueling tankers operated out of Thule during Operation Home Run, a small base not designed for traffic of this magnitude—yet the air and maintenance crews made it work.

"During the first week at Thule," Lloyd Fields continued to describe his participation in Project Home Run, "all of the aircrews underwent Arctic survival training in case we had to bail out or were shot down. We learned how to build igloos and how to obtain water using slow-burning candles. I was surprised how warm an igloo could be. We also found that flight operations at Thule required careful navigation and fuel conservation. The closest suitable alternate airfield in the event of an emergency was approximately 1,200 nautical miles away at Goose Bay, Labrador. Although there was a closer emergency field at a nearby Danish weather station, it was just an airstrip with no supporting facilities of any kind. I was in charge of the 10th SRS aircrew and equipment, but not the KC-97 contingent out of Lockbourne. Major George Brown provided the briefings on assigned overflight targets. Weather support was provided by a SAC team of meteorologists, which was absolutely outstanding. Soon after completing our survival training, we began flying our first missions."

A flight of KC-97 refueling tankers on their way toward the Home Run refueling area.

Thule-based reconnaissance flights over the Soviet Union were long and required abundant tanker support. "At times, we took off from Thule and recovered at Eielson Air Force Base. A few days later we would fly a mission in reverse and recover at Thule," Joe Gyulavics recalled. "'Long' means that the flights were over nine hours in duration. Over nine hours meant that the aircrew had to sit in their ejection seats for that entire period of time. Tanker support was provided by KC-97 refueling aircraft. For a reconnaissance mission flying over the polar ice cap to reach its targets in the Laptev and Kara Seas usually required the support of several KC-97s. Refueling was critical. We launched up to five tankers an hour before we took off, to be able to take the fuel off of at least three of them. One tanker usually developed engine problems and had to turn around before he got to the refueling area. Sometimes two wouldn't make it. I worked out light signals with the tanker crews, since we never used our radios on these flights, so if I met one or two of them heading back prematurely, I would get behind them and get whatever fuel they could offload. At the final refueling point, high over the polar ice cap, they could only give us 10,000 pounds each if they wanted to make it back to Thule themselves. On the return leg we didn't refuel, so we had to have enough fuel to make it back on our own. To rely on a refueling on the way back was too risky because of possible high winds and ice fogs. We loved our tanker buddies, who were always there when we needed them. They could only surmise what we were doing or where we were going, but they knew that after flying ten hours or more we had covered at least 5,000 nautical miles."

Of course everything relating to overflights of the Soviet Union went through the hands of Major General Roger Rhodarmer, then a lieutenant colonel on the Air Staff, the "legman" for overflights wherever they took place, regardless of aircraft type. He recalled at the Early Cold War Overflights Symposium, "It was the spring of 1956, we were expecting to hear about a big overflight from Thule, Greenland, across Siberia, to Fairbanks, Alaska. It was Friday afternoon, late, and I got a call from the Special Security Office telling me that I had a message. I went over, and the message was about a big flight of RB-47 aircraft into Eielson Air Force Base, Alaska. But the numbers of aircraft involved were numbers we had never discussed, beyond anything anyone in the Pentagon had considered. So I called General [Frank] Everest's executive officer to see if the general was still in his office. He was. I went over and knocked on his door, opened it, and Everest was sitting there dictating. He looked up and said, 'What the hell do you want?' I said, 'Sir, SAC is going with fourteen aircraft to Eielson.' He said, 'What?' And he jumped up and headed for the map on the wall so I could show him the route. 'That's way too many, too many. We can't do that.' He punched the red phone and reached General [William H.] Blanchard at SAC headquarters. They jawed for a minute, and Everest got him to cut the number of aircraft in half. The first number scared Everest and me, that the Soviets might go to war over this kind of big overflight. I prepared and sent a code-worded message to Thule, Greenland, where the operation originated from. In a single mission flown on May 6 and 7, 1956, six RB-47s took off from Thule, flew in daylight over the North Pole into northeastern Siberia, and continued at 40,000 feet, exiting Soviet airspace over Anadyr on the Bering Sea. The flight was remarkably successful. We learned a lot from this flight, and not just from the photography. We learned that the Soviet air defenses in the far north were not too well connected. Of course it didn't take the Soviets long to put it together afterward."

"The unique thing about Thule," Joe Gyulavics continued, "was landing on a snow-packed runway. At low temperatures, it really was no problem. You could practically brake on the cold snowpack like it was concrete. Of course, you had to be judicious about it. If you steered too fast, you kept on going, as if you were in a car on ice. Our antiskid brakes helped. In spring, when there was melting, it could get touchy at times. Getting ready to take off one time, I taxied up a little apron near the lip of the runway. There was a slight uphill grade, and two KC-97s had sat on the apron before me, running up their engines, melting some of the snow. When I came up the slight incline, the melted snow had turned to slick ice. I couldn't see the ice from the cockpit. All of a sudden the aircraft started sliding backward and sideways. I had no control. On a tandem gear, this was not a pleasant experience. The nose of the aircraft was rotating, and there were snowbanks all around. I hit the number one and two engines [left outboard engines] and swung around, hoping I would not damage the wingtips or run the tail into a snowbank. I finally managed to swing her around. When we returned from that mission, the crew chief found a sizeable dent in the left wingtip. Things like that only happened at Thule.

"Only once during two deployments to Thule did I meet an Eskimo. It was during Project Home Run. We test-fired our 20mm tail guns as soon as we leveled off, about thirty or forty minutes out. You would think you are out there with nothing but snow and ice below you from frozen horizon to frozen horizon. Because of the total darkness, we couldn't see anything. You can imagine my surprise when after landing one day I was asked if I test-fired my guns. Yeah, I answered, we do on every mission at about the same place. A couple of Eskimos had come in to the Danish Council carrying several 20mm shell casings. 'They fell from the sky,' the Eskimos said. Even near the North Pole, you couldn't be sure there wasn't someone out there."

"Our first overflight mission of four RB-47Es and two RB-47Hs on April 5 was a complete flop," recalls Lieutenant Colonel Lloyd Fields, "and had to be curtailed because our KC-97 tankers developed mechanical problems. Only two KC-97 tankers were at the rendezvous refueling point. Five or six others were very late for takeoff or had aborted for one reason or another. It was pointless to continue, as two tankers could not ever provide half the fuel that was required. So everyone returned to Thule. This prompted General Wheless, the Project Home Run senior officer, to have a face-to-face discussion with the tanker squadron commander to impress upon him the importance of our missions and how he fit into the picture. Thereafter, we never aborted a mission during our stay at Thule for any reason. Our overflights of Soviet territory started in early April 1956, shortly after our Arctic training had ended, and lasted until early May. After the initial tanker-related problem on the first scheduled overflights, we flew a total of 156 flights without a single abort. On one occasion, we had six RB-47s recover into Eielson Air Force Base in Alaska and return the next day. The missions involved both photographic and electronic reconnaissance, with the planes departing in pairs. We mapped not only Novaya Zemlya but also most of the Arctic portion of the Soviet Union including air bases, radar stations, atomic testing sites, and numerous towns and industries.

"One incident happened at Thule that involved one of our most reliable aircraft commanders—John Lappo. John Lappo was about forty-five minutes late returning from a mission. In the command post, I was getting nervous. Colonel Meng was getting nervous. General Wheless was getting nervous. Finally, General Wheless said, 'Lloyd, let's break radio silence. I want you to call John and see how and where he is.' I got on the radio and called John Lappo, saying, 'John, how much fuel have you got?' Lappo got back immediately, 'I have enough.' I repeated, 'John, how much fuel have you got?' And he

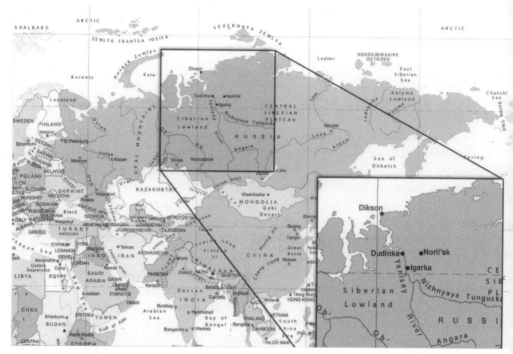

April 14, 1956, overflight of Noril'sk by three RB-47E photo reconnaissance aircraft of the 26th SRW.

repeated, 'I have enough.' I changed my approach and said, 'How many pounds of fuel do you have?' John replied, '8,000 pounds.' That airplane was supposed to have 8,000 pounds of fuel on board when it parked on the ramp and shut down its engines. I knew it took about 6,600 pounds of fuel per hour to fly the RB-47 at his current altitude. So I asked, 'How far are you from base?' 'Forty-five minutes,' he got back to me. I asked him if he wanted a tanker; one was standing by for just such an emergency. He didn't want a tanker. His rational was that if for any reason he missed connecting with the tanker, he would be in real trouble. John, and the other two aircraft in his flight, came straight in and landed. During the debriefing, General Wheless asked John, 'Why were you forty-five minutes late?' 'Well, General,' Lappo responded, 'it was like this. The visibility was not good at the target area when I arrived, and I didn't think you would want to send another flight over to finish the job—so, I made another pass.' To that, Wheless replied, 'Captain Lappo, I wished I had an air division of pilots like you.'"

John Lappo's decision to make a second run against his assigned target was not an idle one. He and his two accompanying aircraft had come a long way—and he was not about to come back empty-handed. Writes the former air

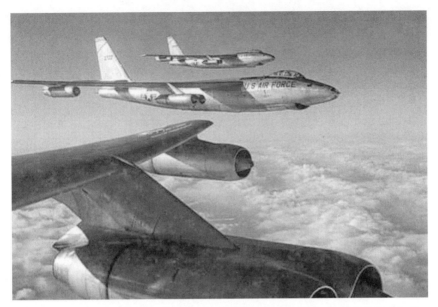

RB-47E photo reconnaissance aircraft during Project Home Run, April–May 1956. Captain John S. Lappo, an intrepid flyer, on April 7, 1959, flew an RB-47E like the ones shown here under the Mackinac Bridge with just 155 feet clearance. That spontaneous decision cost Captain Lappo his wings.

force historian R. Cargill Hall, "Of all the SENSINT missions during Operation Home Run, the one flown on 14 April 1956 was probably one of the most audacious and dangerous—the city of Noril'sk, deep in the interior of Siberia. The city had been founded by Stalin as a slave labor camp, a Gulag, for the purpose of exploiting the rich nickel deposits in the area, and never been open to visitors from the West. John Lappo piloted the lead aircraft, Charles 'Bud' Mundy flew the second and Franklin Roll piloted the third RB-47E. The aircrews knew nothing of Noril'sk's history, to them it was just a name on a map and a set of coordinates. They remembered their flight instructions—one pass and haul ass out of denied territory, a God-like edict in the reconnaissance community, never to be violated. When passing over their assigned target, it was covered with Arctic haze. Lappo decided to make a second pass. On the second run over the target, the haze had lifted, and they turned on their cameras. They had arrived at noon, when the sun angle was just right, casting long shadows in the snow, permitting precise calculations of building sizes, shapes and heights. Then they flew south on the Yenisey River to image the town of Igarka and turned north to photograph the port of Dudinka, from which the nickel was shipped to Murmansk on the Kola Peninsula." Making that extra pass over the target cost Lappo's flight precious fuel, making their return to Thule a very close thing. There were no tankers planned for their return flight, because one could never count on them being there because of possible high winds and ice fogs at Thule. So what they had in their tanks had to take them back home—they made it, but barely. "Once on the ground the aircrews were debriefed in a secure room. The developed film was flown directly to SAC headquarters in Omaha, Nebraska, and to CIA headquarters in Washington, DC."

Lappo had violated the God-like edict for flying reconnaissance and coming home alive of "One Pass—Haul Ass." Lappo's well-meant maneuver soon had the commander in chief of the Strategic Air Command on the ropes. "Lappo's 360-degree turn to make another pass," recalls General Rhodarmer, "caused a flap. I was never quite sure how Washington got word of this deviation, but I do know that the air force vice chief of staff, General Thomas White, came under heavy pressure to respond to this unauthorized coverage. General White called me into his office and told me that there was a great urgency to get a message to General LeMay in Omaha, pronto. He told me what he wanted in the message, and wanted me to hand-carry it 'Eyes Only' to the SAC commander. The letter was short and to the point; it stated that SAC had no discretion to deviate from authorized targets, and that violations of this nature risked the aircrew over denied territory and could jeopardize future authority for conducting overflights. It further stated that General LeMay had to make this extremely clear to the aircrews. We only had one secretary with the clearance to type this letter. When General White read it and signed it, he said, 'You made the point.' As I turned to leave to hand-deliver the letter to General LeMay, General White said, 'You better have your iron suit on when you see him.' I immediately got a T-33 and flew out to Omaha to deliver the letter to General LeMay. Lieutenant Colonel Paul Herring, my counterpart at SAC, already knew I was coming—but not the reason why. As soon as I landed, I was taken to the command section. The SAC vice commander was there and expressed an interest in what I had. I told him the message was Eyes Only for General LeMay. He said, 'Go right in.' It was the first time I had ever met LeMay, and he was not at all what I expected. He was quite cordial, did not bark at me or throw his cigar. He opened the letter and read it. Then he picked up a pen and wrote, 'I have looked into this matter and I support my aircrews.' That was it. I jumped into my T-33, flew back to Washington, and delivered the reply to General White. That was the last I ever saw of that letter."

During Project Home Run, crews fought outside temperatures of 40 degrees below zero Fahrenheit or lower with fur-lined parkas, bulky mittens, heavily padded flight suits, and clumsy mukluk boots. Maintenance had a particularly difficult time with tasks that required them to remove their bulky Arctic mittens. One man held a stopwatch with a second hand, while the other man worked. They completed tasks in stages, switching off to keep their fingers

Noril'sk smelters imaged by a 36-inch focal length camera mounted in Captain John Lappo's RB-47E. A close-up of the smelters is on the left.

from getting frostbitten. Photo- and electronic reconnaissance aircraft frequently operated in pairs. However, the planes did not fly in formation or even in sight of one another. All aircrews were briefed individually, and because of a strictly applied need-to-know security rule, no aircrew knew exactly where the others were going. The Thule missions of 1956 photomapped the islands of Novaya Zemlya and their atomic test site. These aircraft flew behind the Ural Mountains and across Siberia and confirmed that the Soviet Union's northern regions were poorly defended against air attack. Subsequently, many of the SAC bomber routes against the Soviet Union were planned to cross the top of the world. Throughout this difficult operation, not one RB-47 was lost as a result of accident or to Soviet fighters. Not that the Russians didn't try on occasion. Colonel Joe Gyulavics remembered "a bunch of fighters coming up out of Novaya Zemlya. We heard them launch. The Ravens picked up the fighter radars on their receivers. I saw the contrails of the Russian fighters, but they couldn't overtake us. An interesting time. We thought we were invincible and immortal. We never thought of a downside."

Colonel Burton S. Barrett, one of the RB-47H Home Run aircraft commanders, at the Early Cold War Overflights Symposium in 2001, noted that "sub-zero cold does strange things to men and machines. It seldom snows at Thule. The snow at the base is that which blows in off the polar ice cap,

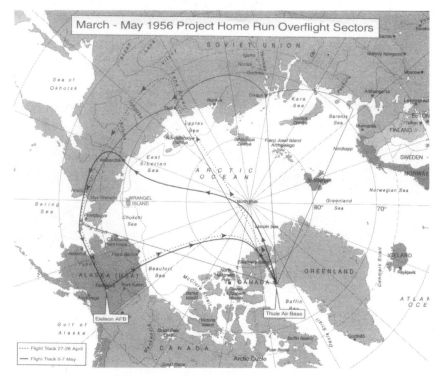

Project Home Run overflight sectors and flight tracks for April 27 and May 6 overflights.

it just never melts and accumulates. Jet fuel in a minus 40 degree environment weighs 7 pounds instead of 6 pounds per gallon, making the aircraft fuel load 107,000 pounds instead of the normal 98,000 pounds. The heavier fuel meant a longer takeoff distance, but ironically the cold air makes the jet engine produce more thrust, causing a shorter takeoff distance. In such cold conditions, engines of motor vehicles were started just once and never shut down, because the engine oil would freeze in five minutes or less. I'll never forget the cold at Thule. I was never so cold in my life.

"Looking back at this operation, I would say that our success depended on two things—navigation and air refueling. Navigation in the Arctic presents a difficult problem as the magnetic compass arrow just turns in circles. All Home Run navigators had to learn the grid system. Grid navigation was first developed by the Strategic Air Command's first operational unit, the 46th Reconnaissance Squadron under Maynard White, back in 1946. Once learned, it was a relatively simple thing to navigate across the pole and get back to where you began. The grid heading for the runway at Thule was about 90 degrees different from the standard heading, so I just told my navigator that

Thule Air Base, Greenland, on a good day in 1956. The runway, the base installation, and the nearby Eskimo village are clearly visible.

after leveling off I would give him control of the aircraft to plot our course. Air refueling was the second crucial item for success of our operation. The KC-97 was a conventional aircraft using high-grade aviation gasoline in its four propeller-driven engines. They had to carry JP-4 jet fuel for our RB-47s, but if they had to lighten their aircraft for any reason they would just pump the jet fuel overboard because they couldn't burn it themselves. As good as the cold was for jet engines, it was very hard on the KC-97's internal combustion engines. The ground crews had to put heaters on these engines at least six hours before takeoff to get them warm enough to start. Normally we took on 20,000 pounds of fuel from a KC-97. When the tanker orbit moved further north, they could only give us 15,000 pounds. A flight of two RB-47s normally required the support of five tankers."

Major George A. Brown was one of two planners for all of the reconnaissance missions flown. He recalled at the Early Cold War Overflights Symposium that "none of the top commanders or operations officers were permitted to fly any of the missions for security reasons. General Wheless understood why, but one or two of the lower-ranking commanders felt that, as during World War II, they should have been allowed to share the hazards encountered by their crews. Air force headquarters had issued that directive for security reasons." As General LeMay liked doing, he flew to Lockbourne Air Force

RB-47H electronic reconnaissance aircraft in 1956 on their way to Thule Air Base, Greenland, for Project Home Run. Four aircraft from the 38th and 343rd SRS participated, piloted by B. Barrett, AC, and D. Waller, CP; R. Campbell/J. Gyulavics; D. Grant/D. Wells; R. Hubbard/C. Aslund.

Base, Columbus, Ohio, soon after the crews had returned from Thule and personally oversaw the award of the Distinguished Flying Cross to each one of the reconnaissance crews who had flown in Operation Home Run. The KC-97 tanker crews, who made the entire operation possible, received Air Medals.

I think that R. Cargill Hall, the National Reconnaissance Office chief historian, succinctly summarizes the achievement of the Home Run operation: "To this day, the SAC Thule missions remain one of the most incredible demonstrations of professional aviation skill ever seen in any military organization at any time." I second that opinion.

FATE IS THE HUNTER: THE SHOOTDOWN OF RB-47H 53-4281 OVER THE BARENTS SEA (1960)

Finally, about six hours after their shoot-down, John McKone sees, low and far away over the waters, the tiny dot of a plane. As it moves closer, he can hear its propellers. Then he can see that it is dark green. Finally he can make out a red star on its fuselage. He frantically waggles his signal mirror, but the plane stays steady on its course. Had it seen him?

—William White, *The Little Toy Dog*

Colonel Charles L. Phillips, then a lieutenant colonel, was assistant director for operations for the 4083rd Strategic Wing at Thule Air Base, Greenland, in 1958. Charlie was a World War II veteran, like so many of the aircrew who served in SAC. In 1945, he flew twenty-nine combat missions against Japan in B-29s out of Saipan, dropping firebombs from altitudes too low for high-altitude antiaircraft guns to be effective, and too high for Japanese automatic weapons fire to reach them. That tactic was one of General LeMay's innovations. In the process, pilots discovered the jet stream, which could almost bring to a standstill a B-29 bomber flying into the wind. Charlie's missions had been grueling fifteen-hour flights, and he sympathized with the RB-47 reconnaissance crews, flying similarly lengthy missions out of Thule. In the B-29, Charlie had been able to get out of his seat and stretch his legs, but the RB-47 aircrews had no such luxury; they were confined to their ejection seats for the duration of their flights.

"While at Thule," Phillips recalled for me during our interview, "I lay on my cot in BOQ 713, listening to the howling winds outside. I thought of my next-to-last combat mission, my twenty-eighth, which I flew on August 6, 1945, the day the first atomic bomb was dropped on Hiroshima. I ran out of fuel after an unexpected encounter with the jet stream and had to ditch my aircraft. I was apprehensive about putting the big bomber in the calm waters of the Pacific. My crew tumbled about considerably when I did, but fortunately only one of us was severely injured. On August 9, the second atomic bomb was dropped by

The 4083rd Strategic Wing base operations facility at Thule Air Base, Greenland. Ice, snow, and minus 40 degree temperatures were the norm during the long winter months.

a B-29 from Tinian. Still, peace negotiations with the Japanese dragged on. On August 14, I launched along with three hundred other B-29 bombers against the Japanese army arsenal at Osaka. I expected to be recalled at any moment because I thought a peace agreement was imminent, but it didn't happen. We dropped our lethal load of high-explosive bombs and watched as the Japanese arsenal below us was reduced to rubble. Shortly after we landed at Saipan, the Japanese surrendered. I know it was August 14, 1945, in the United States—the fifteenth of August on Saipan."

When Thule closed and an aircraft had to divert to an alternate or emergency airfield, few options were available. The most practical choices open to a pilot were emergency airfields on Greenland itself—fields that provided a minimum of support and required a maximum of pilot skill. Recovering aircraft from emergency airfields such as Weather Station Nord became a major operation fraught with risk to the aircraft as well as to the maintenance crews who tried to get the marooned jet airborne again. One such emergency landing occurred in April 1958 at Station Nord, on the northeast tip of Greenland. An RB-47H electronic reconnaissance aircraft, tail number 53-4281, of the 55th Strategic Reconnaissance Wing and piloted by Captain Kenney Addison, was returning from a routine reconnaissance mission off Siberia when Thule closed for Phase III winds. The winds blew across the runway at a right angle and resulted in zero-zero conditions—zero visibility and zero ceiling. Either the severe crosswind or the limited visibility was enough to keep the RB-47 from landing. Only two practical alternatives offered themselves to the tired aircrew. One was Sondrestrom, on the west coast of the southern third of Greenland, with an approach up a fjord and a runway facing a towering ice shelf. The other option was Nord. The crew chose Nord, a barren airstrip adjacent to a Danish weather station that offered only a snow-and-ice-covered 8,000-foot runway. However, Nord had runway lights, the only sure way for a pilot to positively identify the runway in wintry conditions.

"I was startled when my phone rang," Charlie Phillips recalled. "The senior command post officer asked me to try, if I possibly could, to come over. I dressed quickly and as warmly as possible. I pulled the hood of my fur-lined parka around my face and stepped into the Arctic whiteout. It was unusual to be asked for anyone to go outside after a phase had struck. When I reached my destination, my parka was encrusted with a thick layer of ice and frost. I was told that the RB-47 reconnaissance aircraft which had launched the night before had landed at Station Nord, and that as soon as the winds died down, I was to lead a rescue party to get the aircraft back to Thule. I sat down and began planning the recovery of the stranded RB-47H with tail number 53-4281."

Aircraft 53-4281 had made an uneventful landing at Nord. Captain Kenneth Addison of the 343rd SRS, of the 55th Strategic Reconnaissance Wing, and his copilot John Draper had taxied the aircraft to the center of a small parking area near a building that they presumed was the Danish weather station. Before shutting down the engines, Addison blew the approach and landing chutes off to one side. Then, as the engines spooled down with a high-pitched whine, an eerie silence settled over the aircraft. In spite of their helmets, the six-man crew had endured hours of incessant wind noise as they had cut at five hundred miles per hour through the cold skies of the Arctic world at 38,000 feet. One of the three Ravens sitting in the aisle below the pilots opened the entry hatch and let down the aluminum access ladder. The crew emerged slowly, dressed in their bulky winter flying suits, stiff from sitting for hours strapped into their ejection seats. The crew secured their classified logs and tapes and secured the aircraft. Then they turned to their Danish hosts, who greeted them in good English.

It was an occasion to celebrate. Rarely did anyone drop by in the winter months for a visit, emergency or otherwise. The arrival of the Americans was a welcome interruption for the Danish weathermen. The aircrew quickly learned that Danish Aquavit kept ice cold and drunk in one bold gesture was lethal. They enjoyed the cheese that was served and the sleep-inducing drink. Their hosts provided blankets and they slept on the heated concrete floor of the station's laundry room. To fly back to Thule, they knew, they would need outside assistance. They had no way to start their engines. Three days after

A C-47 transport landing on the snow-covered runway at Thule, Greenland. Note that it is almost impossible for the pilot to tell with certainty where the runway is, unless there are some lights along the edges to serve as a guide. In conditions of blowing snow or darkness, even with lights, it is a nearly impossible task to bring in an airplane.

53-4281 had landed at Nord, the winds died down at Thule, and Charlie Phillips and his rescue crew got underway.

Phillips continued: "I took two KC-97 aerial refueling tankers with full fuel loads from the 100th Air Refueling Squadron and sent them off to Nord. The 100th came from Pease Air Force Base in New Hampshire. They were pulling a six-week rotational tour at Thule. Then I had an MD-3 power cart loaded on a Berlin airlift–vintage C-54 transport to power up the RB-47's engines, and I put a maintenance crew on the same plane, and I followed on one of the KC-97s. First and foremost on my mind was the safety of my men and the aircraft we were to rescue. I knew that everything we had to do had to be done carefully and deliberately. I wouldn't have anything bad happen to that reconnaissance airplane. As the team leader, I decided that I would personally handle the potentially most dangerous operation myself—operating the fork-lift in close proximity to the RB-47. I was told that a forklift was permanently positioned at Nord to unload aircraft delivering fuel to Nord in fifty-gallon drums. After our arrival, I had the Danish lift operator explain its operation to me, and then I practiced driving, tilting, and lifting for half an hour before I certified myself as being ready to operate the lift.

"The outside temperatures were in the 40 below zero Fahrenheit range. With the forklift, I lifted the maintenance officer, a major from the 55th Wing,

Colonel Charles Phillips operating the forklift, 1958, at Weather Station Nord, Greenland. Maintenance men standing on the pallet of the lift are connecting a flexible fuel hose to the tanker's extended boom.

up onto the nose of the RB-47 to enable him to connect a flexible refueling hose to the aircraft's refueling receptacle. I carefully drove the lift within inches of the RB-47, lifting the major on a pallet to his icy perch. Once the hose connection was made, the KC-97 started three of its four engines—one to power its brakes, the other two to run the fuel pumps. Since there was no tug to tow the KC-97 into position, the huge aircraft had to be backed in by reversing the propeller pitch. It was a slow and tedious process. Once the first tanker discharged its fuel, it had to be disconnected from the RB-47 and taxied away, and the second tanker had to be backed into position, again very carefully. During the refueling with the KC-97s, the icy wind blast from their running engines frosted up the RB-47. The frost had to come off the jet before it could fly. I had two ropes tied around the waist of one of my men and lifted him with the forklift up on a wing of the RB-47. Two men on each side of the wing held the ropes tied around the wing walker's waist to keep him from slipping off while he brushed off the ice and snow, using a simple push broom. A hazard to the wing walker was a double row of vortex generators sticking up on top of each wing near the wing tips. Each blade was two inches high. A fall onto these knife-like blades could cause serious injury. The operation took over six hours from start to finish. No one was injured, and nothing was damaged. We also installed new approach and landing chutes in the RB-47. Then I wired the command post at Thule for instructions, which came by teletype over the Danish weathernet. Judging from the telegram, the Thule weather forecast wasn't all that good. Conditions varied with blowing snow, winds at 25 knots gusting to 35, and moderate to severe turbulence. We were advised to depart at 0200 Zulu time, Greenwich mean time, on the twenty-eighth, during the best anticipated weather conditions. KC-97 tankers would be standing by at Thule to launch if additional fuel was required.

"When the time came for the RB-47 to launch, everyone at Nord came out to watch. I remember the RB-47 taxiing out to the end of the snow-packed runway and then, as it so often happened, the heat from its six engines generated a huge ice cloud. The cloud settled between us watchers and the RB-47. We didn't know if the cloud also enveloped the RB-47. Then we heard the throaty roar from six jet engines, and suddenly the aircraft emerged from the other side of the ice cloud as it rose into the milky white sky above Station Nord heading for Thule. We all cheered. At that moment it was 'our' plane. We had put our full energy into getting that bird airborne, and we felt good about our accomplishment. There were smiles all around. I shook hands with every-one and thanked them for their hard work and a job well done. After the two KC-97 tankers departed, our Danish hosts invited the rest of us to share some food and drink with them. We did for an hour or two, then exhaustion and the Aquavit overcame us. We slept on the same heated floor in the weather station's laundry room where the RB-47 crew had slept before us. We left the next day in the C-54."

On July 1, 1960, only two months after the shootdown of Francis Gary Pow-ers's U-2 photo reconnaissance plane near Sverdlovsk, an RB-47H reconnais-sance aircraft with tail number 53-4281 took off in the early morning darkness from RAF Brize Norton, United Kingdom, also known as Operating Location 1 of the 55th SRW. The RB-47H, the same aircraft that two years earlier had recovered at Weather Station Nord in Greenland, was on a peripheral recon-naissance mission. Its route was similar to that flown by Captain Harold Aus-tin, except that the plane was not tasked to overfly the Soviet Union. Rather, its mission was a "routine" peripheral reconnaissance flight staying thirty nautical miles off the Russian shoreline. Captain Willard Palm was the pilot, Captain Bruce Olmstead the copilot, Captain John McKone the navigator. The three Ravens flying in the reconnaissance capsule located in the former bomb bay area were Captain Eugene Posa and Lieutenants Oscar Goforth and Dean Phillips. The aircraft was officially declared missing on July 2, and an intensive search was initiated by the US Air Force. Hypocritically, the Soviet Union announced on July 4 that it, too, would join in the search for the miss-ing aircraft—knowing full well that one of its MiG-19 fighters had downed

A Russian MiG-19 supersonic fighter, like the one that shot down Willard Palm's RB-47H, armed with air-to-air missiles, taxiing for takeoff.

A flight of five RB-47H reconnaissance aircraft of the 55th Strategic Reconnaissance Wing flew in a "missing man" formation over Arlington National Cemetery at the burial of Major Willard Palm, the aircraft commander of the ill-fated RB-47H reconnaissance aircraft shot down over the Barents Sea on July 1, 1960, by Russian MiG-19 fighters.

the RB-47 over international waters. The Russians eventually admitted the shootdown and that they had two of its crew in custody, rescued by fishermen who happened to be in the area—Lieutenants McKone and Olmstead, both of whom were promoted to captain while imprisoned in the infamous Lubyanka Prison in Moscow. Captain Willard G. Palm's body had also been recovered and was returned to the United States on July 25, 1960, for burial in Arlington National Cemetery. Palm was promoted to major posthumously. The Russians disclaimed having any knowledge of the three Ravens who were lost—Posa, Goforth, and Phillips—and their bodies were never returned to the United States. The shootdown of the RB-47 turned into a major international incident reminiscent of the Powers shootdown in his U-2 near Sverdlovsk by a salvo of SA-2 surface-to-air missiles. McKone and Olmstead were released from Lubyanka Prison after nearly seven months of imprisonment and interrogation in January 1961, apparently as a goodwill gesture by Premier Nikita Khrushchev to President John F. Kennedy, who had succeeded Dwight D. Eisenhower that January. As the release of McKone and Olmstead was announced, President Kennedy held a news conference at the State Department. "Mr. President, did the Russians ask any quid pro quo, or did we make any concessions?" asked a reporter. The president now referred to the statement "which I read to you earlier, in this matter of overflights." "Does that mean, sir, that they accepted a reassurance of no more overflights as an exchange?" "It is a fact," President Kennedy responded, "that I have ordered that the flights not be resumed, which is a continuation of the order given by President Eisenhower in May of last year."[43] The overflights were to continue, but by other means than aircraft.

THE RB-57D THAT KILLED THE
SENSINT PROGRAM (1956)

SAC did not retain its RB-57Ds very long. Only six remained with
SAC by December 1959. In April 1960 SAC disposed of the last one.
—**Marcelle Knaack,** *Post–World War II Bombers*

Within weeks of the outbreak of the war in Korea, the USAF Board of Senior
Officers began looking at options to replace the aging Douglas B/RB-26
Invader. The board agreed that what was needed was a light jet bomber that
could operate from short runways and unimproved airfields, one with a ceiling of 40,000 feet, a range of about 1,000 miles, and a maximum speed of
around 550 knots. The board looked at what was available, including foreign
aircraft. The Martin XB-51 was the first choice, of course, but it was still undergoing flight testing and probably would not be available for a number of years.
The North American B-45 was looked at but found unsuitable for the tactical
bomber role, limited by a conventional airframe with little growth potential.
The Canadair CF-100 failed on many counts, as did the British Vickers Valiant
and SAC's B-47 medium bomber. The one aircraft that looked as close to an
off-the-shelf combat airplane as one could hope for was the English Electric Canberra. Air force technical intelligence officers attached to the London
embassy were impressed when witnessing its first flight at RAF Wharton in
1949. The Air Staff tasked Brigadier General Albert Boyd, the air force chief of
test and evaluation at Edwards Air Force Base, to take a look. Boyd generally
liked what he saw. But he wanted the Canberra to undergo rigorous tests and
evaluation. Two British Canberras were purchased and flown to the Martin
Company in Baltimore. Although the British aircraft exhibited many shortcomings as they underwent detailed examination and tests, the Canberra
gained more friends than enemies and became a serious contender to replace
the B-26 as an interim night intruder and reconnaissance aircraft for employment in Korea. On February 26, 1951, The senior officer and USAF Weapons

One of the two English Electric Canberras, with British markings, flown to the Martin Aircraft Company in Baltimore for evaluation to become the US Air Force's interim medium bomber. Lots of unpleasant surprises were in store for both the Martin Aircraft Company and its USAF customer.

Board each chose the Canberra as the best interim aircraft available for service in Korea. General Hoyt Vandenberg, the air force chief of staff, signed off on the recommendation. It was a done deal.

The Martin Company, testing the XB-51, the Tactical Air Command's ultimate choice of a tactical bomber, seemed the logical choice to build the American copy of the Canberra. The immediate need was for a bomber in the role of night intruder, and an equally night-capable RB-57 reconnaissance aircraft. Eight B-57A bombers were built before it was realized that this really was not an off-the-shelf airplane. It showed numerous shortcomings that had to be fixed, not the least of which was the J65 engines that took the place of the British Rolls Royce turbojets. The B-57 program stalled. The first flight of a production B-57 did not take place until July 20, 1953. The Korean armistice was signed on July 27. The entire program was nearly killed by a string of spectacular accidents. What saved the B-57 probably more than any other event was the demise of the XB-51. On October 28, 1949, the XB-51 had made its maiden flight. A second airplane was built. In May 1952, during a low-level demonstration at Edwards Air Force Base, California, one of the XB-51s crashed, killing the pilot. The second aircraft soon crashed as well. The contract, for what once was thought of as TAC's ultimate tactical bomber, was canceled. It was clear,

The RB-66B photo reconnaissance aircraft required the pilot to have multi-jet engine experience before qualification in the RB-66 was allowed. The only aircraft available at the time to provide that experience were the B-47 and B-57.

however, that what was needed in the summer of 1952 were airplanes on the ramp rather than more studies. So the B/RB-57 survived its near demise. By July 1954, the first of sixty-seven RB-57s were assigned to the 345th Bomb Wing at Langley Air Force Base, Virginia, and the 363rd Tactical Reconnaissance Group at Shaw Air Force Base, South Carolina. Others were assigned to Hurlburt Field, Florida; Sembach Air Base, Germany; and Laon Air Base, France. The accident rate remained high, yet with all its limitations the RB-57 served as the principal transition aircraft from the B/RB-26 to the yet even newer than the B-57, the US Navy–derived B/RB-66.[44]

While the RB-57A, of which 67 aircraft were built, did yeoman service as a jet trainer for future B/RB-66 pilots, it also served as a high-altitude photo reconnaissance aircraft and continued to evolve into the B-57B bomber, of which 202 were built, and the B-57C two-seat version, a modified B-57B. The D-model was to be different from all the rest with a substantially altered B-57B fuselage, new wings, more powerful engines, and varied reconnaissance configurations. A total of twenty D-models were built. The removal of the fuselage fuel tanks allowed the installation of varied cameras, four of which were located forward of the nose wheel well. The RB-57D's large nose and tail radomes further lengthened the fuselage. The necessary fuel was carried in

An RB-57D shadowed by an RB-57A, showing the enormity of the new wing, which required a new look at hangar space, parking areas, and runways.

the wings, which were of honeycomb construction and had a wingspan of 105 feet—replacing the original wing of 64 feet, nearly twice as large in area, totally changing the appearance of the aircraft. The aircraft was designed to fly at altitudes up to 70,000 feet, and fourteen of the twenty aircraft built were equipped for aerial refueling. The first RB-57D was flown on November 3, 1955, with acceptable results.[45]

The twenty RB-57Ds were ordered in three different versions, twelve of which would be one-man Ds carrying two K-38 and two KC-1 split vertical cameras. Another, also a one-man D, was equipped with a high-resolution side-looking radar for radar mapping reconnaissance. The remaining aircraft were two-man versions equipped for electronic reconnaissance similar to the function of the RB-47H, which would be flown by the 55th Strategic Reconnaissance Wing. Because of the perceived urgency of the program to get the aircraft ready for overflights of the Soviet Union, testing was limited and ended in 1956. The first D-model was delivered to SAC in May 1956. By that September, SAC, the 4080th SRW, had taken delivery of eleven Ds and four C-model two-seat trainers.[46]

Recalls Major General Roger K. Rhodarmer during his presentation at the Early Cold War Overflights Symposium, then a lieutenant colonel and known as the "legman" for Headquarters US Air Force overflight operations:

"I know we got RB-57As in both Europe and the Pacific, but I was not much involved in that program. Those birds could get up to 56,000 feet, some even higher. The RB-57D models built for the SENSINT program also were coming along, and the Air Staff was wondering where we were going to base these things. The air force had already bought the damn things, once they understood the pressure from on high for penetration overflights. The RB-57D had a modified J-57 engine that had a lot of thrust and long, extended wings, and a bigger fuselage than the C-model. So we ended up building a brand new airplane using modification money. Then the RB-57D became a major issue for me. The air force had sent briefers out to USAFE and FEAF to tell them that we had this new airplane coming along. Both USAFE and FEAF just weren't interested. The airplane had unique engines, had new wings, required airfields of different sizes—they just weren't interested. They had their own little airplanes and were very satisfied with what they had and what they were doing. In essence, they turned down the RB-57D for good reasons, and it was even hard for us to see where you could use this thing. I went up to the Glenn Martin plant in Baltimore to look at the airplane. I nearly fell out of my chair. I went to General Everest and told him that this plane was coming and it had to go somewhere. We tried to interest SAC, but General LeMay wouldn't even think of having another airplane in his inventory—he already had the B-36, the B-47, and the B-52 was just getting ready to enter the force. He didn't want to introduce another new airplane, especially a really oddball bird.

"Anyway, someone got a message to General [John Paul] McConnell, who was the director of operations at SAC headquarters. I then was asked to brief him and his staff on what exactly this new airplane was all about. Before I started that briefing, someone told me to go and see a Colonel Robert Smith who was the head of Intelligence at SAC. I gave Colonel Smith a rundown on the RB-57D—and he could hardly stand still. It was exactly the kind of airplane he wanted. What annoyed the folks at Strategic Air Command a little was that we had not put better cameras in the plane. We had used the K-38s and standard cameras. Even though Smith didn't like that part, he got on board and persuaded General McConnell at the meeting. After some impassioned remarks by Smith about the RB-57D, General McConnell finally got up and said, 'OK, goddamn it, if anybody needs to run this thing SAC better take it or it'll go to hell in a handbasket!' It was the best speech I ever heard, because he had influence with LeMay and the SAC staff. They activated the 4080th Strategic Reconnaissance Wing, appointed a commander, and off we went. The aircrews, maintenance, training, everything grew up with that airplane as it came out of the Martin plant front door. By the time they were delivered, everything was ready. We had to have ready all the pressure suits and everything. The wing was activated and moved down to Valdosta, Georgia. Those airplanes took off and damn near went straight up."

While Rhodarmer was selling the RB-57D to SAC, the people in the 4080th tried to make the aircraft do what it was supposed to. The Pratt and Whitney J-57-P-9 engines, Westinghouse autopilots, and some of the more complicated electronic countermeasure systems did not function properly. The greatly enlarged wing kept causing problems. The main wing spar had to be strengthened, as did sections of the wing panels. The Martin-developed honeycomb wing surfaces were subject to water seepage and wing stress. Then there were parts problems, and on and on, all the little things that can go wrong with a new airframe. In time, it was all taken care of, and the aircraft made its first satisfactory flights after twenty failures in June 1957. The last aircraft was delivered from the Martin Company to the 4080th in March 1957.

"Meanwhile, back at the Pentagon, the Sensitive Intelligence, SENSINT, overflight program was going fine," recalls Roger Rhodarmer. "One day in the spring of 1956 I got a call from a guy I knew, asking me to come over to the E-Ring to talk. He told me, 'I need to brief you on a project we've got going here.' And he proceeded to tell me about the U-2, that was going to impact our RB-57D program—because the U-2 engine wasn't working right and the CIA needed the J-57 engines which we used on the D-model. The U-2 was having trouble with airflow through the engine at altitude, and it would not stay lit. This introduced me to a new world and Brigadier General Osmond 'Ozzie' Ritland, the deputy to Richard 'Dick' Bissell, who was in charge of the U-2 project at CIA. Ritland told me that he knew what I was doing with the RB-57D, and to come over and brief Dick Bissell on the SENSINT overflight program. After getting the OK from my boss, General Everest, I worked up a complete flip-chart briefing on the program—I was told they were cleared for God and everything else. On the appointed date I went over, along with General Ritland, to brief Dick Bissell, who was a most charming fellow. Just a few days before this briefing, SAC had flown six RB-47E/H aircraft on May 6 and 7 from Thule, Greenland, over the North Pole into northern Siberia, exiting at Anadyr on the Bering Sea, and landing at Eielson Air Force Base in Alaska. Part of my briefing to Dick Bissell included this particular flight, and it really impressed him.

"Bissell came just about out of his chair; he could hardly believe what I told him. He had this new airplane, the U-2, that could fly at extreme altitudes, and now he knew that it could probably fly unmolested over the Soviet Union. We talked about distances and altitudes; then Bissell, in his enthusiasm, canceled all of his appointments, and we went out for lunch. Someone in Bissell's shop thought it would be a good idea to give my briefing to the president. So the word came back that we needed to prepare a briefing on sensitive intelligence

A NASA WB-57F—a modified RB-57D—at Kirtland Air Force Base, Albuquerque, New Mexico. The D/F series of aircraft performed photographic reconnaissance and flew air sampling missions; some flew for the Air Weather Service, a component of the Military Airlift Command.

operations similar to the one I gave to Bissell, but this time at the White House. When the word came down, I was given the prime job to make sure it was done right. The briefing covered everything from the early years to the present, what the air force had done and how well it was done. Then we waited for a month, and one day we got a call to come over and see General Thomas D. White, the air force vice chief of staff. 'We are going to take this briefing to the White House,' he said. 'Are you guys ready?' Then he added, 'Don't worry. I know President Eisenhower. Now show me the briefing.' We gave General White a quick summary, and then we all jumped into a car and drove over to the White House. Once there, I sat outside the Oval Office, and General White took the charts and the rest and went in. They were in there for some time, longer than I expected, and I was just sweating it out, wondering if I would be called in on some aspect or another. I was never asked to come in. When the door opened, General White stepped out accompanied by the president. General White then said to me, 'Let's go. The president reviewed the program and it's OK.' That was the beginning of my introduction to the CIA and the U-2 program.

"Meanwhile, we were beginning to receive the RB-57Ds and training pilots to fly them down there in Georgia. At SAC headquarters, Colonel Smith set up a photo-processing facility. Everything was ready to go. What they wanted to do was overfly Vladivostok—but before that could happen, we had a meeting with General LeMay, Smith and me, about bringing the RB-57Ds into Yokota Air Base, Japan. We got ready to leave for Japan when I got a call from a guy at CIA to stop by his office. He asked me to take some papers to General Laurence S. Kuter, who commanded FEAF, and to General Lyman L. Lemnitzer, the Far East Theater commander. The papers were a request to base U-2 aircraft at Atsugi Naval Air Station in Japan—and I was not to discuss any of this with my SAC friends involved in the RB-57D deployment. Sometime before that, the CIA people obviously had checked me out as someone who could be trusted with such an assignment. After that, it was like I had been working with the agency forever.

"Upon arriving in Japan, we met with Generals Hunter Harris and Kuter, and we explained the coming bed-down of the RB-57Ds. Then I asked for a private meeting with General Kuter—me, a lieutenant colonel, wanting to have a private meeting with a four-star general. I repeated my request to several gatekeeper generals, leaving them peeved at me, but I got my wish. I delivered the papers to General Kuter as instructed, then asked him to set up a similar meeting with General Lemnitzer, which he did. Both of them gave me an OK on the U-2 matter. General Lemnitzer requested I update him the next time he came to the Pentagon, which I agreed to do.

"Six RB-57Ds arrived at Yokota Air Base, Japan, in November 1956. The code name was Black Knight, suggested by a West Pointer who was involved in the program from the beginning. Earlier overflight projects were named after pretty girls such as 'Slick Chick' and 'Heart Throb.' Black Knight sounded a bit more robust, so we used Black Knight for the RB-57D planned overflight effort."

The target for the first RB-57D mission was Vladivostok and the adjacent airfields, a target that had been overflown by RF-86s and RB-57As in earlier years. General Curtis E. LeMay was there himself to send his newest reconnaissance aircraft on its way. Like other missions planned by the general and his staff, he liked to have his ships arrive in numbers, not necessarily that all of them would be committed, but sending several aircraft at a target tended to have the effect of getting the Russians to turn on all or most of their radars and start talking on the air. All this of course would be picked up by ground stations and other airborne sleuths equipped with the appropriate receivers and linguists if necessary. When Colonel Harold Austin made his lone overflight of the Kola Peninsula in May 1954, LeMay sent three RB-47s into the Barents Sea area; two turned back. During Project Home Run earlier in May 1956, SAC chose to use several RB-47s to overfly Soviet territory. So, in keeping with past practices, this time SAC launched all six RB-57Ds toward the Vladivostok area, three aircraft turning back and the remaining three penetrating Soviet territory. Because the

A shoulder patch of the 4080th Strategic Reconnaissance Wing—later worn by the pilots who flew U-2s over Cuba during the Cuban Missile Crisis of October 1962.

Yokota area was deemed less than secure and open to monitoring, the RBs relocated to Iwo Jima, an isolated and relatively secure location, and launched their high-altitude reconnaissance mission against Vladivostok from there.

"The aircraft, I believe, did a hell of a good job," recalled General Rhodarmer. "However, the Soviets tracked them from the start, and things really hit the fan. We had to go over and brief the State Department. We told them about the flight and then we were left sitting outside of Secretary Dulles's office while the State 'legman' went inside. As I recall, the Russian ambassador to the United States was in there, who had handed the secretary of state a formal protest note over our overflights by the RB-57Ds and earlier flights by RB-47 aircraft. When it was all over and they trooped out, I heard one American say, 'How did you know their tail numbers?' Remember, they were flying at 60,000 feet. The Russian official replied, 'Didn't you ever think of ground observatories?' A telescope! Apparently they were not only tracking the RB-57s with their radars but also were looking at them through a high-resolution telescope. The Russians had no trouble tracking those planes at all. A few days after the Soviet protest, President Eisenhower instructed then Colonel, later General, Andrew J. Goodpaster to relay his order to stop military reconnaissance flights over the Iron Curtain countries—for the time being." That was how the RB-57D ended the SENSINT program.

"From then on, the air force conducted only peripheral reconnaissance flights," Rhodarmer observed. "We had developed an airplane called Sharp Cut, an RB-57C, a two-seater, with a beautiful 240-inch lens on an oblique-looking camera that could look far into the Soviet Union—designed by James Baker and produced at Boston University's Optical Research Laboratory. They could get up high over the Black Sea and see Kapustin Yar damn near from Turkey. There were also long-range oblique photography missions flown by RB-47s out of Eielson Air Force Base, Alaska, along the coast of Siberia, [that] looked way inside the Soviet Union." Control of overflight operations was quite informal until 1956, and they were known only to a few generals, their "legmen," and the president. "In mid-1956, we built an operations center in the basement of the Pentagon; it was a 'Green Door' operation, probably the only one in the Pentagon at the time. Soon after the Operations Center went into business, the SENSINT program was canceled; however, we also incorporated by this time the air force peripheral missions. Then, by 1960, the Joint Reconnaissance Center was set up in the Pentagon. The air force was not alone in this business. The US Navy was flying peripheral missions as well, and had ships and submarines doing reconnaissance of various types. All of this activity and information was pulled together in the JRC. Then, in 1961, the National Reconnaissance Office was created as space reconnaissance entered the picture." The very existence of the NRO was kept secret for years, as was its name. It was also the year, 1961, when the Defense Intelligence Agency, DIA, the host of the 2001 Early Cold War Overflights Symposium, was created.

Rhodarmer continued, "When the U-2 program was getting started, the director of the CIA, Allen W. Dulles, was not supportive of the CIA getting into this business. I think it was Dick Bissell who told me, 'You know the boss. He still likes spies and agents on the ground, that sort of thing.' Dulles had the attitude that aerial reconnaissance should just stay within the air force. The CIA could get all the pictures they wanted without risk to themselves. But President Eisenhower had made up his mind that he wanted a civilian shop in control of this activity. We had gone through some hellacious diplomatic problems as a result of shootdowns of PARPRO aircraft in the Baltic and elsewhere. Those shootdowns involved military people, and it became complicated to deal with this through international diplomatic channels. A civilian-run operation seemed to make things a lot cleaner."

Overflights of super-high-flying U-2 aircraft, 70,000-plus feet up, piloted by civilian pilots, most of whom were all former air force pilots, seemed to

A modern-day Lockheed U-2/TR-1, Dragon Lady, around since 1955 and still earning its pay. The aircraft has grown in size and capabilities. The U-2 is a lasting tribute to Kelly Johnson, who designed not only the U-2 but also such aircraft as the pre–World War II P-38 and the magnificent Cold War Mach 3+ SR-71.

provide the means to safely continue overflights of the Soviet Union. Starting out first from Wiesbaden and Giebelstadt Air Bases in Germany, then flying out of Incirlik, Turkey, and subsequently Peshawar, Pakistan, the CIA U-2s overflew the Soviet Union repeatedly. But 70,000-plus feet wasn't that safe an altitude after all. An RB-57D flown by the Nationalist Chinese out of Taiwan was shot down over China on October 7, 1959—by a Russian-supplied SA-2 surface-to-air missile. On May 1, 1960, a CIA-flown U-2 piloted by Francis Gary Powers was downed by a salvo of SA-2 SAMs near Sverdlovsk, USSR. According to General Rhodarmer, "One vulnerable aspect of the U-2 at that high altitude was that all you had to do was disturb the atmosphere in front of the airplane, and that would make the engine flame out. That May 1960 shootdown put President Eisenhower in a hell of a position, but he had accepted the risk at the outset. It was quite a shock when Powers showed up alive. It would have been cleaner if he had just taken his cyanide shot. Eisenhower had also started other overhead reconnaissance programs, including satellites. By the time President John F. Kennedy arrived on the scene the following January, he just accepted everything and supported it. There was never very much that was ever written down. As General Everest once told me, 'When this SENSINT program ends, it will be like it never existed.'"

THE CUBAN MISSILE CRISIS THROUGH
THE EYES OF A RAVEN (1962)

I survived 1,000 bomber raids as a young boy in Berlin in 1945. I knew
if this thing went nuclear, both my family and I would perish.
—Wolfgang W. E. Samuel

On April 29, 1958, I processed out of the 28th Weather Squadron at Bushy
Park, a suburb of London, and General Eisenhower's one-time headquarters
prior to the D-Day landings, and took a train to Burtonwood in the north of
England. There, I boarded a civilian contract flight to McGuire Air Force Base,
near Wrightstown, New Jersey. At McGuire, I was given new orders assigning
me to Lowry Air Force Base in Denver, Colorado—for discharge from the air
force—and a Greyhound bus ticket home. A ticket to Colorado and my future.
I hadn't done too well that first year at the University of Colorado back in 1953–
1954, so I had joined the air force just in time to qualify for the Korean War GI
Bill—which was going to be my "personal scholarship" to get me through the
University of Colorado and a commission in the US Air Force—and of course
a pilot training slot; that's what it was all about for me. During the dark days
of the Berlin airlift back in 1948, I lived as a refugee kid in a rundown refugee
camp just off the north end of the RAF Fassberg runway. Day and night, the
C-54s carrying coal to Berlin flew over our rotten barracks, maybe 100+ feet
above us. That engine noise to me was the sound of freedom; having lived
under the Communists in the east of Germany, I had no desire to experience
them again. Then, one winter night, one of those freedom planes crashed, fell
out of the sky, right near our camp. Several days later, I went out to the crash
site, which was covered in black oil and coal, an engine sticking up out of
the soft marshy ground, lots of bits and pieces of airplane all over the place.
I wondered about these Americans. Three years earlier they had bombed me
when I lived in Berlin; now they were dying to save that very city. I wanted
to be like them, maybe wear their uniform, fly with them—of course dreams

213

July 1960: my very proud mother Hedy at my commissioning as a second lieutenant in the US Air Force, soon heading off for flight training.

like that never come true for people like me. Well, I got to come to America in 1951. Couldn't speak a word of English, had maybe an eighth-grade education—two years later I graduated from East High School in Denver, Colorado. But I really wasn't ready yet to go to college, which I heard I needed to become an officer in the US Air Force—so I could go to flight training. That first year in high school, I had bought myself a set of second lieutenant bars in a pawn shop—they represented my goal, and nothing was going to keep from getting there and flying with those men of the Berlin airlift.

In May 1958, when I reenrolled at the University of Colorado in Boulder, I felt like I was on top of the world. This time I was ready, and I had the money to get me through school without taking additional jobs as I had to before. Sometimes, failure is the best educator; at least it was for me. Here, I was to make my dream come true. At the Air Force ROTC detachment, they greeted me cordially but had bad news for me. They had no flying slots available of any kind. "The air force is downsizing," I was told. "Sorry." "Does it make any difference if I have prior air force service?" I asked. "Oh, yes, it does. We have slots for prior service students, but all the pilot slots are gone. All we have left is one navigator slot." "I'll take it," I told them. And that was it. No matter what—I had to fly once I got back into the air force. A nonflying job just didn't interest me. May as well go and make some money in the civilian world and buy my own airplane. In two years, I did three years of college work, went through Air Force ROTC summer camp at Hamilton Air Force Base near legendary San Francisco, California, and on a sunny July day in 1960 I graduated with a Bachelor of Science degree; but best of all, I was commissioned a second lieutenant in the US Air Force. My mother and my girlfriend pinned on the lieutenant's bars I had bought back in 1951 in a Denver pawnshop.

Military orders soon arrived terminating my enlisted status in the air force reserve. But most important, a set of orders arrived directing me to report for active duty at Harlingen Air Force Base, Texas. In the weeks that followed, there was little time for me to do anything other than concentrate on what I was there for—learn to navigate air force aircraft in all types of friendly and hostile environments. Our initial training flights focused on the basics of navigation—dead reckoning, sun lines, radio beacons, tactical navigation aids. Our first real challenge was night celestial navigation, a technique widely used to navigate the bombers of the Strategic Air Command, SAC. For our final celestial navigation check ride, we took off at 0100 hours the morning of March 1, 1961, heading for a turning point at Natchez, Mississippi. The weather soon deteriorated. The air became bumpy, making it difficult to keep my sextant focused on a star. The turbulence got worse as the flight went on. I wasn't going to let anything keep me from completing this check ride. While other students gave up and strapped into their positions, I kept on shooting stars, at times holding on for dear life, calculating our position, keeping up with the aircraft. Six hours later, we arrived at the let-down point near Harlingen. I sat back and relaxed. I did it. I was the only student to finish the check ride. Two days later, I received my score—a near perfect night celestial mission. After the instructor returned my charts and logs, he said to the class, "I commend Lieutenant Samuel for his perseverance and the quality of his work. However, the staff has decided not to count his mission because of the inclement weather on March 1. We will fly the mission over again." Everyone cheered. I was less than pleased with the outcome. After celestial navigation, we practiced grid navigation, Loran, pressure patterns, and radar. I passed all of my flight checks with flying colors, was designated a distinguished graduate, pinned on the wings of a navigator, was offered a regular commission vice the reserve commission that I'd held since coming on active duty, and, best of all—I would be able to pick my future assignment. My dream was to fly with the men of the

The C-124, better known to its aircrews as "Old Shaky," was the principal transport for the Military Air Transport Service, MATS, in the 1950s, later renamed Military Airlift Command, MAC, today known as Air Mobility Command. The name changed, but functions remained the same.

Berlin airlift—so I was all geared up to pick the first C-124 assignment available. The C-124 was the principal airlifter at the time, and I figured it was there where I would meet up with the men whom I so idolized.

Both my fellow students and instructors thought I was crazy. "You want to go into fighters or bombers" was their recommendation, "not fly with the 'trash haulers.'" I resented the reference to transport flyers as "trash haulers." They didn't understand my motivation; didn't know or remember that it was these very "trash haulers" who had saved the city of Berlin from the Russians, saved two million Berliners from hunger, cold, and fear of a dark future. But no matter what I wanted, in the end someone other had already made the assignment decision for many members of my class. The Strategic Air Command, SAC, always got what it wanted in those days. SAC wanted the top graduates of navigator training to enter electronic warfare training to man their ever-growing fleet of B-52 bombers. Before I knew what was happening, I held a set of orders in my hands sending me to Keesler Air Force Base in Biloxi, Mississippi. I wasn't ready to give up that easily. I made an appointment with my squadron commander trying to convince him to have my orders changed. He laughed in my face. "Samuel," he said, "this is the best thing that could happen to you. There is no career in flying trash haulers. Get out of my office, and thank your lucky star that you didn't get what you asked for."

When I reported to Keesler, a surprise was waiting for me. Our training aircraft turned out to be converted C-54 transports, which during the Berlin airlift of 1948–1949 had flown coal from Fassberg and Celle Air Bases to

C-54 transports, converted to electronic warfare training aircraft, on the flight line at Keesler AFB, Mississippi, 1961. All of those aircraft at one time participated in the Berlin airlift of 1948–1949 flying coal from RAF Fassberg/Celle to Berlin.

Berlin. The aircraft still had traces of coal dust in their spars, attesting to their earlier use. To me, it was like a reunion with old friends. On my first training flight, I walked around the aircraft and patted its nose, as if it were a living thing. I said nothing to my classmates about how special these airplanes were to me, how they and I once were together in a place and time when I was still a German boy, dreading to have to live under Communist domination. These planes, and the men who flew them, had been my saviors.

After graduating from electronic warfare, EW, training, we were given a choice of assignments. My class was small, and the assignments were written on a blackboard. There was one to the 55th SRW. I was number three in my class, and I thought for sure someone would choose that assignment before me. I sat there with crossed fingers—no one did. On July 1, 1960, an RB-47H reconnaissance jet of the 55th SRW had been shot down over the Barents Sea. Everyone still remembered that shootdown and didn't want to have anything to do with an outfit like that. For me, it made up for not getting to be a C-124 navigator. It was, after all, the kind of assignment I was really looking for. Nothing would give me a greater thrill than flying reconnaissance against the Communists, the Russians. And off I went to Topeka, Kansas, to become a Raven on an RB-47H electronic reconnaissance crew.

I was assigned to the 343rd Reconnaissance Squadron, one of three squadrons in the wing, the others being the 38th and the 338th. The 343rd and 38th

Squadrons were equipped with RB-47H aircraft, each with a crew of six; and several converted B-47E bombers, Tell 2 aircraft, with a crew of five, which were equipped to monitor Russian missile launches. The 338th squadron flew RB-47K photo reconnaissance aircraft, which had the standard B-47 crew of three. On August 20, 1962, I flew my first training mission in an RB-47H north toward the Canadian border, over the near-empty and barren northern states. Lumbering F-89 Scorpion air defense fighters vainly tried to practice intercepts on us as we sliced through the cold, blue northern skies. It was a daytime mission of eight hours' duration in a downward-firing ejection seat, which, someone whispered to me in confidence, was a seat designed not to work. Apparently, the knowledge we Ravens possessed was too sensitive to allow us to be exploited by Soviet interrogators should we be shot down and captured. Electronic warfare officers, EWOs, in a reconnaissance aircraft were referred to as Ravens; those who manned bombers and jammed hostile radars were referred to as Crows; while those flying Wild Weasel SAM-killer missions during the Vietnam War years, flying F-100 and F-105 fighters, would be referred to as Bears. The importance of electronic warfare in future combat operations was a lesson that had yet to be learned, although the Strategic Air Command in 1962 was probably at the leading edge of this poorly understood form of aerial combat.

Three of us Ravens sat in a sealed capsule located in the aircraft's former bomb bay. Our sole mission was to glean the secrets from enemy electronic emissions, our only window to the outside world the electronic equipment we had been taught to operate—direction finders, search receivers, pulse analyzers, recorders. This eight-hour flight, my first, was a short training flight, I was told by my Standardization Board evaluator. "Once you are checked out and certified, your missions will frequently be up to fourteen hours long, requiring air refuelings," the evaluator told me. "You'll fly in places where the bad guys will be waiting for you, waiting to shoot you down. Enjoy your short eight-hour missions while you can." He laughed at me as if he had just let me in on a private joke. Our training program was hectic—fly, critique, plan the next mission. Fly August 20, fly August 23, fly August 24. Every flight was preceded the day before by a lengthy mission-planning process. We were not allowed to use any electronic navigation aids, because they surely would not be available over the places where we were destined to fly. So we planned our routes in great detail, determined the best radar returns, and precalculated our celestial requirements to shoot the stars if visible on a clear night. I had no idea why our pace was so hectic.

On September 26, 1962, I passed my flight check, which certified me as a fully qualified crew member on an RB-47H reconnaissance crew. I received my permanent assignment to crew S-67, a select standardization crew,

Forbes Air Force Base, 1962. More than one hundred aircraft are parked on the apron and the short runway. The dirty spots are the parking areas for KC-97 tankers. The B-47E bombers of the 40th Bomb Wing parked at the northern end of the ramp. Our RB-47 aircraft occupied the ramp area south of our KC-97 tankers.

commanded by Major Howard "Rusty" Rust. My flight check had been a night mission. Upon our return to base, as the aircraft initiated its final approach, we all glimpsed a beautiful sunrise. On takeoff and landing, we three Ravens sat in the aisle below the two pilots to give us a better chance at escape in case of an emergency. The wheels touched down with a jolt, and after eating up much of the runway, we blew the approach and brake chutes off to the side with our jet exhaust, then turned onto a taxiway to find our parking place among more than a hundred B-47 and KC-97 aircraft. Exhausted, we slid down the aluminum access ladder to the oil-stained concrete ramp, glad to be able to stretch aching muscles.

In the distance, I could see one of our RB-47K photo reconnaissance aircraft from the 338th squadron rolling down the runway for an early-morning training mission. All of us watched its takeoff roll out of habit; that's what airmen do. The aircraft gained speed on the runway we had just landed on, disappearing from view as it went over a small rise. The next thing we saw was a black mushroom-like cloud rising into the clear blue Kansas sky; tongues of flame shot through the smoke as if a thunderstorm. Shocked by the suddenness of the tragedy, we stood transfixed, witnessing the death of four of our own—two pilots, a navigator, and a crew chief. A lesson, if it was needed, to emphasize that military flying was very different in its challenges from commercial aviation.

The good news, on October 1, I was promoted to captain; a temporary "spot" promotion for serving on a select crew, a promotion that had to be validated every six months. Yet, after barely two years of service, here I was, a captain in the United States Air Force. Howard Rust, our aircraft commander, was promoted to lieutenant colonel; our navigator, Arlen "Zig-Zag" Howe, to major, as well as our Raven 1, Harry Tull. I flew as Raven 2, and the Raven 3, Chuck Myers, also received a spot to captain. We were a happy crew, you might say. I soon learned why our training pace had been so hectic. The Russians were moving SS-4 medium-range ballistic missiles and IL-28 Beagle light bombers into Cuba, a threat that had been a closely held military secret. For the protection of the missiles and the bombers, the island was being ringed with SA-2 surface-to-air missiles and antiaircraft guns. There were no more training flights for us. The wing's aircraft were entirely committed to flying operational missions in support of the emerging national emergency. During daylight hours, day after day, one of our RB-47H aircraft circled the island of Cuba, searching for SA-2 missile radars and their locations. One day blended into the next, one flight into another. On Monday, October 22, 1962, President John F. Kennedy, in a televised speech to the nation, announced that the Soviet Union was in the process of installing nuclear-tipped missiles ninety miles off our shore. A naval quarantine was to be imposed on the island of Cuba until all missiles were removed. Missile-carrying ships would be intercepted and not allowed to proceed. The quarantine was to take effect on Wednesday, October 24, 1962. By presidential directive, the Strategic Air Command went from Defense Condition 5—peacetime—to Defcon 3: from a routine alert posture for the nuclear-armed bomber strike forces to a readiness posture where all aircraft were loaded with nuclear weapons and ready to launch. There were no more leaves granted, no more training flights. The United States was getting ready to go to war—and a nuclear war at that. On the day the quarantine went into effect, General Thomas Power, the commander in chief of the Strategic Air Command, unilaterally ordered SAC forces from Defcon 3 to Defcon 2. More than a thousand bombers sat on their dispersal bases crewed and loaded with nuclear weapons ready to strike at the Soviet Union. More than a hundred Polaris nuclear-powered submarines went into their final launch positions, ready to execute the order for which they had been built. The nation was on the brink of a nuclear holocaust. It seemed to many of us aircrews that General LeMay's carefully crafted strategy of nuclear deterrence had failed. I had survived World War II and thousand-bomber air raids in Berlin, and I

Crew S-67, Forbes Air Force Base, Topeka, Kansas, 1962. Lieutenant Colonel Howard Rust (pilot); Captain Joe Racine (copilot); Major Arlen "Zig-Zag" Howe (radar navigator); Major Harry Tull (Raven 1); Captain Wolfgang Samuel (Raven 2); and Captain Charles Myers (Raven 3). Harry was a Tuskegee Airman.

knew that neither I, nor my family, would survive a nuclear exchange with the Soviet Union.

It was an apparently routine surveillance mission on October 26. We had taken off from Forbes Air Force Base. Three hours later, at 38,000 feet altitude, we coasted out over Key West, Florida, heading toward the island of Cuba. The sun was just rising in the east; we Ravens in our sealed capsule in the belly of the bomber were not aware of that. We three Ravens searched for hostile MiG fighters and SAM sites. The interior of the aircraft was bathed in a soft red glow of light as we went about our tasks, hour after monotonous hour. The deafening roar of six jets slicing through the icy air strained my ears. I adjusted my helmet to relieve the pressure of an earpiece. Major Harry Tull, the Raven 1, searched the I-band for MiG fighter radar emissions. I, as Raven 2, searched Echo, Fox, and Golf bands for SAM and AAA radars. Captain Chuck Myers, the Raven 3, searched the lower bands for SAM acquisition radars. The monotony was broken when the APS-54 warning receiver went off with a shrill sound in our headsets. Simultaneously, Tull picked up a powerful airborne radar in tracking mode off our tail—somebody intent on shooting us down. The unknown fighter made a tail-cone approach, flying right into our defensive 20mm guns. Joe Racine, our copilot, swung his seat around, locked his radar on the unknown fighter, and reported to Rust that he was ready to open fire.

"It's an unknown," Tull advised Rust over the intercom. "We can't identify him." Rust ordered Racine to "stand down your guns." Joe Racine put his radar in standby, ceasing its emissions, which could be misinterpreted by a trigger-happy friendly fighter. We Ravens knew Soviet radar characteristics, not those of friendly fighters, so by definition the approaching fighter should be one of our own. The unknown continued his approach, his jet wash shaking our RB-47 from tail to nose as he passed over us at close quarters. Several days later, we learned from Intelligence that the unknown fighter making that "dry" firing pass on us was a US Navy aircraft that had been scrambled to intercept us, thinking we were a Soviet Badger bomber. How easy it was to make a mistake at stressful times and moments. A mistake in judgment could have cost a navy pilot his life, or an air force crew of six could have died just as easily off the coast of Cuba. It was all part of doing business—keep your cool; you can't take your bullets back once they have been fired. Our flights around Cuba, labeled Common Cause, continued around the clock during daylight hours, day after day in support of our high-flying U-2 photo reconnaissance aircraft. And we searched for that last ship on its way loaded with SS-4 IRBMs. We Ravens found the SA-2 SAM sites. One of our RB-47Hs, ranging across the open spaces of the North Atlantic, found the elusive Russian ship carrying the offensive missiles. All of us in the 55th Strategic Reconnaissance Wing were proud to have found the needle in the haystack. Once the Soviet vessel was located, navy P-3 antisubmarine warfare aircraft took over shadowing it. American destroyers approached—and, after a brief standoff, the Russian ship finally turned around to return to the Soviet Union. The Cuban Missile Crisis ended on Sunday, October 28, 1962. There was no nuclear war. Premier Khrushchev agreed to remove all offensive missiles and aircraft from Cuba, never again to reintroduce them. In return, the United States, in time, would remove American Jupiter missiles aimed at the Soviet Union from Turkey and Thor missiles from the United Kingdom.

Although no shots were fired in anger, there were losses nevertheless. One of our RB-47H aircraft searching for the missile-laden Russian ship crashed on takeoff from Kindley Air Force Base in Bermuda. Four of our friends and fellow flyers lost their lives. A subsequent investigation determined that the civilian contractor did not properly mix the water and alcohol mixture we used on takeoff to gain additional power. The water/alcohol ratio was supposed to be 28 percent alcohol, 72 percent water; the mix that was pumped into Major William A. Britton's water/alcohol tanks was between 12 and 13.6 percent alcohol, far short of what was required. The aircraft crashed into the rocks just beyond the runway. A totally preventable and unnecessary accident.

A second RB-47H taking off one minute after Major Britton was able to stop in time after seeing the fireball emanating from the crashed RB-47H. A third was in takeoff position. Both of those aircraft also had the bad alcohol/water mixture. Another RB-47H from the 343rd SRS crashed on takeoff from Mac-Dill Air Force Base near Tampa, Florida. All of the crew died. Funeral services were held in the Forbes Air Force Base chapel. We young officers, who had reported to our new duty station only months earlier, were sent on the sad task of escorting our dead brothers in blue to their graves in places like Kansas, Iowa, and Nebraska. Freedom isn't free, never has been. We learned that hard lesson very early in our careers.

Three months later, on January 3, 1963, a cold, blustery, and snowy Kansas morning, my young wife drove me to base operations. I was leaving for RAF Brize Norton in England, to fly the periphery of the Soviet Union to glean secrets the nation desperately needed to counter the Soviet threat. The Kola Peninsula, Novaya Zemlya, Kaliningrad, Klaipėda, and other strange-sounding names few Americans have ever heard of were on our agenda. My wife bade me farewell with a hurried kiss. I swallowed hard. I couldn't let her see my pain. She held our tiny son Charles close in the blustery cold. Our baby boy was ill. We didn't know what he was suffering from, but his temperature was inordinately high. She touched my face with her hand, put the baby into his carry-cot next to her in the car, and drove off toward the base hospital.

Crew S-67—Rusty, Howie, Joe, Harry, Chuck, and Wolf—flew out of England for three long winter months. Our aircraft would lift off from dimly lit runways at night with no radio calls to alert a vigilant foe that we were coming. On one cold February day, we headed north to the far-off Kola Peninsula; a KC-135 aerial refueling tanker flying in trail behind us gave us one last drink of precious fuel near Bear Island off the coast of Norway. Then he turned back for Brize Norton. His mission was done; ours was just beginning. High over the Barents Sea, in the dark of night, we flew nearly wing tip to wing tip with the bombers of Russia's strategic forces as they tested their newest air-to-surface missile. We surprised them. Harry picked up the radars of MiG-19s searching, locking onto their own aircraft, not finding us. As we flew among our foes, we took their secrets with us. Our intelligence officer at the mission debrief pulled us aside, then said, "We watched you going in. Normally, we would have recalled you. But this was such a unique opportunity." We were flying over the same area where, on July 1, 1960, on a daylight mission, Major Palm and his crew, flying an RB-47H aircraft just like ours, was shot down by Russian MiG-19 fighters. We knew exactly where we were and what the Russians were capable of, even though we were flying over international waters, off their coast.

On a daylight mission over the Baltic Sea, we headed for Kaliningrad, the former East Prussia, which had been taken over by the Russians at the end

RB-47H, tail Number 4304, viewed from our accompanying KC-135 tanker in February 1963 on our way to the Barents Sea and the Kola Peninsula, where the Russians conducted much of their R&D testing. On this mission, the MiG-19s tried their best to get us. The ALD-4 pod on the side of the aircraft's fuselage automatically collected all radar emission parameters and site locations— information that was read out at SAC headquarters in Omaha, Nebraska, and incorporated into the Radar Order of Battle. Flights over the Barents Sea, adjacent to the Kola Peninsula, and at the far eastern end of the Baltic Sea frequently brought out Russian fighters.

of World War II. There, the Russians always kept some of their latest fighters and radars. We came in high. Rusty pulled the power back, and the RB-47 dropped out of the sky like a rock. Down and down we went. The Russians went crazy trying to track us. Turning on radars we had not seen before. Sending up a horde of MiG-17s to nail us. But they were too late to catch us. Like the mission high up over the Barents Sea, it was a very productive mission and revealed much about the Soviet air defense system, including their weaknesses. We carried an ALD-4 reconnaissance pod on the side of the aircraft, which automatically picked up whatever we Ravens might have missed—the location of a radar, its frequency, its pulse width and pulse recurrence frequency. The pod had been developed by the E-Systems Corporation, now a part of Raytheon; its data subsequently was read out at SAC headquarters, and in time we would receive a briefing on all we had brought home on every one of our missions—but not those flown by others.

We returned to our home base in April 1963 after flying eighteen lone reconnaissance missions. Each of us was awarded the Distinguished Flying

Cross for the missions flown over the Barents Sea off the Kola Peninsula, and the mission over the Baltic Sea near Kaliningrad. A couple of weeks after we returned from deployment, we were directed to review our mission results at SAC headquarters in Omaha. It was always amazing to see what we had accomplished. It was also gratifying to hear that two of the Russian air defense sector commanders in the Kaliningrad region had been fired because their MiGs didn't manage to catch us and shoot us down. I flew a total of over a hundred PARPRO missions while assigned to the 55th Strategic Reconnaissance Wing at various locations around the Soviet Union. When I left the wing to obtain a master's degree at the Air Force Institute of Technology in 1967, the venerable RB-47 was being phased out and replaced with the more capable RC-135. For me, flying with the 55th Wing was a dream come true—and, yes, a couple of our pilots had flown the Berlin airlift, which had inspired me years earlier as a young refugee boy living in a desolate camp in a devastated Germany. There are times when dreams come true—they did for me.

THE LAST FLIGHT OF RB-47H 53-4290
OVER THE SEA OF JAPAN (1965)

On their third and final firing pass, I thought I scored a hit on the
lead MiG. It nosed up abruptly, then pitched over and descended
straight down in what appeared to be an unrecoverable position.

—First Lieutenant Henry Dubuy, copilot of 4290

On a warm and softly pleasant afternoon in 1961, at the age of twenty, Joel
Lutkenhouse passed through the main gate at Harlingen Air Force Base,
Texas, and became an aviation cadet. Harlingen, then a small agricultural
community in the Rio Grande Valley of Texas, was home to a navigator training base, one of many flying training bases scattered along the Texas-Mexico
border. Here, in the land of blue and empty skies, potential air force navigators spent the better part of a year learning the intricacies of aerial navigation
in twin-engine Convair T-29 aircraft, the military version of the widely used
Convair 240 airliner. The oldest of five children, Joel entered Staten Island
Community College in 1958. One day in the school cafeteria, a classmate
mentioned to Joel that he soon would be leaving to enter the air force's aviation cadet program to train as a pilot. "You don't have a college degree," Joel
replied; "how did you get in?"

"You only need two years of college, Joel," his classmate replied, "not a
degree. You can pick up a degree sometime in the future if you want to do
that. But right now, I want to learn how to fly. I am really excited. I can't wait to
leave. Why don't you come too? If I can get in, you can for sure. You are a lot
smarter than I am." His friend smiled. For days afterward, Joel thought about
what his friend had said. It represented an opportunity to become an officer
in the US Air Force, an opportunity to give his life direction. He decided to
take a closer look, visited with an air force recruiter, and took the required
tests. Although he passed the tests, his score was not high enough to get into
pilot training. When offered, he took the opportunity to train as an air force

navigator. So here he was in January 1961 on a palm tree–studded air base in the remotest corner of the United States. "On an oil-stained tarmac," Joel recalled for me, "I saw row upon row of twin-engined navigation trainers. I suddenly felt excitement rising within me. Those planes were my future. I really wanted to fly. I promised myself I wasn't going to fail at the biggest thing I'd ever attempted in my life."

In November 1961, Joel Lutkenhouse exchanged the shoulder boards of an aviation cadet for the brown bars of a second lieutenant and pinned on the wings of an air force navigator. But instead of a flying assignment to practice what he had learned, his orders directed him to report to Mather Air Force Base near Sacramento, California, to spend another ten months to qualify as an electronic warfare officer, an EWO. Upon graduation in 1962, he was assigned to the 376th Bomb Wing at Lockbourne Air Force Base near Columbus, Ohio. Lockbourne was the same base from where Sam Myers and Hal Austin once flew their RB-45C and RB-47E reconnaissance aircraft on deep penetration missions into Red China and the Soviet Union. Joel's squadron flew B-47E bombers converted to a radar-jamming role, and instead of carrying nuclear bombs, they carried two electronic warfare officers in a capsule in the former bomb bay from where they controlled a number of electronic jammers and chaff dispensers to support attacking bombers—in case "the balloon went up" and nuclear war commenced. Four times during his two years at Lockbourne, Joel "Reflexed" to RAF Brize Norton in the United Kingdom, where he sat alert with B-47 bomber crews for two out of three weeks. Sitting alert meant living in his flight suit in a concrete bunker near his aircraft, cocked to launch at a moment's notice should the klaxon sound. The klaxon never sounded in earnest, and in May 1964 the 376th Bomb Wing disbanded; Joel received orders to report to the 55th Strategic Reconnaissance Wing at Forbes Air Force Base, Topeka, Kansas. Joel was assigned to the 343rd SRS, the same squadron I flew with. Once certified combat ready, he was assigned to crew E-96 as a Raven 3. In the 55th Wing, the EWOs were referred to as Ravens, and he would occupy position three in a capsule located in the former bomb bay of the RB-47H electronic reconnaissance aircraft.

Another young officer was on a career track that for many years nearly paralleled Joel's. Second Lieutenant George V. Back was a little older than most lieutenants, born in 1936 in Syracuse, New York. He joined the Army National Guard as a teenager. By the time he entered aviation cadet training at Harlingen in 1961, he already held a reserve commission as a second lieutenant in the infantry. But George had always wanted to fly, and when the opportunity offered itself, like Joel, he grabbed it. George and Joel were in the same cadet class at Harlingen and were commissioned on the same day. Together, they completed electronic warfare training at Mather and upon graduation were assigned to the same wing at Lockbourne. Once that wing deactivated, both were assigned to the 55th Wing and ended up on the same RB-47H electronic reconnaissance crew—E-96. In George Back's words, "the 55th was considered a closed union, and we were the first brown bars to come into the unit in a couple of years. Most of the crew members were lieutenant colonels, majors, or senior captains—intimidating for us young guys—and we thought we better do things right. Matt—Lieutenant Colonel Hobart Mattison—my aircraft commander, was a no-nonsense kind of officer when it came to flying. Every mission, we lined up under the left wing of the aircraft for inspection—our parachutes on the ground in front of us, our helmets on top of the chutes—and Matt conducted a short premission briefing. After his briefing we did a left face, marched forward until clear of the parachutes, and began our individual preflights. In flight, we addressed crew positions when talking on the intercom—'Raven 2 to pilot' and so on. We said what needed saying, and that's it. No frivolous banter. First names were left at the Officers' Club."

On March 30, 1965, Joel Lutkenhouse and George Back deployed with crew E-96 to Yokota Air Base near Tokyo, Japan. Yokota had hosted various air force reconnaissance elements over the years and at this time served as one of several operating locations around the periphery of the Soviet Union for aircraft of the 55th SRW. I personally flew missions out of Yokota Air Base in RB-47H aircraft in 1965 and again in 1967. Many of the routes flown by the RB-47Hs of the 55th Wing were "canned," meaning they were flown repeatedly along the periphery of the Soviet Union, by their very nature providing the Russian military with tacit assurance that these missions were routine and without hostile intent. All of these missions were flown over international waters, meaning that the United States had every legal right to fly them. However, at times the reconnaissance routes and tactics were modified to cause the Soviets to turn on their radars and possibly reveal wartime techniques and modes of operation, which under normal circumstances they would not do. All radar emissions were recorded for subsequent analysis, and the emitter locations were incorporated in the master Electronic Order of Battle maintained at SAC headquarters. It was a never-ending game, so to speak, of one-upmanship to ensure that air force military tactics and weapon systems remained relevant to the potential threat posed by the Soviet Union. Reaction to such reconnaissance flights over the years had varied, depending on the sensitivity of the information gathered or the whim of a Russian politician or military commander.

Since the early 1950s, a fair number of US Air Force and Navy reconnaissance aircraft had been lost to Russian fighters. Such losses received little publicity from either side unless it proved politically advantageous, such as the downing of Francis Gary Powers's U-2 by Soviet SA-2 surface-to-air missiles in May 1960 over the Soviet Union. The last 55th Wing aircraft lost to hostile action had been an RB-47H shot down by Russian MiG-19 fighters over the Barents Sea on July 1, 1960, only two months after the downing of the U-2 near Sverdlovsk. Although all peripheral reconnaissance missions were flown over international waters, that didn't keep the Russians from sending out their fighters to run intercepts on us. Some of those intercepts were with hostile intent.

The front-end crew of E-96 was led by Lieutenant Colonel Hobart D. "Matt" Mattison, an experienced and skilled aircraft commander; First Lieutenant Henry E. Dubuy served as the copilot and gunner, and Captain Robert J. Rogers was the radar navigator. The back-end crew, the Ravens, were led by Captain Robert C. "Red" Winters, who flew as the Raven 1 and was principally responsible for monitoring airborne threats. First Lieutenant George V. Back flew as the Raven 2 on his first operational deployment, as did First Lieutenant Joel J. Lutkenhouse, the Raven 3. Each of the Ravens controlled a set of similar receivers, analyzers, recorders, and direction finders allowing them to back each other up if necessary. The essential difference between the three positions was that each covered a set of assigned radio frequencies, covering the entire frequency spectrum used at the time by various ground-based and airborne radar emitters. On takeoff, the three Ravens sat strapped into web slings in the aisle below the two pilots. Once the aircraft was airborne and temporarily leveled off at 2,000 feet above the terrain, the Ravens crawled aft, on hands and knees, through a narrow tunnel into their compartment located in the former bomb bay of the aircraft. Their operating compartment was surrounded, front and aft, by fuel tanks. The B-47 aircraft carried no fuel in its wings; all the tanks were located in the body of the aircraft. The Raven 2, the last to enter the compartment, locked the capsule door, and the Raven 3 would then pressurize the compartment. As the aircraft climbed to its assigned altitude, usually somewhere between 30,000 and 40,000 feet, the pressurization in both the front and back end was kept at 14,000 feet, meaning that the crew had to remain on oxygen for the duration of its flight. The two pilots sat in conventional upward-firing ejection seats, while the navigator and the Ravens sat in downward-firing seats. Over the years of B-47 bomber operations, the reliability of the upward-firing ejection seats had been proven many times over; however, downward-firing seats, especially for the Ravens, provided no such sense of operating reliability. Throughout the twenty-two years of operational service of the RB-47H, starting in 1955, of which thirty-five were built, all assigned to the 55th SRW, not once did a Raven choose the option to eject. If given a choice, they preferred a belly landing on a foam-covered runway over ejection from the aircraft.

Colonel Mattison and crew flew aircraft number 4305 over to Japan, but it had autopilot problems and could not hold a heading. On a subsequent test

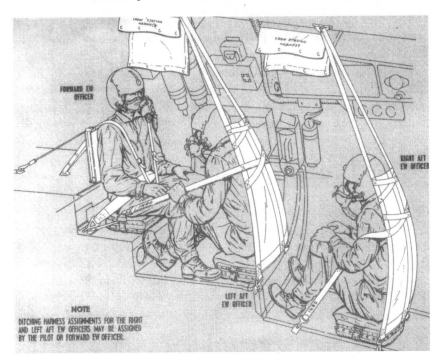

On takeoff and landing, the three Ravens sat in slings in the aisle below the pilots. Their capsule had downward ejection, and there was no chance of escape in a runway emergency situation.

flight over the Sea of Japan, 4305 still couldn't hold a heading; not the kind of aircraft one would want to fly near Soviet airspace. In case of an error in navigation, the Russians would shoot first and ask questions later. The 55th Wing operating location commander at Yokota, Colonel James R. Gunn, asked for an aircraft replacement, which was quickly provided. The new aircraft, tail number 4290, was flown from Forbes Air Force Base to Eielson Air Force Base, Alaska, then on down the Aleutian chain of islands to Yokota. Lieutenant Colonel Howard "Rusty" Rust, with whom I had flown numerous missions in the past, delivered the replacement aircraft, accompanied by the 55th Wing commander, Colonel Marion "Hack" Mixson, who flew as copilot. Hack Mixson of course was an "old head" when it came to flying reconnaissance against the Soviet Union, going back to his days in the RB-45C.

At 0700 hours the morning of April 28, 1965, Lieutenant Colonel Mattison released the brakes on RB-47H, tail number 4290. The sleek jet hurtled down the 10,000-foot Yokota runway, blanketing the base with its thundering noise and black exhaust. The aircraft slowly vanished into the morning mist. The mission was scheduled to be a short seven and a half hours, with no need for aerial refueling. The plane was flying one of the "canned" routes over the Sea of Japan, that would take them close to the southern tip of Sakhalin Island, then along the coast of the Soviet mainland past Vladivostok, the major Russian naval base in the area, and along the east coast of North Korea—and home again. Once the Ravens transferred to their aft compartment, they pressurized and turned on their equipment. By the time the aircraft reached its assigned altitude, the equipment had warmed up and stabilized and the USQ-18 clock was set to Greenwich mean time, putting its tick marks on every audio and video recording. The Ravens settled back, looking at their world of green scopes and red lights, ready to go On Watch once the navigator announced over the intercom that the On Watch point had been reached. They scanned their assigned frequencies with their APR-17 receivers. The automatic ALD-4 external reconnaissance pod as well as other independently operating systems were turned on at the On Watch point, recording pulse width, frequency, location, and other pertinent parameters for every intercepted radar emission. It was, according to George Back, "one of those ho-hum missions."

"Nothing exciting came up, other than the usual Soviet early warning radars. Occasionally a height finder would give us four or five scans to confirm our altitude. The Russians knew what we were doing. They knew the 'canned' route we were flying as well as we did. They knew we were no threat to them as long as we didn't deviate from our route. Therefore, there was no need for them to turn on any of their threat radars [SA-2 surface-to-air missile or Firecan AAA–associated radars] or use any unusual techniques. But the Russian operators monitoring our aircraft probably passed our route information via landline to their North Korean comrades."

"As we passed Vladivostok," recalled Joel Lutkenhouse, "I picked up Russian shipborne gun and missile radars. Our pilots looked for them, but couldn't see the ships because of a low-lying cloud layer. Bob, our navigator, saw the ships on his radar. They were tracking us with their antiaircraft and SAM radars, but the ships were in international waters and no obvious threat to us."

"We were six hours into our mission," recalls Bob Rogers. "Only another ninety minutes and we would be back at Yokota enjoying a hot shower and a good meal. We turned to a south-southeasterly heading abeam of Wonsan harbor on the east coast of North Korea. Then we tracked down the Korean peninsula and initiated a 180-degree turn at 37 degrees north latitude, heading north-northwest, back toward Wonsan, back the way we had come." At that time, copilot Hank Dubuy recalled, "we were routinely monitoring our instruments. Everything looked normal. The autopilot was tracking, temperatures, fuel flow, everything was within tolerance. Matt and I scanned the horizon out of habit. Nothing but clouds above and below us. We had an unobstructed view from wing tip to wing tip, but not the low rear quadrant, which was obstructed by the aircraft fuselage and wings. There was a layer of strato-cumulus clouds below us, preventing us from seeing the water below or the coastline of North Korea. Another layer of gray stratus clouds was above our cruising altitude of 36,000 feet."

"We rolled out of our turn and headed north again," Bob Rogers, the aircraft navigator, recalled for me, "and stabilized the aircraft on its new heading, when suddenly a loud single-sideband warning came blasting into our headsets over HF radio. It was a message broadcast in the blind from a secret American monitoring station somewhere in South Korea or Japan, warning aircraft of bogeys in the area around Wonsan. It was a strange warning for a reconnaissance aircraft flying over international waters off the coast of one of the more hardline and belligerent communist countries. I had never received such a warning on any other mission. Briefly, I wondered if the monitoring station had overheard a radio call of intent to shoot us down. But I was busy navigating my aircraft, and as quickly as the cautionary thought entered my mind, I pushed it aside." Raven George Back put it this way: "No matter how much preparation I had, how much I knew about the bad guys, I never thought that some North Korean would try to kill me on my first operational deployment. But the North Koreans were deemed unpredictable and their actions frequently irrational. After that mission, I knew this for a fact."

The two pilots, Mattison and Dubuy, continued to scan the horizon, seeing nothing but empty sky. Copilot Hank Dubuy, who in the RB-47 sat directly behind the pilot, swiveled his seat around. "I raised my camera and took a couple of shots off the wings. I had switched the A-5 fire control system to warmup soon after our departure from Yokota. In the off and warmup position, our two 20mm tail guns remained stowed, pointing upward. Over open water I had switched the system to standby, the two guns then pointed straight back. I switched to operation, firing a couple of short bursts over open water to ensure the guns were working properly—if not, it was a condition for which we would have to abort the mission. Maintenance before a mission taped over the gun barrels, to make sure we did not fly a mission with inoperable guns. Everything looked good to me, and I had put the system back into standby." The ammunition load for each 20mm gun was 350 rounds. Normally, in an aircraft's standard combat load, every fifth round was a tracer, to give the gunner a visual indication of where he was firing. But Hank didn't carry tracers in his ammunition load. General Curtis E. LeMay, when in command of the Strategic Air Command, had prohibited the use of tracers for his bombers, and that ruling had not been changed after his departure.

The gun radar system was designed to automatically track rear-hemisphere attackers approaching within 45 degrees of azimuth to either side of the aircraft, and 37 degrees of elevation up or down. Targets outside this automatic tracking window had to be fired on by going to emergency manual operation, using the antenna control handle, manually positioning the gun system's tracking antenna on the target azimuth, and then spotlighting the target in elevation. The antenna control handle was spring loaded to position the guns at zero elevation and azimuth, which gave the gunner, the aircraft's copilot, the ability to quickly baseline his guns and know where they were pointing. As the warning message still echoed in the crew's ears, the Raven 1, Red Winters, picked up the distinctive scan of an airborne intercept radar on his APR-17 receiver. The signal was weak and faded quickly, but Red had heard it and seen it long enough on his receiver trace to identify it as an airborne threat signal emanating from the rear of the aircraft. It sounded to Red like the scan of a MiG-17 radar in search mode—squak, squak. Red Winters notified the crew and simultaneously started his recorder in case the signal reappeared, but it didn't. George Back at that time was working a North Korean GCI radar (Ground Control Intercept used to guide fighters to their target). "I was unaware of what was happening. I had turned my intercom switch to the 'private' position to eliminate crew communications and was in the process of annotating the signal I was working to aid in subsequent analysis and evaluation." Raven 3, Joel Lutkenhouse, was similarly engaged: "Although I was aware that there were probably MiGs prowling around in our piece of sky. I did check that I was properly strapped into my ejection seat. The first I knew that we were under attack was when I felt the aircraft shudder." What Joel felt was the impact of 23mm cannon shells exploding into the aft main fuel tank, right behind their capsule, and into the chaff chutes.

"I felt the aircraft shudder, pitch nose down, and begin losing altitude," George Back recalled. "My first thought was that the autopilot or trim had failed, but a split second later, as I went back to the normal intercom position, I learned that a couple of MiG-17s were serious about shooting us down. I noted that the altimeter, reading about 27,000 feet when I glanced at it, was rapidly unwinding. In an instant, my mind seemed to go into a thousand different directions. It was the first time in my life I thought I was really going to die. The irony was that I had no control over what was happening. Panic and fear paralyzed my thought processes, and I think I sat dumbfounded for what seemed an eternity, trying to figure out what the hell was going on and what to do. When Colonel Mattison said over the intercom, 'We are hit, and going down,' I thought it was the end. I started the ejection sequence. My mind was still racing, and everything I had ever done seemed to go whirling by in a kaleidoscope of my life. At the same time, a different part of my brain seemed to be saying, 'Don't panic. You have been trained for situations like this. Do your job, and follow the checklist.' I calmed down and realized that the aircraft was still well above 14,000 feet and that my likely time of survival in the 50-degree water of the Sea of Japan was less than thirty minutes. So I didn't pull the D-ring between my legs. I was still scared but starting to think rationally. 'Get your oxygen mask on. Check the flow. Tighten your parachute harness. Remember, you are sitting on an armed seat. Watch out for the D-ring.' During the subsequent MiG firing passes, I could feel the cannon shells impacting the aircraft. I remember thinking that at any time there would be a tremendous explosion, a rush of cold air, and that would be the last I would remember."

Mattison, the aircraft commander and pilot, exclaimed, "They are shooting at us. We are hit. I'm going down." George Back, who had just come back on intercom, overheard only part of Mattison's comment, "We are hit . . . going down." Mattison was telling his copilot, Captain Hank Dubuy, that he was going down to a lower altitude and taking evasive action—a comment that George Back misinterpreted because he had not been on intercom full time—and by arming his ejection seat, automatically depressurized the Raven compartment, rapidly dropping the back-end crew from 14,000 feet pressure altitude to the actual altitude of the aircraft, somewhere around 25,000 feet. Joel, the Raven 2, saw George pull up his leg braces, felt the rapid decompression, and immediately lowered the visor of his helmet in preparation for ejection. He assumed the practiced ejection position—back straight against the seat, head against the back headrest, feet in the seat stirrups—but he didn't do anything further. He waited for instructions from the pilot.

George and Joel sat side by side in their ejection seats, facing aft, their inner turmoil not apparent to each other. Joel listened on the intercom to the front-end crew's conversation as they tried to cope with the situation. He glanced over at George, sitting there ready to eject, looking calm. "Thoughts raced through my mind. How could this be happening to me? My heart was pounding in my mouth. I thought I could feel my blood coursing through my body, my nerves tingling. Suddenly, I was intensely afraid of losing my life. I could feel tears running down my cheeks. I decided to say a prayer, the Act of Contrition. As suddenly as the fear had surged through my body, just as suddenly it subsided. I felt calmer, and listened to the ongoing battle over the intercom, feeling shells from the attacking MiGs slamming into our aircraft."

The two North Korean MiG-17s, approaching through multiple cloud layers and probably guided by the GCI radar George Back was recording and analyzing, had reached the RB-47 unseen from behind and below, the plane's blind spot. The MiGs kept their radars off, or they would have been picked up by the RB-47's APS-54 airborne warning receiver and by the Raven 1. When they commenced their attack they were still low, directly behind the B-47, firing upward, trying to stay out of the cone of fire of the B-47's 20mm tail guns. Copilot Hank Dubuy watched the MiGs as they positioned themselves behind his aircraft, taking a couple of pictures of them. The rules of engagement for the RB-47 were to continue to fly the assigned route and to abort the mission only if the intercepting aircraft showed clear hostile intent, such as turning their gun-laying radars from search to track mode or firing their guns. The lead MiG suddenly initiated the attack by firing its cannons. It was war. Hank dropped his camera. As the shells slammed into his aircraft, he requested permission from his pilot to fire. "Shoot the bastard down," exclaimed Mattison while calling "Mayday," the internationally recognized call of distress, on his single-sideband radio. As he proceeded to drop the aircraft toward the lower cloud layer, Mattison called for the navigator to give him a heading "to get the hell out of here."

Captain Bob Rogers, the navigator, sat hunched over his radar scope in the nose of the aircraft, busy ensuring that the plane remained on its planned track when the attack occurred. "At first I thought Mattison was joking when he said we were under attack. I thought he was joking until I heard and felt the hits." Bob's calm response to Mattison's request for a heading, "Take a 90-degree turn to the right, and I'll refine it in seconds." Then Bob put his radar cross hair on the coast of Japan and asked Matt for second station. In second station, the pilot puts the aircraft on autopilot, and the navigator manually controls the aircraft in azimuth—it was a system devised to provide for the best possible bombing results for B-47 bombers. Mattison couldn't release control of his stricken aircraft to his navigator at such a time, but Bob's request demonstrated the crew's mettle and competence. Matt had no idea which aircraft systems were still operational. He needed to hand-fly. "After Matt called out 'Mayday,' everyone in the air was told to clear our frequency, because everyone, including some KC-135 tankers, was offering to help," Bob Rogers recalled.

Unknown to Mattison and his crew, a captain on an airborne Looking Glass C-135 SAC airborne command post aircraft circling near SAC headquarters in Omaha, Nebraska, picked up their HF radio transmissions of distress. The captain immediately notified the brigadier general on the aircraft, an aircraft designed to take over control over nuclear forces should SAC headquarters be destroyed by a surprise attack. While the general and his crew listened to one of their aircraft under attack by North Korean fighters thousands of miles away, they downlinked the radio intercept to the SAC command post at Offutt Air Force Base. The Looking Glass crew and the command post staff listened to the unfolding drama over the Sea of Japan but could do nothing to help.

In the meantime, Hank Dubuy was trying to defend his damaged plane against two persistent MiGs. "When I tried to return fire, I couldn't get the MiGs on my radar. They were too close and outside the elevation and azimuth limits for the guns to lock on in automatic mode. I immediately went to manual mode to engage the MiGs. We carried no tracer ammunition for me to see where I was firing, and to increase my probability of hitting the MiGs, I continually reset the guns to zero azimuth, zero elevation—I knew then where the guns were pointing—and I was able to aim the guns at an attacking MiG fighter. I punched the firing button and repeated the process of aligning the guns and firing. The first MiG approached from behind and below, assumed a nose-up position, and fired. Then the MiG-17 fell off on one wing and dove to regain airspeed and altitude for a second pass. While the first MiG recovered, the second tried to down us using the same awkward tactic. The Raven 1 released a steady stream of chaff [aluminum strips designed to break the lock of enemy fighter radars] into the face of the MiG trying to get into firing position behind and below us. At one time, the attacker was totally obscured in a cloud of aluminum chaff and broke off his attack."

The two MiGs made three passes each. Although their flying was clumsy and their gunnery abysmal, their 23mm cannon shells brought the B-47 close to disaster. In George Back's words, "The hydraulic system failed, boost pump lights illuminated, and the aft fuel tank was hit and burning. During subsequent attacks, the number three [left inboard engine] was hit as well. Shrapnel from broken turbine blades damaged the number two engine, but both engines continued to operate, although at reduced power. The number three engine vibrated like an old car with no universal joints. Out of six engines, only the two outboard engines [numbers one and six] remained undamaged and performed at full power."

"Both hydraulic systems were damaged," recalled copilot Hank Dubuy. "The pumps operated but there was no fluid. The aircraft was sluggish in its response when I pulled on the yoke, like a truck that lost its power steering. In addition, we had to deal with an ever-deteriorating center of gravity [CG]. As the main rear fuel tank continued to lose fuel, on fire when the fuel spray exited the aircraft through the shell holes, the diminished weight in the rear of the aircraft due to the loss of fuel slowly shifted the aircraft's CG forward. The nose came down. It wasn't that much of a problem flying at 425 knots, but we were concerned about our possible landing back at Yokota— having to deal with a nose-down attitude, which we couldn't overcome with trim and flap adjustments. Landing on the nose gear of the aircraft was a sure recipe for disaster. Matt knew the landing would be difficult—if we made it that far. I continued to engage the MiGs, while Matt did evasive maneuvers and assessed the damage we sustained. Throughout the engagement, Bob, our navigator, continued to provide headings to lead Matt out of the area to Yokota. On their third and final firing pass, I thought I scored a hit on the lead MiG. It nosed up abruptly, then pitched over and descended straight down in what appeared to me as an unrecoverable position. Matt observed the MiG disappearing through a cloud deck at 12,000 feet, heading for the water. Then my guns ceased firing—jammed or damaged, I didn't know. I picked up my camera and took a couple of quick shots before the remaining MiG broke off his attack and turned back toward Wonsan. After the last MiG disappeared, Matt yelled over the intercom, 'Hank, get the Dash-1 out and go to the emergency procedure pages.'

"'Which page?' I asked. 'Any page will do,' was Matt's laconic answer."

The RB-47 had taken a lot of punishment. The aircraft was vibrating badly, but Matt felt that it was responding to his control. He could still fly it. Hank could see that the aft fuel tank was still emitting smoke, but the fire seemed to have diminished in intensity, and the color of the smoke had changed from black to white. A lack of fuel and wind blast had probably put out the fire. But the CG problem was irrevocably with them and would have to be dealt with once they got ready to land. The pilots had no idea if their tires were shot up, if the approach and landing chutes were in shreds, or if there was other damage that might doom their landing attempt. But the aircraft was flying, and they had ample fuel to get back to their base. Hobart Mattison was an experienced 8th Air Force combat veteran who in 1944 had bailed out of a stricken B-17 bomber over Hungary, made his way through southern Germany to France, and then escaped to England with the help of the French underground. For him, to abandon a still-flying aircraft was not an alternative. After leveling off at 10,000 feet and bringing the three Ravens forward, Matt asked his crew what they thought about punching out over Tokyo Bay or over the runway at Yokota. According to George Back, "When Matt inquired if anyone wanted to bail out, there was a unanimous 'No, Sir.' All fear had left me, and I had the utmost confidence in Matt's flying ability—and somehow knew that God didn't get us this far just to see us splattered all over the Yokota runway."

In similar situations, nose-down landings by B-47s most often resulted in a funeral pyre. A shredded brake chute or a blown tire could easily spell disaster on landing. As a result of Mattison's radio calls, there was no lack of radio assistance—but no American fighters had appeared. Interceptors launched from Yokota Air Base were much too far away to provide timely assistance. And once they arrived on the scene, they could only visually confirm the external damage sustained by 4290. Matt turned down a suggestion by the SAC command post at Yokota to land at a base in South Korea; instead, he initiated his descent into Yokota. As they approached Yokota, Colonel Gunn, the 55th SRW detachment commander, came up in a T-39 Sabreliner and looked them over. He couldn't add any new information to what Matt already knew to assist in the upcoming landing at Yokota. "Rusty" Rust, the pilot who had delivered 4290 only a couple of days earlier, was up in the Yokota control tower making his expertise available if Matt needed advice. Rusty had been

One of the cannon shells entered the main aft fuel tank nearly in the center of the US Air Force star adorning the side of the aircraft. The resulting fire was eventually blown out by the air stream generated by the aircraft.

stationed at Yokota for four years earlier in his career, and he knew the area's peculiarities well. "Matt was coming in from the south, heading north to make his first landing attempt. From that direction, visibility was half a mile in haze. I wanted to tell him to come in from the north, heading south. Visibility in that direction was three miles. Although I could see him coming in, I had no way of reaching him. He was talking on the radio, first to the SAC command post, then to the GCA radar operator. All I could do was watch. The B-47 was built like an automobile, with one UHF radio. There were no backups."

On approach to Yokota, Raven Red Winters manually lowered the landing gear. "One gear stuck and didn't want to lock positively," Hank recalled. "Red Winters was afraid he was going to break off the handle. 'Do it, Red,' I told him. We had no other choice. Finally, the recalcitrant gear gave, and we got a positive lock indication." The Ravens sitting in their web slings in the aisle below the pilots simply waited. Matt and Hank determined that they could use flaps half down, without getting the aircraft in an unrecoverable nose-down position. Matt said a final few words before he initiated his landing attempt. He knew the aircraft was going to porpoise, bouncing back into the air after a hard landing on the forward gear, a situation that frequently led to loss of directional control. "The landing will be rough. We will come down hard on the forward main due to our nose-down attitude. Henry, you deploy the [brake] chute and stand on the brakes after the second bounce. I will keep the wings level and maintain directional control." Colonel Gunn cleared the runway for them. Everything was as ready down below as it could be—fire trucks, firefighting helicopters, medical teams. The crew did its prelanding check list.

"Crew discipline and training were important in how we handled the situation," Hank observed. "Crews have scenarios come up in a flying career, and by good fortune the majority make it through. In some cases they don't. Maybe more discipline and training would have made the difference in those cases. It probably did for us. On our first landing attempt, we tried to follow standard procedures of descending 4,000 feet per minute and keeping the airspeed below 290 knots. As we slowed, the nose of the aircraft began to dip because of our forward CG. We reduced our rate of descent as we approached the runway and continued to experiment with the airspeed and the flaps. We didn't want the nose to drop on us, because we had no idea if we could get it back up. As we continued to bleed off airspeed, approaching the runway, the aircraft's nose continued to drop on us. We couldn't get low enough in time and had to opt for a go-around. Matt put the power to the engines as we crossed the runway threshold, and slowly the nose began to rise again. On our second attempt, we got her down to five hundred feet," Hank reflected pensively, "then three hundred, then two hundred, and as soon as Matt pulled the power off, the aircraft nose came down and the forward gear slammed into the runway." Rust, watching through high-powered binoculars from the Yokota control tower, said, "When I saw him after his go-around he had a good landing attitude. Then, suddenly, the nose of the aircraft dropped down and went straight into the runway. He took a tremendous first bounce, nearly up to the level of the rescue chopper, and then he hippity-hopped down the runway until he came to a stop. Recovery from this unusual attitude took great skill and coordination by Matt and Hank."

George Back sat helplessly in his sling below the pilots. "The landing was as rough as Matt said it was going to be. We porpoised about eight feet into the air, where we nearly hit the fire-suppression helicopter hovering above us. I thought the fuselage was going to break right behind the copilot, but it held together. Matt brought the aircraft to a stop, and we exited, heading for the edge of the runway. I squatted down next to Red Winters, watching the pandemonium around the damaged and smoking aircraft. Red turned to me and said, 'You know George, we are now living on borrowed time.' I wondered what Red meant by that. Then I saw Red, our ever-conscientious crew leader, disregard the potential threat of fire, sprint back to the aircraft, climb up the aluminum ladder into the forward crew compartment, and crawl as fast as he could through the narrow tunnel into the Raven crew compartment to retrieve the classified mission logs and other classified material we had left behind."

After landing at Yokota Air Base, 4290 revealed numerous 23 mm hits inflicted by the cannons of the attacking North Korean MiG-17s. A main aft fuel tank was punctured and shifted the CG forward due to fuel loss; other critical systems such as tires and approach/brake chutes were not damaged. Captain Jim Brookie, a 343rd SRS Raven, points at one of the many shell holes survived by the crew of 4290.

Copilot Dubuy recalled, "During the final landing attempt, I watched the airspeed throughout our descent. We were below 160 knots when we touched down. I pulled the brake chute at the top of the bounce. The chute wasn't damaged, thank God. It blossomed and slammed us to the ground and kept us there. I stood on the brakes as Matt had ordered me to do. If the chute had failed? I don't even want to think about that." Navigator Bob Rogers recalled, "After the brake chute deployed, we hit like a ton of bricks. Everything loose came flying forward, toward my position in the nose of the aircraft. Once the aircraft came to a stop, something else was uppermost in my mind. Get out, of course, but not before I secured the O-15 radar film. I held onto it for dear life because I knew there would be a lot of questions regarding our position."

When the aircraft was inspected, it was found that a cannon shell had knocked one of the 20mm tail guns off its mount. Still, Hank Dubuy had fired more than three hundred rounds, nearly half the ammunition the plane carried, and his skillful handling of the guns probably ruined the day for one MiG-17 pilot. Shortly after the crew evacuated the wrecked aircraft, they were summed to Colonel Gunn's office and debriefed. Were they on course? Yes, the O-15 camera film confirmed that. Who shot first? The MiGs did. The usual questions were thrown at the flyers. Then they were off to see the flight surgeon. He wanted to see all of them and examine their fitness to fly. All were fine, were served the customary glass of Old Methuselah combat-ration whiskey, and released. That evening, after long, hot showers, the crew met at the bar of the Yokota Officers' Mess. They decided that the North Koreans must have sent up two of their worst pilots that day. None of the flyers could understand how the two MiGs failed to down 4290—a sitting duck.

It did not make economic sense to repair 4290. "I remember counting the holes in the airplane. I forgot the exact number, but it was in the hundreds," Colonel Rust recalled. The aircraft was used for parts, and then cut up. Its loss was not significant, since the advent of a new reconnaissance system was only two years in the future. The new RC-135 aircraft, which would relieve the combat-tested RB-47Hs, did not carry guns. In spite of Vietnam, the Cold War was getting a little less frigid between the two nuclear superpowers. Two days after the North Korean attack on 4290, crew E-96 flew again, this time in aircraft 4305, an aircraft in which I had flown earlier missions over the Barents Sea, the Baltic Sea, and other places less visited by most. This time, while taking radar scope photography in the Gulf of Tonkin, the two fighters with them belonged to the US Navy.

Crew E-96 returned to the United States on May 17, 1965. The following month, they reported to SAC headquarters at Offutt Air Force Base in Omaha. It was standard procedure for reconnaissance crews to receive a debriefing from the intelligence people on the quality of their take. General Richard O. Hunziger met with them. Lieutenant Dubuy recalled General Hunziger looking at several pictures Hank had taken of the attacking MiGs after the guns quit firing. "How did you have time to take these pictures, Lieutenant?" the general inquired. Hank responded, "I had to shoot at them with something, General, and the camera is all I had left."

Matt Mattison, the competent and courageous pilot with nerves to match his flying skills, died in the early 1990s. George Back was right when he said, "I had the utmost confidence in Matt and somehow knew that God didn't get us this far just so we would end up splattered all over the runway." Military flyers may see the hand of God more often than most mortals, but without the consummate flying skills and self-discipline of a Colonel Mattison, the flight would have ended in tragedy. In a twenty-six-year air force career, Matt served in World War II with the 8th Air Force, flew C-54 transports during the Berlin airlift in 1948–1949, tested RB-45C reconnaissance aircraft at Eglin Air Force Base in Florida, and then survived a midair collision at Eglin while testing an F-86D fighter. After his retirement, Matt settled in Florida and worked for another twenty years for the FAA. Copilot Hank Dubuy left the air force in

Flight and maintenance crews in front of their RB-47H reconnaissance aircraft at Yokota, Japan, March 1967. Left to right, Simpson, Aiken, Thrasher, Oaks, Samuel, and Lutkenhouse. Captain Lutkenhouse flew as Raven 2 on the ill-fated RB-47H tail number 4290.

1969 to fly for Continental Airlines. He settled in the greater Los Angeles area. Bob Rogers, the navigator, continued to fly for years with the 55th Wing and after retirement settled in the greater Boston area.

In contrast to the often very descriptive award citations issued to World War II and Korean War veterans, Crew E-96's awards of the Distinguished Flying Cross contain not a word about what specifically the awards were given for. Such factually sparse citations were the norm for awards presented to those of us who flew reconnaissance during the Cold War years. Reads the citation that accompanied the award of the Distinguished Flying Cross to Lieutenant Lutkenhouse: "First Lieutenant Joel J. Lutkenhouse distinguished himself by extraordinary achievement during aerial flight as an Electronic Warfare Officer, from 30 March 1965 to 20 May 1965. During this period he participated in a program of vital international significance and demonstrated outstanding effectiveness and courage in the accomplishment of missions conducted under exceptional flight conditions. The professional competence and aerial skill, and devotion to duty, exhibited by Lieutenant Lutkenhouse reflect credit upon himself and the United States Air Force."

The Distinguished Flying Cross and/or the Air Medal (as shown in the figure) were the usual awards for reconnaissance aircrews. If shot down, crew deaths did not qualify for the Purple Heart, a medal awarded for injury or death suffered in wartime. The Silver Star was reserved for wartime heroism, ergo reconnaissance crews were not eligible for that award, either. Although an act of Congress resulted in the award of the Silver Star to the two survivors of the RB-47H shot down over the Barents Sea on July 1, 1960, it was a rare exception. General Curtis LeMay, the commander of SAC in 1954, awarded Colonel Austin and his crew two DFCs each for their May 8, 1954, overflight of the USSR. Even LeMay did not have the authority to present anything higher than the DFC to his courageous aircrews. Reconnaissance operations post–World War II up to 1960 actually constituted a secret war between the United States and the Soviet Union, and all the men who died during these operations should in fact be awarded the Purple Heart retroactively—only fair for a nation that sent them into harm's way. The bullets and shells that terminated their lives in the service of their country were as real as any fired in a formally declared war.

AN UNINTENTIONAL OVERFLIGHT
OF EAST GERMANY (1964)

Pilots of course are warned not to enter thunderstorms, but if they do how should they behave?
Flight Test at Wright-Patterson went out looking for a thunderstorm in a B-66. Their findings:
Maintain an airspeed of 250 knots. The power setting and pitch attitude for this airspeed should
be established before entering the thunderstorm. To paraphrase what they are saying: Once
you enter a thunderstorm all hell will break loose and you can't trust your instruments.
—**Wolfgang W. E. Samuel,** *Glory Days*

When President Dwight D. Eisenhower ended the U-2 overflights of the
Soviet Union in 1960, he in no way limited the Peacetime Aerial Reconnaissance Program, known in Pentagon jargon as PARPRO. The RB-47s of the
55th Strategic Reconnaissance Wing continued to fly the borders and coast-
lines of the Soviet Union and its satellites, monitoring Soviet missile launches
and conducting other specialized operations to ferret out the secrets of Soviet
combat aircraft as well as missile and radar systems. It was in the peripheral
reconnaissance role, while flying over international waters, where Soviet fighters were most prone to lash out at American aircraft. On July 1, 1960, only
two months after the shootdown of a Central Intelligence Agency U-2 aircraft
near Sverdlovsk, an RB-47H of the 55th SRW was downed over the Barents
Sea by MiG-19 interceptors.

As early as April 8, 1950, the Soviets downed an American aircraft over the
Baltic Sea off the coast of Latvia, a US Navy PB4Y2 with a crew of ten. Over
the years, American reconnaissance aircraft of all types had been downed
by Soviet fighters over the Sea of Japan, the Baltic Sea, the Sea of Okhotsk,
the Bering Strait, and the Black Sea, as well as off the Kamchatka Peninsula.
Ben Rich, the director of Lockheed's legendary Skunk Works, wrote: "Had the
American public known about the ongoing secret air war between the two
super-powers they would have been even more in despair than many already
were about the state of the world."[47] By 1964, little had changed. Soviet military

commanders of PVO Strany, their air defense command, remained paranoid about intrusions into Soviet airspace. On January 28, 1964, a T-39 Sabreliner from Wiesbaden Air Base on a routine flight through the southern Berlin air corridor strayed beyond the twenty-mile limit and was shot down by Russian fighters. The crew of three perished.

Captain David I. Holland reported for duty in 1963 with the famed 19th TRS, the squadron that in 1955 had flown three of its RB-45C reconnaissance aircraft from RAF Sculthorpe deep into the Soviet Union, at Toul-Rosières Air Base, France. "After flying a number of training missions, I was declared combat ready. I was assigned a brand new navigator straight out of navigator training, Second Lieutenant Harold Welch. Hal Welch was eager, alert, and a pleasure to work with. After flying a dozen training missions together, I was pleased to have him as my partner. The time for Hal's combat qualification check arrived—March 10, 1964. Captain Melvin J. Kessler was the instructor-navigator who would monitor and evaluate Lieutenant Welch. A few minutes after noon on March 10, the three of us preflighted our assigned RB-66B photo reconnaissance aircraft, taking off at 1300 hours. We proceeded to fly the mission as briefed—a high-low-high profile to include a low-level photo run of several bridges in northwest Germany near Osnabrück. The flight was scheduled to last about two hours and twenty minutes. It was our practice on a check ride to leave radio navigation aids tuned to Toul-Rosières, because the navigator was being evaluated and he could see the pilot's instruments from his position. When we were about a hundred or so miles from Toul, the VOR/TACAN was out of range. We leveled off at 33,000 feet. I engaged the autopilot and reported my position to the Frankfurt air traffic controller. We were flying in clear skies above an undercast. Captain Kessler sitting to the right of Lieutenant Welch could read the Doppler latitude and longitude, showing that we were on course. In reality, we were flying into the central Berlin air corridor, one of three such corridors providing access for Allied flights to and from Berlin. Lieutenant Welch gave me a new heading and time to descend for our low-altitude photo target. I made the turn, began the descent, and extended my speed brakes. We had gone down about 2,000 feet when I felt a slight jolt and heard what sounded like a 'crump.' I looked outside and saw at ten o'clock a fighter streaking away and jettisoning his external tanks. At first I thought it was a NATO fighter that had jumped us and come a little too close. When my airspeed began to increase and my hydraulic pressure was going to zero, I realized that the aircraft was seriously damaged and this was no ordinary event.

"I was on a westerly heading, I thought, with a standard penetration angle and speed brakes extended. With the loss of hydraulic pressure the speed brakes retracted, and elevator and aileron response was zero. I attempted to

RB-66B photo reconnaissance aircraft of the 10th Tactical Reconnaissance Wing, 19th Tactical Reconnaissance Squadron, landing at Toul-Rosières Air Base, France, after returning from a training mission. The shooting star on the tail of the aircraft was the 10th Wing emblem. An aircraft just like this one was flown by Captain David Holland and shot down by Russian MiG-19 fighters.

raise the nose of the aircraft and the left wing, applying 100 percent power to the left engine, but if there was a response it was negligible. When I heard Captain Kessler tell me that we were passing through 15,000 feet and I had no control over the aircraft, I ordered the crew to eject. I heard two loud bangs, saw the airspeed indicator passing through 400 knots, and then went through the ejection sequence myself—left preejection lever up, right preejection lever up, squeeze trigger in right preejection lever. I believe I went out at about 10,000 feet as the plane cartwheeled downward in flames. I then blacked out and didn't wake until I felt a terrible pain in the groin from my parachute straps. I tried to unbuckle my chute, then realized I was still several thousand feet above the ground. One thing I remember clearly, how quiet it was as I was floating to the ground. It turned out to be a very soft landing with the tree branches catching the chute just right to allow me to touch down gently on my feet. My first thought after touching ground was, 'Oh, shit, what have I done.'"

On March 10, 1964, Russian senior pilot Captain Vitaliy Ivannikov, at Wittstock Airfield, was on alert duty at readiness level two. "At 1646 Moscow time

Captain David Holland in the cockpit of an RB-66B while assigned to the 10th Reconnaissance Wing at Toul-Rosières, France, in 1965. Note the white helmet—painted camouflage during the Vietnam war years. Holland was an excellent pilot and found himself in a situation created by an errant N-1 compass, which led his aircraft into East Germany. In subsequent years during the Vietnam War, Holland flew 146 combat missions in EB-66 aircraft.

I was given orders by my fighter division command post to assume readiness level one. I started my engines, took the runway, and took off at 1649, assuming a heading of 330 degrees. As I was climbing to 15,000 feet, the controller informed me that my target was on a heading of 090 degrees at 30,000 feet. Four minutes later, to the left and about 6,000 feet above me, at an approximate range of about six miles, I spotted the intruder, pulling contrails for about 1,500 to 2,000 feet behind him. I also saw the aircraft of Captain Zinoviev. Without losing sight of either aircraft, I completed a hard left turn into the target. I saw there were no guns in the back of the B-66—otherwise we would have been immediately destroyed. Captain Zinoviev fired, the target turned left to a heading of 270 degrees, and while he was turning Captain Zinoviev fired again, but I couldn't tell if he hit anything. Halfway through the turn, I assumed an attack position behind the violator at a distance of about 1,000 feet, he extended his speed brakes, and my distance decreased to 600 feet. At 1657, after Captain Zinoviev finished his attack, he turned left and away from the target. I received a command from the controller to fire my C-5 rockets from a distance of less than 500 feet. The rockets were programmed to fire singly. I saw the rocket leave my plane, hit the target; its left engine began to smoke. I fired no more rockets, because I was too close, and the rocket's proximity fuse would not have armed in time, so I used my 23mm cannons from a distance of about 300 feet. I observed hits in the vertical stabilizer and lower part of the fuselage and speed brakes. I reported the results to the command post of my fighter division. I broke off my attack and climbed away to the right. I inadvertently flew past the aircraft into the debris zone, and as a result punctured one of my wing fuel tanks, something I didn't know until after landing. The target rolled to the left, entered a steep spiral, and I saw three red-and-white parachutes, which I reported to the command post. I was then ordered to land at Altes Lager Airfield, because Wittstock was below minimums. The entire flight from beginning to end lasted about twenty-five minutes."

"It seemed only minutes after I had disconnected from my chute and taken off my helmet," Captain Holland recalled, "that a jeep-like vehicle appeared with three people in it. Two in uniform, one in civilian clothes. They indicated through gestures that I should get in and accompany them. I didn't think I had a choice. Where I came down was near the small town of Gardelegen in East Germany. I later learned that there were six thousand Soviet troops in the area on maneuvers. I inquired about my crew, but no one talked to me—this being the way things remained for the next seventeen days. We arrived at a hospital, where I was made to disrobe, put in a bed, and examined by medical personnel. I indicated to them that I had pain in my left arm, and they X-rayed it. I was frightened. I remembered the U-2 shootdown in 1960 of Gary Powers. I also thought about the three USAF officers on the T-39 from Wiesbaden who had been shot down and died on January 28, just a little over a month ago. One of the nurses whispered to me, 'I so wish you were not here,' adding to the drama. Sometime during the middle of the night I was put into an ambulance and taken for a bumpy ride to a Russian hospital in Magdeburg. My private room was small, a guard was at the door, and the food was far from gourmet. I enjoyed pickled herring, but what I thought was a piece of delicatessen fish turned out to be just raw fish. The borscht wasn't too bad.

"The following day, interrogation began. The Russians clearly believed we were on a spy mission and tried hard to have me admit it. I was worried about Hal and Mel, but the Russian interrogators wouldn't give me any information about them. I had no idea whether the air force really knew what happened, whether my family knew about my plight. I was kept in total ignorance. Although I knew nothing about what was going on in the outside world, my relatives were notified of our missing status, and the incident became a media event in *Time*, *Newsweek*, and all the dailies. Headlines continued until the Alaska earthquake overshadowed our predicament. There was of course no way for me to know that [people in] my government—President Lyndon B.

Johnson, former ambassador to the Soviet Union Llewellyn Thompson, and Secretary of State Dean Rusk—were making every effort to secure our release.

"During the seventeen days of detention and isolation there were five interrogations, some threats of a trial in Moscow, and questions about 'Madrid Control.' The Russians had salvaged the wire recorder from the crashed RB-66, which evidently still contained recordings of a pilot talking to Madrid air traffic control when proceeding to or from our fair-weather base near Tripoli, Libya. Standard procedure became to be awakened at three or four in the morning, to sign a paper, which of course I refused to do. The days passed slowly. No radio. No newspaper. No one to talk to. I had attended survival training at Stead Air Force Base near Reno, Nevada, prior to reporting to Shaw. The training I received was effective in preparing me mentally for this period of detention. I have the greatest admiration for those who survived long periods of imprisonment as prisoners of war. The one thing that sustained me during that relatively short period of detainment was my faith in my government making every attempt to obtain my release.

"After the sixteenth day, I was led to a bathroom and allowed to take a shower. The next morning, to my great surprise, I received a breakfast of scrambled eggs with bacon. Something was up, but I didn't know what. After breakfast, a Russian officer entered my room with what he called a 'clothing list' and asked me to sign it. It was in Russian and I refused to do so. He argued but finally left. Another person arrived later with my flight suit, underwear, socks, and boots. I began to get my hopes up not to be going to Moscow. What happened next was puzzling. A Russian major escorted me to a room on the first floor. There, we sat and waited. Then he escorted me to a waiting car with a driver. When I asked where we were going, he put his index finger to his lips. I got the message. We drove into Magdeburg; it was about noon. I was struck by the lack of traffic and people in the streets. The Russian said something to the driver, who pulled over to the side of the street and parked. It seemed that whatever we were involved in had something to do with timing. Apparently we were ahead of schedule. Then the major turned to me and asked me if I believed in God. I said, 'Yes.' Answering his own question he said, 'Nyet.' We arrived at the Helmstedt crossing the same time another car, with Captain Kessler, arrived. Prior to getting out of the car, the Russian major told me not to shake his hand when he turned me over to a US Army officer.

"Kessler and I boarded an army staff car, which took us to Hannover. The media was relentless, attempting to get newsreels and photographs of two US Air Force officers being released from Soviet captivity. In Hannover, Kessler and I boarded a C-54. A flight surgeon gave us a cursory physical examination, then we flew to Wiesbaden Air Base. We were driven to the large air force hospital in Wiesbaden. When I entered my room, I was met by General

Gabriel Disosway, the commander of the United States Air Forces in Europe, USAFE. 'I'm glad you are back,' he said, shaking my hand. He cautioned me not to talk to anyone about my experience except the OSI—Office of Special Investigations—officer assigned to me. And he added that this was ordered by President Johnson. I was also ordered by General Disosway not to speak with Lieutenant Welch, who had the room next to mine, or to Captain Kessler. While the general was giving me instructions, an airman ripped the telephone out of the wall.

"I was allowed to say hello to my crew mates, learning for the first time of the extensive injuries suffered by Lieutenant Welch during his ejection. His left leg was broken in two places, and his right arm was broken as well. He had a neck fracture, which was not discovered until he was X-rayed at the Wiesbaden hospital. While in the East German hospital, Hal Welch had been allowed a visit by an air force flight surgeon, who, after examining him, asked for his immediate release so he could get proper care. Lieutenant Welch was released after ten days of captivity. The next five days I spent almost entirely with the OSI—daily interrogations; a polygraph test; a visit to a psychiatrist, who questioned me and then administered a Rorschach test. Finally, it was over, and I boarded a T-29 for Toul-Rosières to meet the inevitable flying evaluation board."

The shootdown by a Russian Mig-19 fighter on March 10, 1964, of the straying RB-66B, 53-451, piloted by Captain David Holland, reverberated through the 19th Squadron, the 10th Wing, Headquarters USAFE in Wiesbaden, the State Department, right up to the White House. Lieutenant Welch's navigation combat qualification test was a disaster. It was one of the notable Cold War incidents ranking right up there with the shootdown of Francis Gary Powers's U-2 on May 1, 1960, and the subsequent downing of the RB-47H electronic reconnaissance aircraft over the Barents Sea that same year. Within four days of the shootdown of the RB-66, Headquarters USAFE established an Air Defense Identification Zone, ADIZ, and Brass Monkey procedures for flights along the inner East German and Czechoslovak borders were implemented to preclude any further such incidents from happening. Any aircraft entering the ADIZ without authorization was contacted on Guard channel, a radio channel monitored by all aircraft at all times, and directed to immediately reverse course. These procedures, although implemented after a shootdown that could have been prevented, solved the problem, and there were no further intrusions into East Germany after Brass Monkey procedures were implemented. While flying EB-66 aircraft in the early 1970s with the 39th Tactical Reconnaissance Squadron over West Germany, more than once I heard a Brass Monkey call on Guard channel, a procedure that should have been implemented years earlier.

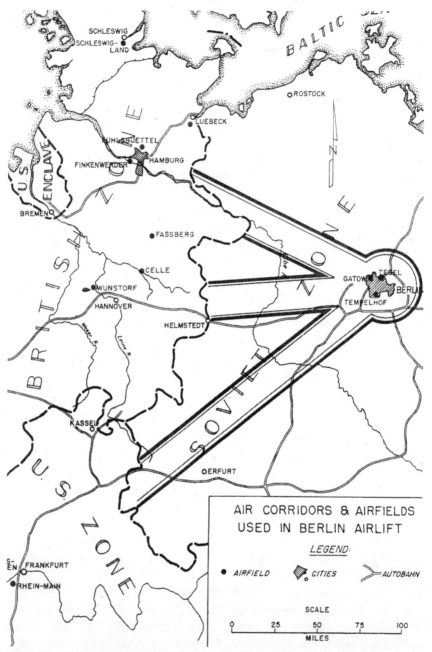

The three air corridors leading into Berlin: the central corridor was used for flights heading west, while the two others were entry corridors to the Berlin airfields of Tegel, Gatow, and Tempelhof.

The *Stars and Stripes* military newspaper, *Newsweek*, and *Time*, among many other publications, carried lengthy articles about the loss of the RB-66. "One of the trickiest games of the Cold War is a sort of airborne electronic 'chicken,'" speculated *Time*, "in which a high-speed aircraft without warning dashes headlong for the enemy's border, turning away just in time. The game is played by both East and West, and not just for fun. From such phony forays has come a wealth of crucial information about one another's defense capabilities. . . . . In the past two years, according to one official source, Soviet jets have poked their noses into Western airspace 95 times—mostly on just such sniffing missions. But when a Western plane goes into Communist territory, innocently or not, the Russians do not hesitate to shoot. Since 1950, 108 U.S. airmen have died or disappeared within Communist airspace, the last three only seven weeks ago when an unarmed—and demonstrably innocent—T-39 jet trainer was blasted from the leaden skies over Vogelsberg," *Time* magazine wrote. "Last week," the weekly magazine continued its story, "a U.S. Air Force RB-66B reconnaissance bomber bellowed off the runway at Toul-Rosières Air Base in France, then sloped east by northeast on a routine, 2½ hour 'navigational training mission.' The flight plan called for the 700 m.p.h., twin-jet bomber to swing over Germany's beautiful Mosel Valley to Hahn Air Base, then bank north to Bremerhaven before returning with zigzags and altitude changes to Hahn and home. . . . The big swept wing Douglas jet crossed into Communist East Germany in the vicinity of the central Berlin air corridor. Moments later, two swift blips rose on the radar screens—Soviet MiGs in deadly pursuit. The slower moving blip that marked the RB-66 leaped suddenly into wrenching, zigzag evasive maneuvers, [and] four minutes later disappeared from the screen well within East German territory. On the ground a German school boy watched the last moments of the flight: 'The fighter closed on the bomber from behind and fired on it. The American plane burst into flames. I saw a fireball on one wing. The crew of three came out by parachute. The first two came out together. The third one came a bit later.' . . . Whatever the nature of the RB-66's mission, the Russians had all the ingredients for a fat, propaganda-loaded 'show trial' like that of U-2 pilot Francis Gary Powers." Although East and West played games aplenty, as the *Time* magazine article chose to speculate, the RB-66 was clearly a victim of circumstance of an overly aggressive Soviet regime.

Kermit Helmke, one of the more experienced navigators at Toul-Rosières, remembers the day well: "I was about to start a top secret briefing concerning a change to our war plans. It was about one o'clock or so on the tenth of March. The command post called the briefing room and asked for Lieutenant Colonel McCormack, my boss and the chief of plans. We waited for about ten minutes. Then I got a call to scrub the briefing and come down to the CP. When I got there, I learned a border violation had occurred and that a 19th Squadron airplane was suspected. We called Bill Schrimsher, who was flying one of the Brown Cradles in the same area where Dave Holland was supposed to be, to see if he had heard from Dave. Nothing. In the next hour or so we learned that Holland had been shot down. Then things got quiet for a while. Colonel McCormack obtained a radar plot of the track of Holland's aircraft and asked me what I made of it. It's a compass malfunction, I told him.

"'How do you know that?' The track is a very smooth curve leading me to believe that a gyro was steering the aircraft. An open rotor or stator lead in the system would cause a precession of this nature. My answer was based on experience with selsyns as a remote-control turret mechanic on the B-29. Verne Gardina was listening to our conversation. Vern was the 19th Squadron senior navigator."

Early that evening, the wing commander, Colonel Arthur Small, arrived from Alconbury and had dinner with Major Gardina. "We discussed the possible causes," wrote Major Gardina. "I told him that something happened to me seven years earlier that may have happened also to Dave Holland. In 1957, Captain Henley and I flew from Shaw to the Douglas plant in Long Beach, California, test-hopped an RB-66, then flew it back to Shaw. We were on autopilot. Halfway to Shaw I gave Henley the heading and ETA—estimated time of arrival—to the next checkpoint, then slid my seat back and went to sleep. It had been a long day. I woke up about thirty minutes later and looked at the radar scope and couldn't believe what I saw. I checked the N-1 compass immediately, and it was reading as it should, 90 degrees, but there was the Mississippi River running east and west, directly under the radar heading marker, which was on 90 degrees. We flew into Shaw using the standby whiskey compass. I described the symptoms to maintenance. The next day, they told me that one leg of a delta-wound coil had failed and caused the compass to precess at a rate of two to three degrees per minute to maintain the 90-degree heading.

"Colonel Small then instructed me to select the people I needed to pursue this possibility. By daybreak I was in the compass mockup area in the armaments and electronics shop. I told the maintenance men that I wanted to fail each leg of the delta-wound coil of the N-1 compass alternately. There were three 120-degree legs in the coil located in the left wing of the aircraft. I wanted to check the precession rate and duration especially on headings between 000 degrees and 010 degrees, the heading from Hahn Air Base to Nordholz. We found the compass mockup too crude for a convincing test. So I had an RB-66 ground test run with maintenance failing one, then another of the coil legs with all equipment operating. We timed the precession and effects on all associated equipment that directly used the N-1 inputs. This test showed that the B-phase of the coil failed when the aircraft was trying to maintain a northerly heading; it would cause the aircraft to turn toward 090 degrees in order to maintain a 360-degree heading on the compass."

The N-1 gyro-stabilized magnetic compass system in the B-66 aircraft was its primary directional reference. The navigator and pilot alike relied on it. The N-1 had a high level of reliability, so much so that few ever questioned the system. The whiskey compass in the pilot station, installed as an emergency backup, was notoriously unreliable as a meaningful cross-check reference. Not only because of the distorted magnetic field in the cockpit but also because of a serious problem with a magnetized nose wheel in many of the B-66 aircraft. The N-1 was the only directional input to the Doppler-driven ground position indicator, GPI, system. The GPI provided continuously updated latitude and longitude to the navigator station, and stabilized the navigation radar display to true north. Colonel Don Adee taught the N-1 compass system to basic navigator-bombardier students at Mather Air Force Base, California. Adee remembers teaching his students that the power failure warning light on the N-1 would illuminate whenever alternate current was lost on the system. Only after David Holland's shootdown was it discovered that the warning light measured only one phase of the three-phase AC power. The phase lost on aircraft number 53-451 flown by Holland was not the one being monitored, so Lieutenant Welch, Holland's navigator, had no warning of the N-1 compass failure. "In tactical radar navigation, the navigator was required to obtain periodic radar fixes. The beginning of the fix process was to obtain an initial position, in this case Hahn Air Base, which would routinely have been obtained from the GPI counters or by manually taking time, speed, and direction from a last-known position. Next, the navigator would have looked at his navigation map using the initial position he established as his starting point, then tried to determine the radar return pattern for his next fix. In the German environment, where there are so many cultural radar returns, it is quite easy to find a similar pattern of returns that matches those expected from your next position, then checking an incorrectly oriented radar display, the consequences were predictable. The crew flying over a total undercast, however, thought everything was alright.

"After running a test on a squadron aircraft to prove the N-1 precession theory, Major Gardina hurriedly drew charts and graphs of all equipment affected by the N-1—autopilot, radar, APN-82 Doppler system, and RMI—and briefed Colonel Small. We also drew a prediction of the track from Hahn to Nordholz if the compass failed. At a precession rate of two and a half degrees per minute, the prediction led the aircraft from Hahn into the central Berlin corridor. We had no previous word of where the aircraft crossed the border, only our prediction. Colonel Small in the meantime was under unbelievable pressure to find the cause of what happened. He sent me and a standardization and evaluation pilot to brief the Headquarters USAFE staff on what I had come up with on Wednesday evening, the eleventh of March. USAFE accepted us and my briefing like we were raw meat in a lion's den. They were totally negative to anything technical and spent their time berating and condemning us and the entire 10th Wing.

"We picked up our briefing charts and tattered remains, and returned to Toul late Wednesday night. I proposed to Colonel Small that we fly a test with the B-phase disconnected and photograph and record the instruments and the ground to establish our actual track, using checkpoints to simulate Hahn and Nordholz. We soon learned that our test had to be approved by Edwards Flight Test Center. We spent hours on the phone with them. Since we were the world's center of attention at this time, they gave us their approval. The Headquarters USAFE staff was totally negative toward us doing the test, so we bypassed them and went directly to friends in the Pentagon. Major Gardina, flying in the gunner's seat of an RB-66B photo-reconnaissance aircraft exactly like the one flown by Dave Holland, jury-rigged a cutoff switch on the N-1 compass leads in the C-2 compass transmitter housed in the left wing of the aircraft. That allowed him to interrupt AC current flow, inducing the same error that led 451 into East Germany." Norm Goldberg flew as navigator. "We headed north out of France toward the UK," recalled Goldberg. "Verne disconnected the C-2 sensor lead when we got over the English Channel. After about twenty-five minutes of flight, we were heading due east toward the Dutch coast. The picture on my radar scope was photographed with an O-15 camera, standard equipment to record B-47 and B-66 radar presentations."

"When we landed," Major Gardina stated, "the film was immediately processed. The test proved that the entire navigation suite of the aircraft, including the RMI, range measuring equipment, gave false indications. Even an experienced navigator wouldn't have been able to recognize the misplaced returns encountered by Lieutenant Welch in a heavy industrial environment. We took this information, the photographs, and a better-prepared set of charts and graphs, back to Wiesbaden. Again, we were received like the plague. They condemned our reasoning and discredited our test flight. We returned to Toul in the wee hours of Friday morning, March 13. Reflew the test Friday morning to overcome some of the USAFE objections. Again hurriedly put the data together, and Colonel Small and I returned to Wiesbaden. When we arrived, the situation was worse than before. There was pressure from the very top for an explanation—President Johnson and Secretary of Defense McNamara, the air force chief of staff General Curtis LeMay, and too many others to mention. Scores of general officers were inbound to Wiesbaden to join in the melee. Before the big meeting between Generals LeMay, McConnell, Disosway, and a jillion other nervous generals, I briefed Major General

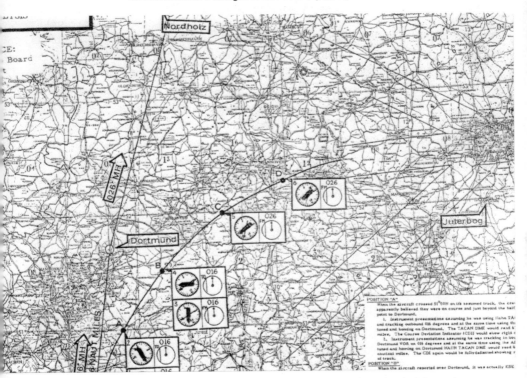

The route of Captain Holland's ill-fated flight into East Germany. The planned route is shown on the left, passing over Dortmund and heading for Nordholz. The actual route shown on the right leads the aircraft into the central Berlin air corridor and a fateful encounter with two Russian MiG-19s.

[Henry Garfield] Thorne, the USAFE Director of Operations, and Lieutenant General [James V.] Edmundson, the 17th Air Force commander. Then Colonel Small and I tried to brief Major General [Romulus W.] Puryear, the 3rd Air Force commander, to make certain he was knowledgeable (the 10th Tactical Reconnaissance Wing fell under the 3rd Air Force, headquartered at South Ruislip, a suburb of London).

"Colonel Small and I were not permitted to be present in the general officer meeting—we were persona non grata, so to speak. I began to brief Puryear. He threw Small, me, and all our charts out of his office and told us he wouldn't brief that bullshit, and wished he was a thousand miles away. General Edmundson then got us two sharp generals who would be in the briefing, and I brought them up to speed and gave them my charts so that the two could at least make a half-assed presentation. They were very nervous, not technically oriented, and not convinced we knew what we were talking about. While the meeting was going on, Small and I were in a large room outside the briefing room with a score of others. I was a major; everyone else was either a bird-colonel or a general. Every one of them was giving me and Colonel Small hell. Small was getting most of it. About 2100 hours that evening, Small was called to a command post telephone. Major Miller, from the 10th Wing Headquarters detachment at Toul, was on the line. 'Colonel,' he said, 'I have the best news you ever heard.' Poor Small was under so much pressure that his first thought was, 'They found out that Holland was a defector.' Instead, Major Miller informed him that they had located the film from the GCI radar site that had been tracking Holland's aircraft. It, and Gardina's plot, was no more than two or three miles off the whole way into East Germany. Small came back and handed me the coordinates he had taken down from Miller. I had gotten up at five o'clock on Wednesday morning, flew two test flights, made numerous ground tests, prepared and made briefings, and made three trips to Wiesbaden. I was exhausted. Flying back, wouldn't you know it, the weather was bad at Toul, and we had to divert to Laon. I finally got to bed on Saturday morning."

Colonel Arthur Small was relieved of command effective March 24, 1964, by General Disosway, the USAFE commander—a position held by General Curtis LeMay in 1948. As always, there had to be a scapegoat, and Colonel Small, as the 10th TRW commander, fit the bill. As General LeMay was quoted to have said when responding to the firing of several B-47 bomb wing commanders when they failed to properly execute a "no notice Cocoa" alert, practicing their assigned wartime mission, "I cannot differentiate between the incompetent and the unfortunate." The border violation was due to a technical malfunction, and Colonel Small was indeed unfortunate, and anything but incompetent. Yet he was the wing commander, the man at the head of a combat wing who usually paid the price for failure, no matter the cause. Major David Holland attributes his exoneration by the Flying Evaluation Board to the extraordinary efforts of Major Verne Gardina. Holland continued to fly and serve his country in Southeast Asia, flying 146 combat missions in EB-66 aircraft. He was awarded five Air Medals and retired in the rank of major—his overflight experience a definite factor in limiting his progression within the air force rank structure. Major Gardina suffered no ill effects from his courageous investigation to save one of his own. In 1976, Gardina retired from the United States Air Force in the rank of colonel. His last duty assignment was as vice commander of Langley Air Force Base, Virginia, the location of the headquarters of the Tactical Air Command.

As a patriotic teenager in 1942, wanting to serve his country, Verne Gardina carried a letter of commendation from his high school principal to the army enlistment center. His principal described Verne as "a young man of good character, manly bearing, and excellent poise. He is sincere and straightforward, and in my judgment he possesses the qualities of leadership necessary in military service." He served in the Pacific Theater of Operations, was shot down, but survived. Colonel Gardina served in the best traditions of the United States Air Force and certainly was all his high school principal said of him, and more. He passed away on January 24, 1995. Lieutenant Harold Welch, upon his return from Soviet detention, was unable to recall any events after takeoff from Toul-Rosières. Welch did not return to the 19th TRS.

Things didn't end with that star-studded meeting of March 13, 1964, at Headquarters USAFE in Wiesbaden. American overflights of the Soviet Union, and the occasional shootdowns by Russian fighters or surface-to-air missiles, was an ongoing topic of discussion and formal exchanges between East and West. The March 10 shootdown of the RB-66, soon after the shootdown of an errant T-39 trainer over the GDR, the German Democratic Republic, also referred to as East Germany, was obviously grist for the Soviet propaganda mill. At an April 4, 1964, meeting between Ambassador at Large Llewellyn E. Thompson and the Soviet ambassador to the United States, Anatoly F. Dobrynin, Dobrynin handed Ambassador Thompson the Russian-language text of a letter from Chairman Khrushchev to President Johnson. As expected, the letter was long-winded and self-serving, stating: "The fundamental position of the Soviet Union is the improvement of Soviet-American relations and strengthening peace, and we would prefer, of course, not to engage in demonstrations of force, of hard firmness, and in the elimination of the consequences of incidents provoked by the acts of American military forces, but to concentrate, with you, our efforts toward guaranteeing for the people of our two countries a durable peace." Such verbiage came from a man who only eighteen months earlier tried to put nuclear-tipped missiles on the island of Cuba aimed at the United States.

Chairman Khrushchev continued, referring to the T-39 shootdown, "In spite of the warning and the order to land, the aircraft continued to fly deep into the GDR until it was shot down. The American side stated that this violation was unintentional, that this was not a military plane but a training plane which had lost its bearings. It is difficult to agree that even a training plane could stray off course in such clear weather and over territory which is quite familiar to flying personnel.... But hardly six weeks had gone by and on March 10 there occurred a new violation of the frontier of the GDR. This violation was committed by a military aircraft, a reconnaissance bomber equipped with air cameras as well as radio reconnaissance facilities which were in operation at the time of the flight.... Can we fail to reach the conclusion, Mr. President, that the RB-66 intentionally violated the air space of the GDR and did so in order to engage in air reconnaissance? ... I believe that the flight of the RB-66 was arranged without instructions from the President of the United States of America. But I declare to you that I do not accept the idea that this was an accidental border violation." The letter continued at length in the same spirit, counseling President Johnson that he had a runaway military on his hands.

Khrushchev chose not to take the route of a show trial. On April 17, 1964, President Johnson responded in a direct and brief letter, "I can quite well understand your concern that within a short period of time two American airplanes crossed the demarcation line. There is little I can say about the incident involving a training plane, since the crew were killed and we are unable to ascertain what actually happened. I am disturbed that in both cases, however, there does not appear to have been justification for the rapidity with which there was a resort to force by Soviet planes. The American planes should not have been there, but I believe that this fast and violent reaction is quite unjustified. . . . I recognize that this is an astonishing series of errors, and upon my instructions the American military authorities have established the most rigorous procedure possible in order to prevent any repetition of such incidents." Chairman Khrushchev had less than six months left in power when he received President Johnson's reply.

Don Adee, who in later years taught young aspiring air force officers the intricacies of aerial navigation at Mather Air Force Base, wrote: "I arrived at Toul-Rosières in April 1964 and was assigned to the 42nd TRS. I became a navigator flight examiner at Toul before we moved to Chambley in 1965. After the two shootdowns over East Germany, all of us new guys had briefings running out of our ears before we were allowed close to an airplane."

General LeMay, who flew into Wiesbaden after Captain Holland's shootdown on March 10 to whip his generals into line, had less than a year remaining as chief of staff before retiring. With his departure, an era in American military aviation ended. In early August 1964, a fateful meeting between the destroyer USS *Maddox* and North Vietnamese torpedo boats changed the American political and military landscape. A rallying Congress passed the Gulf of Tonkin Resolution on August 7. The once secret war in Southeast Asia was out in the open. Few understood what the United States was letting itself in for. Fewer still understood how unprepared we were to fight a conventional air war halfway around the world. We had neither the iron bombs on hand to sustain an air campaign nor aircrews trained for anything other than nuclear weapons delivery. Air-to-air combat of the World War II and Korean War variety had been declared obsolete, and our newest fighter, the F-4C Phantom, came armed only with air-to-air missiles. The technologies necessary to further the development of conventional weapons had long ago been put on the back burner by senior air force leaders focused on nuclear war. Although precision-guided munitions achieved a high level of development and success toward the end of World War II—such as the US Navy's Pelican and Bat bombs, the Army Air Forces' Axon and Razon glide bombs, and the German Fritz X and Henschel 293—such weapons and their continued development were deemed irrelevant in the nuclear age. In 1964, the air force had little more

Major David I. Holland and his navigator, Captain Alex Mazzei, at Tan Son Nhut Air Base, South Vietnam, 1965. Major Holland, a good friend, went West in 2017 to that special place in the sky reserved for military aviators.

than old-fashioned general-purpose bombs, and not enough of them, to take out a bridge the way it had been done in World War II. If an aircraft didn't break the sound barrier or was unable to carry a nuclear device, it apparently wasn't needed in a world of absolutes defined by megatonnage. A nation and an air force were about to be given a costly lesson by a "Third World country."[48]

THE REASONS WHY (1948–1960)

I was just a dumb 23-year-old fighter jock, which is exactly what the Air Force was looking
for back in 1957. All they told me was "How would you like to fly at very high altitude in a
pressure suit?" I immediately thought rocket ships! Buck Rogers! Count me in.
—**Buddy Brown,** U-2 pilot, in Ben Rich and Leo Janos, *Skunk Works*

In late 1957 a fifty-foot Christmas tree was erected at Offutt Air Force Base, the headquarters of the Strategic Air Command. It was an enlistment gimmick. Commanders could light a bulb on the tree when meeting their enlistment or reenlistment quotas. A status board was erected next to the tree to show the names of the commanders and their units who had met their goals. A painter was to affix a sign to the status board reading: "Maintaining Peace Is Our Profession." That seemed a bit wordy to the painter—he couldn't fit all the words on the board—so he removed the word "Maintaining." "Peace Is Our Profession," the sign proudly proclaimed for all to see. A visiting officer liked the sign and the message it tried to convey, and once he got back to Westover Air Force Base in Massachusetts, he had a similar sign made and displayed at the main gate, adding the SAC shield displaying blue sky, an olive branch, white puffy clouds, and a mailed fist. "Peace Is Our Profession" caught on among others and soon was the slogan that came to define the Strategic Air Command. In 1958, SAC bristled with over 1,700 B-47 and B-52 strategic nuclear-capable bombers and nearly 200 RB-47 reconnaissance aircraft, supported by more than 900 aerial refueling tankers. The powerful offensive capability the United States possessed in 1958, especially its strategic bomber force, held an expansion-minded and predatory Soviet Union in check. Not the case ten years earlier, in 1948, when the United States and its western allies struggled to maintain even a semblance of military force.

The rapid disarmament after World War II left the United States no option other than an airlift when Joseph Stalin made his move on Berlin in 1948. That potential disaster barely avoided, when the Russians in August 1949 exploded an atomic device. The atomic bomb, which had given the United States a unique weapon to checkmate potential Soviet military threats against western Europe, now became part of their arsenal of weapons as well. And they had the bombers, the TU-4, a copy of the American B-29, to deliver them. A quick analysis showed that the most vulnerable places to the Soviet atomic threat, other than Europe, were Alaska and the west coast of the United States. If Russian military progress was not enough, the Chinese Communists in 1949 declared victory over the Nationalists, completing the occupation of mainland China. Only a small island, Formosa, renamed Taiwan, remained to finish the job, and they intended to do that shortly. The United States had barely time to digest all of this bad news when in June 1950 the North Koreans, with the blessings of the Soviets, invaded South Korea. The United States was at war again, regardless of it being referred to by the United Nations and the Truman administration as only a "police action." The Eighth Army was saved from disaster by the F-51s and A-26s that decimated the attackers by day and night. A spectacular landing at Inchon drove the North Koreans north into their own mountain country, up against the Chinese border. The North near defeat, General Douglas MacArthur split his forces in pursuit and, smelling victory, declared to the troops that they would be home by Christmas. That neat little plan all changed that November when the Chinese Communists committed nine armies to save their North Korean ally. Now it was the Eighth Army, for the second time during this "police action," trying to extricate itself in brutal winter conditions from the vulnerable position an overconfident General MacArthur had led it into. The Eighth Army, and elements of the US Marine Corps, managed to do it, under conditions only previously experienced by Germany's Sixth Army in World War II, and they didn't survive.

President Truman, taken aback by events, like everyone else, voiced his frustration to reporters on November 30, 1950, saying that he "would use the atomic bomb, if necessary, to assure victory." Of course, such a statement scared the daylights out of our British ally, and Prime Minister Clement Attlee, a staunch supporter of the Berlin airlift in 1948–1949, quickly flew to Washington to get things straightened out. "Getting things straightened out" meant for the United States to confer with the United Kingdom before making rash moves with nuclear weapons. With the United States vulnerable in Korea, the Soviet Union, with its vast tank armies deployed along the West German border, was viewed with suspicion. Are they going to take advantage of American vulnerability? We had no intelligence, no reliable information on what they were doing, not to mention what their intentions might be. After conferring with Attlee in early December, Truman authorized "overflights of denied territory" in the Far East—meaning Communist China and the Soviet Union. Additionally, the fourth production model of a B-47 bomber was pulled from the production line to be given photo-reconnaissance capabilities to overfly eastern Siberia to see if the Soviets had deployed any of their strategic bombers, potentially threatening Alaska and the west coast. Truman also recalled General Dwight D. Eisenhower to active duty, who assumed the duties of NATO Supreme Allied Commander Europe (SACEUR), with its headquarters in Mons, near Brussels, Belgium. All of this didn't do anything to alleviate the Western lack of military capability, nor did we have the information—intelligence in other words—to make informed decisions about what we needed to ensure the safety of our people. In Europe, along the borders of the Soviet Union, the US Air Force and US Navy had already begun flying peripheral reconnaissance—PARPRO missions in Pentagon jargon—as early as the Berlin airlift days, and suffered their first loss to Russian fighters over the eastern Baltic Sea in April 1950. The British were also busy selecting aircrews to fly reconnaissance over European Russia using American planes—RB-45Cs. The stage was set. The Soviet Union was a closed society to outsiders, but not much longer. America was going to get the information it needed to build an appropriate force structure to oppose the Soviet threat—and the best and easiest way to accomplish that was by direct overflights of the Soviet Union to gather information on military deployments, production facilities, and of course target information for our own bombers.

The result of all the uncertainty faced by America's and Great Britain's political leadership and their military planners quickly resulted in overflights of denied Chinese and Russian territory by RF-80, RF-86, and RB-45 jet reconnaissance aircraft. Much of the information gathered, however, was to support the ongoing war effort in Korea. The information brought back by reconnaissance flights over Chinese ports was passed to the B-29 bomber crews flying out of Kadena Air Base, Okinawa, and Yokota Air Base, Japan, who then tried to catch the ships as they were unloading in North Korean ports. On the European side of the Soviet Union, the British were the ones who initiated the overflight program in 1952, when they flew three American RB-45C reconnaissance aircraft deep into European Russia. Six months later, two American RB-47Bs flew over eastern Siberia, adjacent to the Bering Sea, to see if by chance the Soviets had moved TU-4 bombers onto Siberian airfields. The year that followed saw the death of Stalin, the turmoil that accompanies a dictator's passing, and the swearing in of a new president for the United States—Dwight D. Eisenhower. Eisenhower, within a short period of time, not only sanctioned Truman's overflights initiated during a national emergency and a period of war but expanded on them with what became known as the Sensitive Intelligence Program, SENSINT, in 1954.

If anyone understood the value of having up-to-date, accurate information on one's adversaries, intelligence in other words, it was General Eisenhower, who had led the Allied armies in World War II from the shores of Normandy

General Dwight D. Eisenhower in December 1943 with President Franklin Roosevelt at La Marsa, Tunisia.

to the Elbe River. Eisenhower remembered Pearl Harbor—an intelligence failure that all who experienced it vowed was never going to happen again. And yet it did happen again just five years after V-J Day. We were totally surprised when North Korea overran South Korean and American forces, nearly running them into the Sea of Japan. And then again later that same year, strategic surprise came when the Chinese Communists intervened that November in the Korean conflict. When it came to knowing what our potential adversaries might be up to, we seemed to be totally ignorant. Eisenhower vowed to fix that problem once and for all, instituting a "compartmented" intelligence collection effort where "Need to Know" became the mantra. "Need to Know" meant that the fewest people possible were to be privy to information gathered by overflights of denied territory. And only a handful needed to know about such flights at all. Even the aircrews directly involved would know nothing about missions flown other than their own, and they were briefed to never talk about their overflights—to anyone. Requests for overflights originated with the most senior military commanders, were vetted by the Joint Chiefs of Staff, the Department of State, and the CIA, and approved, without exception, by the commander in chief. Eisenhower, like others before him, knew that such undertakings as overflying denied territory, although a necessity for the United States, were at best a violation of international law and at worst could be interpreted as an act of war. Therefore the planning, approval, and execution of such flights were restricted to a handful of people; the fewer people who knew about any of this, the better. Top secret compartmented intelligence information (SCI) became a rigorously enforced concept and provided the framework to limit access to sensitive national programs.

Under the auspices of the SENSINT program, RF-86Fs, RB-47E/Hs, RB-57A/D/F/Ws, and supersonic RF-100As entered the inventory and were employed in Europe and the Far East. The truly amazing thing is that we experienced no losses. We kept on flying higher and higher—at 40,000 feet, plus or minus a few thousand feet, the MiG-15 struggled and wasn't a threat to our reconnaissance aircraft. The MiG-17 improved on the lack of performance of the MiG-15, but we bested it, too, by moving up to 50,000 feet—then the MiG-19 came along, pushing the envelope. We kept on going higher and higher with lightweight, better engines and large winged aircraft such as the RB-57Ds and Ws, and eventually the U-2, which flew above 70,000 feet. What Eisenhower gained from numerous overflights was an insight into the economy of the Soviet Union and its military and nuclear force structure and deployments. It allowed him to make rational and economic decisions as to our own military needs, including putting the brakes on the nonstop expansion of SAC's bomber force. So, when on May 1, 1954, the Soviets put on their version of Thanksgiving with a huge military parade in Red Square, including a flyover of purportedly one hundred new Bison jet bombers, political Washington went into an uproar and spoke of a "bomber gap." Actually, if there was a bomber gap, it was in our favor, and Eisenhower knew that. He had up-to-date information on the subject provided by his fearless aviators who overflew the Soviet Union. The same scenario played out in October 1957 when the Soviet Union launched Sputnik 1—this time, it was a missile gap. Well, we had experienced setbacks with our Vanguard rockets, which kept blowing up on the launchpads. But Eisenhower knew where we stood in missile development and what the Soviet threat actually was—and, like the bomber gap, the missile gap proved illusionary, a gap that existed only for the uninformed. Nevertheless, Eisenhower was not about to share publicly the critical information he gained through the SENSINT and U-2 overflight programs.

All good things have to come to an end sometime, one way or another. For the super-successful SENSINT program, the mass overflights by RB-47s in early 1956 got the Soviets' attention, and they let us know in private that they didn't care for us to continue such efforts. But it was the flight of three RB-57Ds over Vladivostok, the huge Russian naval base adjacent to the Sea of Japan, that really upset them. In a note of December 15, 1956, they voiced their displeasure: "The Government of the Union of Soviet Socialist Republics considers it necessary to advise the Government of the United States as follows:

According to precisely determined data, on December 11, 1956, between 13:07 and 13:21, Vladivostok time, three American jet planes, type B-57, coming from the direction of the Sea of Japan, south of Vladivostok, violated the national boundary of the USSR by invading the airspace of the Soviet Union." Followed by several more paragraphs expressing their displeasure, the note concluded, "In case of any repetition in the future of violations of the airspace of the USSR by American planes, the Government of the United States of America will have to bear the full responsibility for the consequences of such violations."[49] The American response was brief and polite, but President Eisenhower got the message—and ended the SENSINT program. Many of the airframes, such as RF-100s, that had flown shallow penetrations over Eastern Bloc countries, as well as RF-86 and RB-57 aircraft, were passed on to the Nationalist Chinese for flights over Communist China. Farsightedly, back in 1954, President Eisenhower had approved the development of the U-2, a powered lightweight glider that could reach altitudes where no fighter could go, beyond 70,000 feet. The designer? Clarence "Kelly" Johnson, of course. The impetus for the U-2 program was to preclude strategic surprise, Eisenhower's mantra. No more Pearl Harbors or Korean surprises while Eisenhower was president. He assumed the presidency with that overriding thought in mind, and he was going to leave knowing that the nation was equipped to preclude military surprise of any kind. In addition to the development of the U-2, Eisenhower pushed the CIA into assuming the overflight role of the Soviet Union, using contractors, in other words, highly paid US Air Force fighter pilots, to get the military out of the spy flight business, with its potentially military ramifications.

Writes R. Cargill Hall, in his article "Clandestine Victory: Eisenhower and Overhead Reconnaissance in the Cold War": in a November 23, 1954, "meeting in the Oval Office with the secretaries of state and defense and senior CIA and Air Force officials, Eisenhower approved the program under CIA management. Because the intelligence agency possessed no infrastructure or personnel to bring it into operation, the president ordered the Air Force to furnish all of the assistance needed to train, base and operate the new reconnaissance aircraft."[50] Among the chosen few to get the CIA into the overflight business, not really supported by Allen Dulles, the director of the CIA, was Marion "Hack" Mixson, who had trained the Royal Air Force contingent to fly the RB-45C in 1951. "Kelly Johnson promised delivery of the first of the spy planes in eight months." True to form, Kelly Johnson delivered not only on time but also below program cost. The U-2 flew its first test flight on July 21, 1955. So, when the SENSINT program ended in late 1956, the U-2 had already assumed the role of overflying the Soviet Union. "Between June 20 and July 10, 1956, U-2s launched from West Germany—Wiesbaden and Giebelstadt Air Bases—made eight overflights inside the Iron Curtain, five of them over the Soviet Union.

Among other sites, they imaged downtown Leningrad and Moscow. Earlier, the US Air Force had claimed that the USSR possessed over a hundred Bison long-range heavy bombers, but the U-2 photography belied that claim. The U-2 missions covered nine Soviet long-range bomber bases in European Russia, including the Fili airframe plant near Moscow that produced the bombers, and they failed to uncover any of them." The SENSINT shutdown initially also shut down the U-2 overflights, but Eisenhower quickly reconsidered, allowing continued overflights of the Soviet Union by U-2 aircraft.

"Eisenhower approved a flight from Pakistan to Norway, across the Soviet Union. Scheduled for late April 1960, it did not take place until May 1, the communist 'All Saints' Day,' just fifteen days before another Four Power Summit Conference. The pilot, Francis Gary Powers, flew north over Stalinabad, the Tyuratam missile test center, and then proceeded northwest toward Yurya and Plesetsk, the submarine shipyard at Severodvinsk, the naval base at Murmansk, with recovery scheduled in Norway late in the day. While operating at its design altitude of 70,000 feet, over the city of Sverdlovsk, Powers's plane was brought down by a salvo of SA-2 surface-to-air missiles. The pilot survived." According to Ben Rich, the longtime director of Lockheed's famed Skunk Works, "a Soviet missile battery had launched in shotgun fashion 14 SA-2s at the approaching U-2, a sign that they were waiting for his arrival. One missile had knocked down a Russian fighter trying to intercept Powers, and the shock waves from the exploding missiles had knocked off the U-2s tail."[51]

Premier Khrushchev took full advantage of the opportunity at the summit conference in Paris, demanding a personal apology. The U-2 shootdown ended the overflight program for good, including a follow-on program called OXCART, which produced the CIA-flown Mach 3+ A-12 spy plane. An air force two-seat version flew for the remainder of the Cold War years at altitudes over 80,000 feet along the periphery of the Soviet Union—but never over the Soviet Union or Communist China, the current PRC, Peoples Republic of China. However, the SR-71 cameras were of such high quality that they could look for hundreds of miles into the Soviet Union while flying offshore. President Dwight D. Eisenhower handed over the national reigns in January 1961 to President John F. Kennedy, leaving him not just with an interstate highway system that brought the US infrastructure into the twentieth century but also with a nascent Corona satellite reconnaissance program that no longer came with the downside associated with aircraft overflights, even if flown by quasi-civilians. As for the Soviet Union—in 1960 it no longer was a closed society as it had been in 1948. The Open Skies proposal that Eisenhower broached to Khrushchev in 1960, rejected of course, in fact was implemented with the launch of the Corona spy satellite.

The highly successful U-2 program had its teething problems like any other new aircraft design. By 1958, twelve U-2s had been lost due to accidents. "The CIA had paid for 20 aircraft," writes Chris Pocock, an authority on the U-2, "and the USAF had taken delivery of another 30. Kelly Johnson offered the government a sweet deal to produce another five aircraft, partially built from spare parts left over from the earlier contracts. The USAF took up the offer, and five additional aircraft were delivered by March of 1959."[53]

The overflights program of the United States during the early Cold War years was a survival measure that provided the information needed to preclude strategic surprise in the nuclear age. Noted Richard Helms, the director of the CIA from 1966 to 1973, "The U-2 overflights of the Soviet Union provided us with the greatest intelligence breakthrough of the 20th Century. For the first time, American policy makers had accurate, credible information on Soviet strategic assets.... Those overflights eliminated almost entirely the ability of the Kremlin ever to launch a surprise preemptive strike against the West. There was no way they could secretly prepare for war without our cameras revealing the size and scope of those activities."[52]

There were, however, some authors who maintained, on the flimsiest evidence, that at times General LeMay, the SAC commander, initiated overflights on his own accord. Those stories were false and did injustice to a program that was tightly controlled at the highest level of the US government, the president of the United States. However, General LeMay pretty much ran the PARPRO reconnaissance program, in which I personally participated. Peripheral reconnaissance missions were flown over international waters along the shores and borders of the Soviet Union and its satellites, as well as the PRC and North Korea. An issue that arose as early as 1948 was what constituted the national limit of offshore sovereignty. International law called for an offshore limit of three miles. Russia, and later the Soviet Union, extended that limit to twelve miles, and in July 1948 our State Department, to be supersafe, called for a forty-mile limit, which didn't sit well with our military, which continued to lobby for a twelve-mile limit. Our cameras weren't that good at the time to provide useful imagery beyond the twelve-mile limit. By August 1948, State relented and agreed to a twenty-mile limit in the Pacific. Things changed with the outbreak of the Korean War in 1950, but peripheral reconnaissance flights worldwide stayed beyond the twelve-mile limit. With the advent of high-flying jets and a significant increase in camera effectiveness and film resolution, peripheral reconnaissance proved very productive. In addition, reconnaissance began to capture electronic emissions over a broad frequency spectrum from offshore locations. It is here, in the peacetime aerial reconnaissance program, flying over international waters, where we suffered significant losses in aircraft and crews.

From September 1962 to September 1967, the air force's ground-to-air missile units shot down five KMT (Kuomintang) U-2 reconnaissance aircraft. The picture shows four U-2 aircraft exhibited at the Chinese People's Revolutionary Military Museum.

THE PRICE WE PAID (1945–1993)

> On July 27, 1953, Ralph Parr, flying an F-86F Sabre, shoots down a Russian IL-12 Coach
> transport, with 21 passengers and crew aboard, just hours before the Korean Armistice
> is signed. Two days later, on July 29, 1953, an RB-50G of the 343rd SRS is shot down in
> retaliation over the Sea of Japan, near Vladivostok. Captain John Roche, the copilot,
> was rescued. The bodies of two crew members were recovered. Most of the crew were
> rescued by the Russians. . . . They had immediately been whisked away to the KGB.
> **—Laurence Jolidon,** *Last Seen Alive*

It sounds like an oxymoron that peripheral reconnaissance flights along the borders of the Soviet Union, North Korea, the People's Republic of China, and other Cold War allies of the Soviet Union should have been more dangerous than overflying Mother Russia. But such was the case. The 55th Strategic Reconnaissance Wing, for which I flew during the volatile 1960s, at the time was equipped with RB-47H aircraft configured for electronic reconnaissance. Some of our aircraft monitored Soviet missile shots as well, and others yet were configured to address new and unique issues. We flew our missions from five principal locations: Yokota Air Base, Japan; Incirlik Air Base, Turkey; Eielson Air Force Base, Alaska; Thule Air Base, Greenland; and several Royal Air Force bases in the United Kingdom. However, it wasn't unusual to fly from other locations, all depending on what the situation called for. Other SAC reconnaissance units flew out of Kadena Air Base, Okinawa, and from the windswept island of Shemya at the extreme western end of the Aleutian chain of islands monitoring communications and missile-related events.

The 55th Wing came into existence in February 1947 at MacDill Air Force Base, Florida, equipped with dated World War II–type aircraft to perform photo mapping. It was soon disbanded and in 1949 came to life again flying RB-29, and later, RB-50 aircraft. All slow and low flyers, easy prey for aggressive attackers. But of course they would be flying PARPRO missions over international waters, outside the twelve-mile limits of whatever nation they were flying against. It turned out that aircraft flying over the Barents Sea, the eastern Baltic, the Black Sea, the Sea of Japan, and the Sea of Okhotsk would find themselves frequently under attack. The fact that they were flying over international waters seemed to have no relevance. The rationale for that sort of aggressive action is hard to understand. Possibly it reflected a sense of Russian impotence in the face of the frequent overflights by American aircraft of the Russian motherland, flights that they were never able to shoot at because they were either flying too high for their fighters or they were detected too late, or both. But much more likely is that commanders of PVO Strany, their equivalent of our Air Defense Command at that time, had a great amount of latitude in how they dealt with perceived intruders—even if the "intruder" was in fact not flying over Soviet territory nor heading in that direction. When intercepted by Russian fighters, which was a frequent occurrence for us, we continued to fly our missions as briefed. If we aborted every time the Russians sent up a fighter or two, we would have never been able to accomplish our tasks. Our rules of engagement in the 1960s, and they hadn't changed over the years prior to or after the 1960s, were to take evasive action if the hostile aircraft fired on us or went from a radar search mode to lock on—meaning that the hostile fighter was getting ready to fire its guns, cannons, or missiles. We only fired our own guns in self-defense and never initiated such action, but only responded to the aggressor.

One other very volatile area was access to and from Berlin, flying through the three Berlin air corridors. As early as 1946, we configured A-26 aircraft to fly photo reconnaissance in the Berlin corridors and many other places in Europe. In subsequent years, we used reconnaissance-configured B-17, C-54, C-97, and C-130 aircraft to fly electronic and photo reconnaissance missions in the Berlin corridors. Under the Four Power Agreement, such missions were not authorized, but they were flown anyway, cameras and antennas for receivers carefully hidden or disguised. However, aircraft straying outside the twenty-mile-wide air corridors to and from Berlin were risking a shootdown by Russian fighters. On occasion, they would attack or harass aircraft even while flying within the confines of the corridors. There is an interesting story that occurred during the Berlin airlift of 1948–1949. Colonel Harold "Hal" Austin, then a young lieutenant, was piloting a C-54 from Rhein-Main Air Base to Berlin. "It was night, and we were on our second run to Berlin, me and my copilot, Darrel Lamb. Both of us were sleepy. We didn't call in over the Berlin beacon. When I awoke, I saw Darrel was sound asleep. The bird dog, our radio compass, was pointing toward the tail. There were not many lights on the ground below. Everything was pitch black. I really got scared. I woke Darrel. He cranked in Berlin radio. It was weak. We had no idea how long we had been asleep, but we promptly did a 180. It took us thirty minutes to get back to Berlin, about ninety or so miles. We were probably over

Stettin, or somewhere over the Baltic Sea, when we made our turn. The corridor wasn't always full of aircraft, so we waited until someone called in over
the Berlin beacon. We waited three minutes, then called in our own number
and rejoined the stream of aircraft flying into Berlin. We sweated blood for
a couple of days, expecting the hammer to come down at any time. Nothing
ever happened." Austin, in May 1954, would fly his RB-47E photo reconnaissance aircraft over the Kola Peninsula and come home nearly unscathed. The
luck of the Irish, or something like that. I never asked Hal if he had Irish
blood in his veins—probably did.

The table in this chapter is a listing of not only reconnaissance and observation aircraft shot down in the course of their missions but also airliners
misidentified by Russian pilots and ground controllers and shot down with
heavy loss of life. The 1978 and 1983 attacks on South Korean airliners revealed
the continuing disarray of the Soviet air defense system. The 55th SRW by
that time had converted to RC-135 aircraft, a derivative of the KC-135 tanker
and the 707 airliner. The Russians apparently believed that it was one of those
reconnaissance aircraft that had flown off course, and they were shooting
down. Although it is difficult to mistake a 747 airliner with flashing red and
green lights for an aircraft that looks very much like a Boeing 707 flying with
no lights on. Russian radar controllers generally determined a fighter's action,
even the weapons he was to use, as in the case of the RB-66B shootdown. The
pilot of the Russian jet just executed the orders given.

Not shown in the table are the many unsuccessful attacks by Russian
fighters on American reconnaissance planes, and there were plenty of those.
Attacks against American aircraft began in late 1945 and picked up as the years
went by. For the Russians, the confrontation with the West clearly began as
soon as World War II ended; for the West, it took a while to have that fact
sink in, but by 1948 the Cold War was in full bloom and recognized as such
by everyone.

Looking at the loss statistics in the table, the high number of U-2 aircraft
lost by the Chinese Nationalists is a standout. There may have been more
losses than those shown in the table, plus a number of accidents that added
to the total. How did that happen? The PRC, the Chinese Communists, had
obtained SA-2 surface-to-air missiles from the Soviet Union, the same missiles that downed Francis Gary Powers's aircraft on May 1, 1960. The Taiwanese
U-2s that overflew China were principally employed to photograph China's
secret nuclear test and development facilities at Lop Nor, two thousand miles
inland, "and a very tough round trip for even the most experienced U-2 pilot."
The loss of several of the U-2s flying over China made Kelly Johnson suspi-
cious. "Kelly long suspected that the electronic counter-measures black box
we installed on the tail section of Powers's U-2 may have acted in an opposite

Aircraft Shot Down by Russian Fighters, 1950–1983

Date	Aircraft Type	Operator	Location of Loss/Means	Dead/Missing
04/08/50	PB4Y-2	USN	Baltic Sea near Latvia/MiG-15	10
12/04/50	RB-45C	USAF	Russia/Yalu River area/MiG-15	4
11/06/51	P2V-3W	USN	Sea of Japan/La-11	10
11/18/51	C-47	USAF	Hungary/MiG-15	3
06/13/52	RB-29	USAF	Sea of Japan/off Hokkaido/MiG-15	13
06/13/52	RC-47	Sweden	Baltic Sea/MiG-15	7
06/16/52	Catalina	Sweden	Baltic Sea/MiG-15	0
10/07/52	RB-29	USAF	Kurile Islands/La-11	8
11/29/52	C-47	China Air/CIA	China	2
01/12/53	RB-29	USAF	Manchuria (leaflet mission)	3
01/18/53	P2V-5	USN	Formosa Strait/AAA	6
03/10/53	F-84G	USAF	Czechoslovakia/MiG-15	0
03/12/53	Avro Lincoln	RAF	East Germany/Berlin/MiG-15	7
07/29/53	RB-50G	USAF	Sea of Japan/MiG-17	16
08/17/53	T-6	USAF	Korean DMZ/AAA	1
07/22/54	DC-4	Cathay Pacific	Hainan Island/La-9	10
09/04/54	P2V-5	USN	Sea of Okhotsk/MiG-15	1
11/07/54	RB-29	USAF	Sea of Japan/off Hokkaido/MiG-15	1
01/19/55	L-20	USAF	Korean DMZ/AAA	1
04/17/55	RB-47E	USAF	Off Kamchatka Peninsula/MiG-15	3
06/22/55	P2V-5	USN	Bering Strait off Siberia/MiG-15	0
07/27/55	Constellation	El Al	Bulgaria/MiG-15	40
08/17/55	T-6	USAF	Korean DMZ/AAA	1
08/22/56	P4M-1Q	USN	Formosa Strait	16
09/10/56	RB-50	USAF	Sea of Japan/MiG-15	16
12/23/57	T-33	USAF	Albania	0
02/18/58	RB-57A-1	Taiwan	Over China/MiG-19	1
03/06/58	F-86	USAF	Over North Korea	0
06/27/58	C-118A	USAF	Over Armenia/MiG-17	0
09/02/58	RC-130A	USAF	Over Armenia/MiG-17	17
10/07/59	RB-57D	Taiwan	Over China/SA-2	1
05/01/60	U-2	US/CIA	Over Russia/SA-2	0
05/25/60	C-47	USAF	Over East Germany/MiG-19	0
07/01/60	RB-47H	USAF	Over Barents Sea/MiG-19	4
09/09/62	U-2C	Taiwan	Over China/SA-2	1

Date	Aircraft Type	Operator	Location of Loss/Means	Dead/Missing
10/26/62	U-2A	USAF	Over Cuba/SA-2	1
05/17/63	OH-23	USA	Korean DMZ/AAA	0
08/06/63	C-130	USAF	Over North Korea	6
11/01/63	U-2C	Taiwan	Over China/SA-2	1
01/28/64	T-39	USAF	Over East Germany/MiG-19	3
03/10/64	RB-66B	USAF	Over East Germany/MiG-19	0
07/07/64	U-2C	Taiwan	Over China/SA-2	1
01/10/65	U-2C	Taiwan	Over China/SA-2	1
12/14/65	RB-57F	USAF	Black Sea	2
09/09/67	U-2C	Taiwan	Over China/SA-2	1
04/15/69	EC-121	USN	Sea of Japan/MiG-17	31
08/17/69	OH-23	USA	Korean DMZ/AAA	0
10/21/70	U-8	USA	Over Armenia	0
07/14/77	CH-47	USA	Korean DMZ/MiG-21	3
04/20/78	707	KAL	Near Murmansk/Su-15	2
09/01/83	747	KAL	Sea of Japan/Su-15	269

way from the one we intended," wrote Ben Rich, the former director of Kelly's Skunk Works. "It was possible that the Russians had changed these frequencies by the time we incorporated them into our missile spoofer, so that the incoming missile's seeker head was on the same frequency as the beams transmitted off our tail and acted as a homing device. A few years later a similar black box was installed in the tails of CIA U-2s piloted by Taiwanese flying highly dangerous missions over the Chinese mainland. One day three of four U-2s were shot down, and the sole survivor told CIA debriefers that he was amazed to be alive because he forgot to turn on his black box. To Kelly, that clinched the case. But we'll never really know."[54]

The majority of shootdowns occurred in the 1950s, many over the Sea of Japan and adjacent areas such as the Sea of Okhotsk, all areas I flew many times in the 1960s in RB-47H jet aircraft. Losses over the Sea of Japan were inflicted not only by overly aggressive Russian fighters but by the North Koreans as well; North Korea was well known for its unpredictability. The most egregious act committed by the North Koreans being the capture of the USS *Pueblo*, an electronic reconnaissance ship posing as a research vessel, on January 23, 1968, off the east coast of North Korea. Both the United States and the Soviet Union used vessels of that nature to monitor each other's military exercises and communications, a practice tolerated by both sides. However, this

The eighty-two survivors of a crew of eighty-three of the USS *Pueblo*, led into captivity by its skipper, Lieutenant Commander Lloyd Bucher. After an apology by the US government on December 22, 1968, insisted on by the North Koreans even though the ship was in international waters, the crew was released.

was not the Soviet Union the *Pueblo* was facing, but a North Korea that had frequently attacked and shot down unarmed American observation aircraft over or near the Demilitarized Zone, and three years earlier, in 1965, nearly shot down an RB-47H flying over international waters off Wonsan. Neither the RB-47H electronic reconnaissance aircraft, attacked by MiG 17s, nor the USS *Pueblo* in 1968, attacked by MiG-21s and North Korean armed speedboats, received American fighter support. Nor did the slow-moving and low-flying RB-29/50 aircraft, or similar US Navy aircraft, during the 1950s. All too many of which perished. To me, it is totally inexplicable that we did not have properly armed fighter aircraft sitting alert on our air bases in northern Japan to provide appropriate protection for our vulnerable reconnaissance aircraft, and of course fighter escort could have been provided over areas deemed especially vulnerable. Once the *Pueblo* was captured, we moved large numbers of combat aircraft from Southeast Asia into Japan facing Korea. But for some reason our senior military leadership couldn't figure out beforehand that our continued reconnaissance operations over the Sea of Japan might elicit another violent response from a volatile North Korea, even though it had happened with the Russians many times before. In retrospect, what is difficult for me to understand is our senior military leadership's apparent obliviousness to a situation calling for action. They sent us on these dangerous flights for good reason, yet fighter support apparently was never a consideration, regardless of place or situation. We also had KB-29/50 air refueling tankers based in Japan, and later KC-97 and KC-135 tankers became available, which easily could have supported fighter aircraft over the Sea of Japan when reconnaissance aircraft, or a ship such as the USS *Pueblo*, approached vulnerable areas. There were many options available—none were exercised, which, as a senior air force officer, I find not only inexplicable but frankly irresponsible.

As if the attack on an RB-47 in 1965, and the subsequent attack on the USS *Pueblo* in 1968, didn't provide sufficient warning for our senior commanders to adjust the way we conducted reconnaissance off North Korea, or in the Sea of Japan area as a whole, a bitter lesson was yet to come. Just a little over a year after the *Pueblo* capture, on April 15, 1969, a US Navy EC-121 electronic reconnaissance aircraft was shot down by North Korean fighters over the Sea of Japan. All thirty of the crew perished. That should never have happened after what had come before.

As for the Russians, shootdowns diminished drastically after the downing of Powers's U-2 on May 1, 1960, and the Khrushchev/Eisenhower confrontation at the Paris summit, which terminated the U-2 overflights of the Soviet Union. Khrushchev had played a masterful hand at the Paris summit, greatly embarrassing the president of the United States, Dwight D. Eisenhower. Recalled General Andrew J. Goodpaster at the Early Cold War Overflights Symposium in 2001, "I have to tell you that the handling of that critical international situation—and it was critical—was about as clumsy in my opinion as anything our government has ever done. I can say that because I had a hand in that clumsiness. We had absolutely failed to consider the many 'what-ifs' of the U-2 overflights in a thorough, realistic, and searching manner. The shootdown was a lesson that was burned into us by the way we mishandled it. In any case, the shootdown ended all aerial overflights of the Soviet Union.... It just so happened, however, our 'blindness' was temporary. Four months later, in August, the Corona project, the nation's first photo reconnaissance satellite authorized by the president back in 1958, became operational. Corona satellites overflew and returned imagery of the Soviet Union in incredible volume, far more than was ever possible with the U-2. And that was accomplished in outer space without risking the lives of any pilots or aircrews."

After embarrassing Eisenhower at the Paris conference, Khrushchev was going to play an even bigger hand, a heady gamble one might say, two years later confronting the United States with nuclear-armed IRBMs based in Cuba, less than a hundred miles offshore from the United States. In spite of the Corona satellite circling the earth, it took an RB-47H reconnaissance aircraft

An RC-135E, *Lisa Anne*, of the 4157th Reconnaissance Wing, flown by Brigadier General Regis Urschler. General Urschler spent his entire career flying, commanding, and directing reconnaissance units and operations. He flew every model of the RB-47 and RC-135, starting as a lieutenant in the 1950s, and years later ended up as commander of the 55th Reconnaissance Wing.

Left to right, Brigadier General Regis Urschler; Colonel Thomas Shepherd, RB-47 navigator; Colonel Wolfgang Samuel; and Hank Dubuy, copilot of RB-47 #4290, at the funeral of Colonel Bruce Olmstead at Arlington Cemetery in 2017, whose aircraft was shot down over the Barents Sea on July 1, 1960.

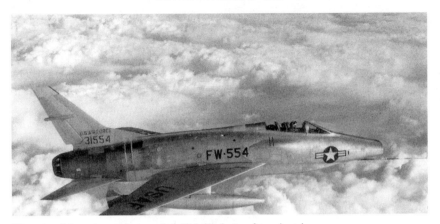

RF-100A serial number 31554, one of six Slick Chick aircraft produced.

Early Cold War U-2 recovering at Incirlik Air Base, Turkey.

to find the missile-carrying ship in open ocean. This time, the shoe was on the other foot, so to speak, and to avoid a nuclear showdown Khrushchev ordered the ship to turn around. The Cuban Missile Crisis resolved itself not in Khrushchev's favor, and he soon was put out to pasture.

Aggressive shootdowns continued over East Germany, taking down aircraft straying from the approved air corridors or experiencing navigational issues. None of which had anything to do with reconnaissance, nor did the shootdown of the South Korean airliner in 1983. That was to be the last, and the Soviet Union ceased to exist as an entity ten years later. Aerial reconnaissance was not an option for the United States in the early Cold War years, if it wanted to survive in a nuclear-armed world. It was a matter of life or death. Yet the implementation of our reconnaissance program, and the protection of the vulnerable aircraft, left much to be desired. For those who lost their lives serving our country, we, in the reconnaissance community, remember them as Silent Warriors as well as their Incredible Courage. Men and women of the fabled 55th Reconnaissance Wing, still based at Offutt Air Force Base in Omaha, Nebraska, continue to serve our nation in the many ongoing conflicts in our current world. The fabled U-2 reconnaissance plane, renamed TR-1, then back to its original name, still flies dangerous skies to help record and decipher the intentions of the newest crop of world tyrants. I cannot imagine their services not being needed in future years.

NOTES

1. Matthew B. Ridgeway, Soldier: The Memoirs of Matthew B. Ridgeway (Westport, CT: Greenwood Press, 1974), 141–46.

2. R. Cargill Hall, ed., Early Cold War Overflights Symposium Proceedings, vol. 1, Memoirs (Washington, DC: Office of the Historian, National Reconnaissance Office, 2003), 45–46.

3. George C. Marshall, "General Marshall's Victory Report: Biennial Report of the Chief of Staff of the United States of Army, 1943 to 1945, to the Secretary of War," War Department of the United States of America, Washington, DC, September 1, 1945, 6.

4. Wolfgang W. E. Samuel, Glory Days: The Untold Story of the Men Who Flew the B-66 Destroyer into the Face of Fear (Atglen, PA: Schiffer Publishing, 2008), 15.

5. Wolfgang W. E. Samuel, I Always Wanted to Fly: America's Gold War Airmen (Jackson: University Press of Mississippi, 2001), 181–82.

6. Wolfgang W. E. Samuel, American Raiders: The Race to Capture the Luftwaffe's Secrets (Jackson: University Press of Mississippi, 2004), 429.

7. Martin E. James, Historical Highlights: United States Air Forces in Europe, 1945–1979 (New York: Headquarters USAFE, Office of History, 1980), 3–7.

8. Theodore von Karman, "Toward New Horizons: Science, the Key to Air Supremacy; A Report to General of the Army H. H. Arnold" (Washington, DC: Headquarters Army Air Force, 1945), iii–vii.

9. Vannevar Bush, Modern Arms and Free Men: A Discussion of the Role of Science in Preserving Democracy (New York: Simon and Schuster, 1949), 85.

10. Kenneth Chilstrom and Penn Leary, eds. Test Flying at Old Wright Field (Omaha, NE: Westchester House, 1993), 82.

11. Chilstrom and Leary, Test Flying, 92–93.

12. Samuel, American Raiders, 257.

13. Samuel, American Raiders, 147.

14. Samuel, American Raiders, 152.

15. Samuel, American Raiders, 154.

16. James, Historical Highlights, 11.

17. Curtis E. LeMay with MacKinlay Kantor, Mission with LeMay: My Story (Garden City, NY: Doubleday, 1965), 411.

18. John T. Bohn, The Development of Strategic Air Command, 1946–1976 (Omaha, NE: Office of the Historian, Headquarters Strategic Air Command, 1976), 9.

19. Bohn, The Development of Strategic Air Command, 2.

20. LeMay, Mission with LeMay, 432–33.

Notes

21. R. Cargill Hall, "The Truth about Overflights," Military History Quarterly 9, no. 3 (Spring 1997): 26–27.

22. Ridgeway, Soldier, 191.

23. Samuel, I Always Wanted to Fly, 151.

24. Samuel, I Always Wanted to Fly, 158–59.

26. Samuel, I Always Wanted to Fly, 175–89.

26. Hall, Early Cold War Overflights Symposium, 1:153–59.

27. Samuel, I Always Wanted to Fly, 188–89.

28. Wolfgang W. E. Samuel, In Defense of Freedom: Stories of Courage and Sacrifice of World War II Army Air Forces Flyers (Jackson: University Press of Mississippi, 2015), 229–30.

29. Bohn, The Development of Strategic Air Command, 35.

30. Hall, Early Cold War Overflights Symposium, 1:1.

31. Samuel, I Always Wanted to Fly, 119.

32. Bohn, The Development of Strategic Air Command, 39.

33. Marcelle S. Knaack, Post–World War II Bombers, 1945–1973 (Washington, DC: Office of Air Force History, Headquarters US Air Force, 1988), 297–301.

34. Knaack, Post–World War II Bombers, 303.

35. Samuel, I Always Wanted to Fly, 151–52.

36. Samuel, I Always Wanted to Fly, 151–52.

37. Samuel, I Always Wanted to Fly, 151–52.

38. Bruce M. Bailey, "We See All": Pictorial History of the 55th Strategic Reconnaissance Wing, 1947–1967 (Omaha, NE: 55th ELINT Association, 1982), 47–48.

39. Samuel, American Raiders, 153.

40. Hall, Early Cold War Overflights Symposium, 1:248.

41. Samuel, I Always Wanted to Fly, 198.

42. Hall, Early Cold War Overflights Symposium, 1:15–32.

43. William L. White, The Little Toy Dog: The Story of the Two RB-47 Flyers, Captain John R. McKone and Captain Freeman B. Olmstead (New York: E. P. Dutton, 1962), 293.

44. Knaack, Post–World War II Bombers, 297.

45. Knaack, Post–World War II Bombers, 333.

46. Knaack, Post–World War II Bombers, 336.

47. Ben R. Rich and Leo Janos, Skunk Works: A Personal Memoir of My Years at Lockheed (Boston: Little, Brown, 1994), 123.

48. Samuel, Glory Days, 151–64.

49. Hall, Early Cold War Overflights Symposium, 1:23.

50. R. Cargill Hall, "Clandestine Victory: Eisenhower and Overhead Reconnaissance in the Cold War," in Forging the Shield: Eisenhower and National Security for the 21st Century, ed. Dennis E. Showalter (Chicago: Imprint Publications, 2005).

51. Rich and Janos, Skunk Works, 160.

52. Rich and Janos, Skunk Works, 163.

53. Chris Pocock, The U-2 Spyplane: Toward the Unknown; A New History of the Early Years (Atglen, PA: Schiffer Publishing, 2000), 129.

54. Rich and Janos, Skunk Works, 162–63.

BIBLIOGRAPHY

Acheson, Dean. Present at the Creation: My Years at the State Department. New York: W. W. Norton, 1960.

Bailey, Bruce. "We See All": Pictorial History of the 55th Strategic Reconnaissance Wing, 1947–1967. Omaha, NE: 55th Elint Association Historian, 1982.

Bohn, John T. The Development of the Strategic Air Command, 1946–1976. Omaha, NE: Office of the Historian, Headquarters Strategic Air Command, 1976.

Bush, Vannevar. Modern Arms and Free Men: A Discussion of the Role of Science in Preserving Democracy. New York: Simon and Schuster, 1949.

Butcher, Harry C. My Three Years with Eisenhower: The Personal Diary of Captain Harry C. Butcher, USNR, Naval Aide to General Eisenhower, 1942 to 1945. New York: Simon and Schuster, 1946.

Chilstrom, Kenneth, and Penn Leary, eds. Test Flying at Old Wright Field. Omaha, NE: Westchester House, 1993.

Dupuy, Ernest, and Trevor Nevitt Dupuy. The Encyclopedia of Military History from 3500 BC to the Present. New York: Harper and Row, 1970.

Ferrell, Robert H., ed. The Twentieth Century: An Almanac. New York: World Almanac Publications, 1985.

Hall, R. Cargill. "Clandestine Victory: Eisenhower and Overhead Reconnaissance in the Cold War." In Forging the Shield: Eisenhower and National Security for the 21st Century, edited by Dennis E. Showalter. Chicago: Imprint Publications, 2005.

Hall, R. Cargill, ed. Early Cold War Overflights Symposium Proceedings. Vol. 1, Memoirs. Washington, DC: Office of the Historian, National Reconnaissance Office, 2003.

Hall, R. Cargill, ed. Early Cold War Overflights Symposium Proceedings. Vol. 2, Appendices. Washington, DC: Office of the Historian, National Reconnaissance Office, 2003.

Hall, R. Cargill. Military Space and National Policy: Record and Interpretation. Washington, DC: George C. Marshall Institute, 2006.

Hall, R. Cargill. NRO History: Early Cold War Strategic Reconnaissance. Washington, DC: Office of the Historian, National Reconnaissance Office, 1997–1998.

Hall, R. Cargill. "The Truth about Overflights." Military History Quarterly 9, no. 3 (Spring 1997).

James, Martin E. Historical Highlights: United States Air Forces in Europe, 1945–1979. New York: Headquarters USAFE, Office of History, 1980.

Jolidon, Laurence. Last Seen Alive: The Search for Missing POWs from the Korean War. Austin, TX: Ink-Slinger Press, 1995.

Karman, Theodore von. Toward New Horizons: A Report to General of the Army H. H. Arnold, Submitted on Behalf of the A.A.F. Scientific Advisory Group. Washington, DC: Headquarters, Army Air Forces, 1944.

Kennan, George F. Memoirs, 1925–1950. Boston: Little, Brown, 1967.

Knaak, Marcelle S. *Post–World War II Fighters, 1945–1973*. Washington DC: Office of Air Force History, US Air Force, 1986.

Knaak, Marcelle S. *Post–World War II Bombers, 1945–1973*. Washington DC: Office of Air Force History, US Air Force, 1988.

LeMay, Curtis E., with MacKinlay Kantor. *Mission with LeMay: My Story*. Garden City, NY: Doubleday, 1965.

Marshall, George C. "General Marshall's Victory Report: Biennial Report of the Chief of Staff of the United States Army, 1943 to 1945, to the Secretary of War." War Department of the United States of America, Washington, DC, September 1, 1945.

Natola, Mark, ed. *Boeing B-47 Stratojet: True Stories of the Cold War in the Air*. Atglen, PA: Schiffer Publishing, 2002.

Pocock, Chris. *The U-2 Spyplane: Toward the Unknown; New History of the Early Years*. Altglen, PA: Schiffer Publishing, 2000.

Rich, Ben R., and Leo Janos. *Skunk Works: A Personal Memoir of My Years at Lockheed*. Boston: Little, Brown, 1994.

Ridgeway, Matthew B. *Soldier: The Memoirs of Matthew B. Ridgeway*. Westport, CT: Greenwood Press, 1974.

Samuel, Wolfgang W. E. *American Raiders: The Race to Capture the Luftwaffe's Secrets*. Jackson: University Press of Mississippi, 2004.

Samuel, Wolfgang W. E. *Glory Days: The Untold Story of the Men Who Flew the B-66 Destroyer into the Face of Fear*. Atglen, PA: Schiffer Publishing, 2008.

Samuel, Wolfgang W. E. *I Always Wanted to Fly: America's Cold War Airmen*. Jackson: University Press of Mississippi, 2001.

Samuel, Wolfgang W. E. In Defense of Freedom: Stories of Courage and Sacrifice of World War II Army Air Forces Flyers. Jackson: University Press of Mississippi, 2015.

Smith, Jean Edward. Lucius Clay: An American Life. New York: Henry Holt, 1990.

Webner, Neil E. He Was a Hero. N.p.: n.p., 2008.

White, William L. The Little Toy Dog: The Story of the Two RB-47 Flyers, Captain John R. McKone and Captain Freeman B. Olmstead. New York: E. P. Dutton, 1962.

Winchester, Jim. American Military Aircraft: A Century of Innovation. New York: Barnes and Noble, 2005.

INDEX